The Havana Conspiracies

Rights of Passage of a Master Spy

Based on a True Spy Story

Dr. Julio Antonio del Marmol

The Cuban Lightning

© Copyright 2016 Dr. Julio Antonio del Marmol.

All rights reserved. No part of this publication may be reproduced, stored in a retrieval system, or transmitted, in any form or by any means, electronic, mechanical, photocopying, recording, or otherwise, without the written prior permission of the author.

ISBN: 978-1-68588-010-1 (sc)
ISBN: 978-1-68588-009-5 (hc)
ISBN: 978-1-68588-011-8 (e)

Because of the dynamic nature of the Internet, any web addresses or links contained in this book may have changed since publication and may no longer be valid.

Any people depicted in stock imagery provided by Thinkstock or found elsewhere are models, and such images are being used for illustrative purposes only.

Certain stock imagery © Thinkstock. All other copyright credits given individually on the end page.

Cuban Lightning Publications, Int rev. 12/07/2016

Introduction

At the age of twelve, the author, Julio Antonio del Marmol, found that his destiny had taken him through extraordinary circumstances that happen only a few times in history during widespread social chaos—like those seen in the deranged turmoil of the Cuban Revolution in 1959. The supreme leader, Fidel Castro, nominated this young boy to be the Commander-in-Chief of the new army for the future.

As Fidel Castro went through his own changes of heart at the start of this tumultuous time, the youth went through his own conflict as he watched his childhood friends abandon the island, discontented with the complete disruption of democratic establishment and the institution of Marxist ideology by the new leaders. Julio Antonio del Marmol, the Young Commander, sadly remained behind and daily observed the freedom of the Cuban people evaporate as promise after promise was broken. In spite of the commitment to equality for all without distinction based on political or religious belief, the Castro brothers and Che Guevara ruthlessly hunted down and exterminated all opposition. His admiration towards the leaders turned into disappointment and frustration, as he watched the Castros' forces execute their enemies and commit the most horrendous crimes humanity had ever seen in their ambition to maintain power.

He concluded that this is not what the Cuban people had fought their revolution for and decided, before sharing these horrible experiences with anyone, including his father, to abandon the country as his friends had done. When he did share these intentions with his uncle, he received the most shocking surprise: his relative was a veteran master spy. His uncle proposed that he be trained to be the next in line, and Julio Antonio del Marmol became the youngest spy in modern history at the age of thirteen.

In this volume, Julio Antonio uses Che's newfound trust in him to penetrate the most secret of submarine bases and terrorist training camps. He discovers that some of the assassination blueprints he had uncovered were in a more advanced operational stage than mere planning. When suspicion arises that a mole has infiltrated his group's inner circle, he develops a new contact. To protect him, they must now isolate him from those few he had already come to trust. He must learn to trust the new contact, even as he discovers a sinister and terrifying scheme to kill thousands and blame the United States, not only breaking down relations between the U.S. and Cuba, but making millions through insurance fraud.

The author tells the story not merely as a narrator; he was an active participant in these events as part of his first steps in his life as a thirteen-year-old spy, retrieving important documents for his friends in his intelligence network. Only when they reviewed the data did he realize the sheer magnitude of what he had accomplished as he exposed what really lay behind the Havana conspiracies.

The Cuban Lightning

Volume II of Rites of Passage of a Master Spy

Acknowledgements

I am a very lucky man because I have a great group of people by my side that I not only consider my friends but also who are the most capable, sacrificing professionals equal to the ones I've risked my life with over the past 50 years in their dedication and values. This group has made possible the publication of this book. To them, with all my heart today, I give the best of my love, gratitude, and sincerest thanks to every one of these fantastic warriors. In order of seniority, I would especially like to thank O'Brien: a great friend, a great individual with extraordinary values, thank you for your contributions you have made in many different ways to this project, as well being loyally by my side and watching my back for almost all of my career. I know for a fact you have never done that before for anyone. To my right arm and great friend, Tad Atkinson: for your dedication to every detail in research and many hours of hard work with me, never hesitating to sacrifice even your personal and private family time in order to make this happen. To Steve Weese: thank you for the many pieces of computer and graphic work as well professional enhancement of photos to improve the quality of the book. To Carlos Mota: my thanks for your dedication and multiple contributions and sacrifices you have made in order to make this happen. To Gervasin Neto: for your constant loyalty and many hours standing on your feet or hiding between cars in order to maintain our security with your group of people you've coordinated to watch our backs, continually keeping us informed of any suspicious activity that occurs in our surroundings. To Chopin: for your great companionship, loyalty, and support for the last 50 years with me in our fight for freedom and that beautiful, generous letter you wrote in behalf of the project. To our editor, Jen Poiry-Prough: who managed to make this book as easy to read, using her magic touch to polishing this piece of coal and bring to you, the readers, what I consider to be a very rare diamond. It makes all of us very proud to be involved in this project. Your professionalism, vast knowledge, and dedication, has made this book a great piece for future generations. To all of you, my friends who remain in the shadows, who contributed in one way or another in making this book and help me to bring the truth to the public, you have given the best of yourselves, putting forth your best effort to educate future generations. God bless you all. I embrace you as the Christian warriors that you all are.

Dr. Julio Antonio del Marmol

Prologue: Versus Evil Innocence

116 Avenue Cabada
Pinar del Rio, Cuba
1958

I walked into the living room where my friend, Alfredo, was waiting when Mima stopped me. "Julio Antonio, I need you to go to the church now. I promised Father Lara that you would go to his office to clean it today."

"But, Mima," I protested, "I'm about to go play marbles with Alfredo. I can go over afterwards."

"Julio Antonio del Marmol!" she said in a reproving tone. "This won't take long, and you can play marbles with Alfredo afterwards. Be a good boy and let your mother fulfill her promise by running along to the priest to help him. Maybe if Alfredo helps you clean, it will take less time."

Alfredo and I exchanged unhappy glances, but I

nodded obediently. "Yes, Mima," I said, managing to keep the sigh out of my voice. "Come on, Alfredo."

Alfredo and I went outside to where our bicycles lay on the porch. We rode them to the church. The task before us wasn't too immense, and as Mima had predicted, it did not take the two of us very long to get the cleaning done. In fact, I decided to take a little extra time to organize Father Lara's office so that it would be even cleaner for him than before.

"Padre!" I called out. "Padre, we're done. Come and see!"

Father Lara walked into the room and looked around in undisguised joyful surprise at the thoroughness of our work. "My, you boys have done a spotless job, like your Mima said you would, Julio Antonio! I'm so proud of you both."

He walked over to a cabinet on the wall and opened the door. He pulled out two small, iron crosses on delicate chains and handed them to us. "These are for my two special young men who helped me put my study back in order."

"Thank you, Padre," I said in gratitude, "we are honored."

"Thank you, Padre," Alfredo echoed.

Father Lara made the sign of the cross as he blessed us. "Now hurry home before it gets dark, or your mothers will be worried."

Indeed, as we went outside, it was getting a little too dark for our marbles game. We agreed to get together again tomorrow, and so I raced Alfredo to his house through the darkening streets on our bicycles, the crosses around our necks flopping against our shoulders and chests in the violent motion. As we skidded to a halt outside Alfredo's house, I could see his father, Mr. Valdes, talking with some of the local tobacco workers outside.

He smiled as he saw us and waved. "There you boys are!"

"Hi, Papa!" Alfredo called out.

Mr. Valdes' expression changed to one of rage as he spotted the cross around Alfredo's neck. He strode over as he threw his cigar down on the ground and furiously yanked the cross with one hand, while the other shoved Alfredo hard. The chain snapped, and Alfredo fell to the ground.

"What is this, you stupid boy?" he demanded of his son. "How many times do I have to tell you? No false idols in my house! I just threw away an image of the Caridad del Cobre one of my waitresses brought into my restaurant! What kind of example are you setting? You're my son—you cannot believe in this crap!"

Alfredo looked up at his father and then at me with embarrassed tears in his eyes, his expression a mixture of fear and anger. "It was only a gift for my hard work, Papa!"

I rushed forward to help Alfredo up just as Mr. Valdes wound up to throw the cross. His elbow caught me in the eye, blackening it, and I reeled back and away. He hurled the cross into the dirt and ground his booted heel upon it, as if he were crushing out a cigarette. He glowered at me and snarled, "You should not interfere in family matters, Marmolito. Stay away!" He turned back to Alfredo. "When Castro takes control, I will also destroy all the Lady of Charity churches for the tobacco workers! We Marxists are beyond this superstitious crap. All we need is ourselves. You hear me?"

I held my cross as I picked up my bicycle and got back on it. I looked compassionately at Alfredo and nodded in understanding and disgust at my friend's situation. I stared pityingly into Mr. Valdes' eyes as I said, "They were only gifts for cleaning Father Lara's office. I cannot understand why you're getting so mad, letting such a tiny thing upset you so much. Are you afraid of God?"

Mr. Valdes looked at his friends in embarrassment, and when he looked back at me, his face grew black with hatred. I did not wait for an answer but pedaled away quickly. Tears started to stream down my face, and I did not want that bully of a man to see them.

Behind me, I heard Alfredo start to sob and Valdes bellow, "Alfredo! Get inside the house right now, you stupid boy!"

I rode as fast as I could back to my house. In my distress, I lay my bicycle on the porch and walked into the house and to the living room. I went straight to the piano, sat down, and began to bang out notes. It was just a rudimentary tune, but as I repeated the phrase, I made adjustments to it. My musical studies were not yet very advanced, so it remained fairly elementary in spite of my alterations. I concentrated intensely on the song that wanted to burst out of my heart, and I allowed my pain and anger to flow through my fingers onto the keys.

I heard Mima walk in from the kitchen. "Julio Antonio, what are you doing?" I looked up at her, and she saw my blackened eye. "Julio Antonio! What happened to your eye? Who did this to you?"

I stopped and turned to her. "Mr. Valdes," I replied, "but it was only an accident. Alfredo got a lot worse." I held up the cross. "Father Lara gave us these as presents, and when Mr. Valdes saw the one Alfredo was wearing, he went crazy." I looked at Mima and noticed her eyes moist with tears. "What's wrong with him, Mima? Is he crazy or sick or what?"

Mima sat down next to me and embraced me, holding me to her. "Oh, my son—these communists don't believe in anything. They have no values at all. They're no good, my dear boy. We must pray, Julio Antonio—not just for them, that they wake up from what they think is a dream, but also for people like Alfredo who have to live with them, and for the world, that they don't one day control it."

I pulled away gently and nodded, then turned back to the piano. "And maybe the word will spread about them, as well. That's what I'm doing now—I'm creating a song, protesting how they treat people who believe differently than they do."

Mima smiled fondly at me. "And what will you call this song?"

That gave me pause for a moment, and I thought about it carefully. "Ave Maria. Lizt and Schubert both have one, so this shall be the Ave Maria of Julio Antonio."

"Very good. Now you work on your song while I get something for that eye."

San Juachin Catholic Church

Greed is the worst parasite any human being could have in his or her mind.

Dr. Julio Antonio del Marmol

Chapter 1: False Idols of History

I took the hand of the elegantly-dressed man before me to shake it. It was not until later that I realized the tremendous importance this man had to Che and his Soviet partners' dreams to rule the world.

"Mucho gusto," he said. "Jacob Leon Rubenstein. But my closest friends call me Jack Ruby."

"Very well, Jack," I said. "Thank you." I leaned back and considered this strange-looking man, who looked like a cross between an FBI agent and an Italian gangster.

He took a couple of steps and hugged Che as if they had known each other all their lives. "My friend," he said to Che, "what a great pleasure it is to see you again. I've a lot of good news for you."

After Che greeted Marko, Jack put his hat on a hat rack in the room. He took off his raincoat and draped it over a chair near him. He wore a beautiful shoulder holster with a pistol that was clearly custom made—

chrome with a white lacquer grip. He had a cleft chin and a pronounced widow's peak. His eyes were deep-set and stared penetratingly at everyone he looked at. It was the stare of a criminal, I thought.

We all sat down around the table, and Che asked, "Well, Jack—what are your bits of good news? I hope at least one of them is the one I've been waiting for."

Jack straightened his hair and grinned. "Yes, my friend, and a lot more. Everything has been taken care of. It's not easy, because these goddamned Kennedys have screwed everyone after we put money in their campaign. They promised us the world, and now they're turning against every single one of us, including my friends in law enforcement. And we haven't even got the S.O.B. elected yet. God knows what he'll do once in office! It's made everyone really nervous, so it's not easy—they all want more. What used to cost me ten thousand dollars now costs me fifty because of all the harassment from the Justice Department. I've already managed to get half the money we agreed on, and I assured them, since I know your word is gold, that at the end of the operation they'd receive the other half."

Che grinned from one ear to the other, stretched out his legs, and put his feet up on the table. "Oh, my friend! That is one of the best pieces of news I've received lately! What about the passports for Marko and Yuri?"

Jack smiled and shook his head. "Well, that is resolved, too. But there's a small inconvenience."

"What is the inconvenience?"

"It's going to cost a lot more than we anticipated."

Che scratched his head unhappily. He looked at Jack dubiously and quietly asked, "How much more, Jack?" He rested his chin in his hand in irritation.

Jack noticed Che's demeanor and shifted uncomfortably in his chair. "Believe me, if it were up to me, I would do it for free. Unfortunately, there are other parties involved. We have to understand that things need to be done differently now than from how we did business before."

"OK, Jack," said Che in growing exasperation. "How much more?"

Jack hesitated, as if bracing himself for an explosion. Finally, he said, "Fifty thousand more for each one of the passports, and an additional thirty thousand for each officer and policeman that'll be involved in this operation—in total, six."

Che waived both hands in the air as he leaned forward angrily. He shook his head violently. "Two hundred eighty thousand dollars more than we talked about, Jack? This is unacceptable! How has this shit happened?"

"I know," Jack said placatingly, "I know. But, believe me, Che, each one of these men is worth this and more, because they are solid. I've tested them before. That doesn't have any price. Not one of them will say a single word, even under pressure."

He stretched his legs into a more comfortable position. "We have to take into account the magnitude of this operation. If we want it to be successful, we cannot give to these people less than what they want. We should even give them a bonus if they do a good job, especially considering that we'll be cutting off the head of the snake and at the same time, eliminating the executioner. There will never be any possibility of someone deciphering the enigma we'll leave for history. To protect the hands behind all of this, I think this is money very well invested."

Che listened unhappily, still shaking his head. He had, however, calmed down after Jack was finished. He was trying to convince himself that the reasons Jack had laid out were solid, but he was obviously still dubious. "Two hundred eighty thousand dollars—it's a lot of money. A lot more money than we had budgeted, especially when you consider we've already invested two and a half million in this operation."

Che continued to shake his head in doubt. "This project is becoming a Frankenstein monster." He placed his hands behind his head and leaned back in his chair. "I hope nothing goes wrong. This will be a huge fiasco and a tremendous embarrassment I don't want to share with Fidel if something goes wrong, after all this money got pumped into it."

Marko had been silent the entire time. "Well, we have to think about it from this perspective. The money is coming from the government—it's not our money. We shouldn't be so worried."

I had to speak up at that point. "I beg your pardon, Marko, and I'm sorry to interrupt. This government is the Revolutionary government—of the people and for the people. That money doesn't come from the government, but from the pockets of the people. We're not in the same dictatorship we had before, where they were stealing from the people for themselves. We have to be worried about how much we're spending, no matter what, and make sure it doesn't go to waste."

Jack leaned over the table and looked at me as if he were mocking me. A sarcastic smile crept across his face, mixed with a little incredulity. "Excuse me, how old are you?"

I didn't like the way he asked that question, as if he were making fun of me for my lack of experience. I leaned back in my chair, crossed my legs. Rather than answer him, I instead asked him, "How many times have you had a machine gun shooting over your head—not one, not two, but three times—and maintained your calm to react properly, not only to save your life, but the lives of your friends, as well? Without filling the air with the smell of crap and piss in your pants?"

I stopped there. No one said a word, but Che smiled, as he knew what I was talking about. I broke the silence and continued in a serious tone, "Common sense, bravery, and convictions you cannot measure with age or time. Only experience and nothing else. That means that my age is an irrelevant subject in this conversation right now." I emphasized my final point by tapping the table with my forefinger.

Che looked at me very seriously. He took out a cigar, passed it under his nose as he smelled it, and offered it to Jack. Looking very embarrassed, Jack pocketed it. He then offered one to Marko, who took it, smelled it, and lit it with a match held by of one of the escorts. For a few minutes, I thought I might have gone overboard in my act of defending the Cuban people. I knew these men were trying to benefit themselves and squeeze Che for more money. I was surprised when Che raised his hand to point at me and speak in my defense.

"You see this kid here who doesn't even shave yet? You need an eighteen-wheel semi to carry his balls. He put himself in the middle of the three-machine-gun shower of bullets to pull me down and save my life today. He has more cojones than his age."

Jack looked at me in astonishment.

I felt proud by Che's defense, but at the same time a little embarrassed. He was exaggerating a bit, and I didn't care for that kind of compliment. Jack and Marko both looked at me in surprise, and Marko exclaimed, "Oh—you are the Commandantico! I've seen you by Fidel many times in his speeches in the Plaza de la Revolución and other places."

I just nodded.

Jack's demeanor changed from one of arrogance and intense scrutiny to a much more pleasant and relaxed one. Perhaps he thought my presence was to represent Fidel and supervise the whole operation. Che told me later that the two of them had developed a little friction earlier.

Jack smiled broadly as he tried to apologize. "I didn't mean to offend you when I asked your age. I was only curious."

I held up a hand and nodded in waving away the offense, but kept my face serious.

Che moved his chair towards me a little, reached out, and patted my shoulder. His hand remained resting there. "You see this boy here? He organized our Juvenile Commandos for the Rebel Army. And he's now going to organize not only the Young Communists but also a group to be the International Young Communists. Those are the ones that will invade America and then the rest of the world with our Marxist philosophy!"

Che took a long puff on his cigar and looked at Jack. "Don't worry—even though this is out of the budget, I will find a way to justify it, someway or somehow." His expression grew emphatic, even a trifle menacing. "But—I want you to warn your friends that if this shit goes wrong, they can go beneath the ocean two thousand miles, and I will still find them, bring them out, and execute every single one of them. As the Commandantico says, no one can fuck around with the Revolution and the money of the people for their own purposes and not what it is destined for. That will make us really angry—everyone will be angry, but particularly me."

I smiled in satisfaction, because there was no doubt that Che had swallowed my pill completely, even to the point of repeating my words.

"Well, gentlemen," he said to Jack as he stood and shook the hands of both men, "you will receive the money on the way out. If everything goes the way it's supposed to, you will have a generous bonus as my personal gratitude for all your service."

Jack smiled as Marko said, "This is a master plan. There cannot be any mistake—everything will follow the course we've charted."

Both men left the conference room after we said our goodbyes and were followed closely by Silvano, Che's large, mustachioed right-hand man. Outside the conference room, Silvano opened a briefcase for Jack, who nodded. I didn't know if that was the entire amount or a goodwill deposit.

It was by now after midnight, and Che asked everyone if we wanted anything to eat or drink. We shook our heads, and he said, "Well, then we should all go to bed. It was a hectic day today, and we have to get up early in the morning to depart for Caibarién and the most important objective of this trip."

We said goodnight to each other and each retired to his own room.

Typical street in Caibarien

Early the next morning after breakfast, we got into our cars and left the city of Santa Clara towards the port of Caibarién. We arrived at what appeared to be a naval base with several warships and some light aircraft carriers. Our caravan drove to a gate that opened into the base. There was an additional checkpoint with a sign next to it that read, "Restricted Area: Authorized Personnel Only."

After the guards identified who we were, one of them

The Havana Conspiracies

ran to open the gate and wave us through. As we passed, they saluted us. The paunchy driver, Fausto Pijirigua, returned the salutes very sloppily and arrogantly, his manners and respect even worse than the cheap cologne that had made the long drive seem even longer. He turned to us and grinned sarcastically, showing his rotten teeth.

We continued behind the first car into the restricted area. We drove into some hills where there was a training camp of marines running an obstacle course—tires, climbing ropes, crawling under barbed wire through mud, drilling with communications equipment, and so on.

We drove through this and entered an aircraft hangar. We stopped at another guard post similar to the previous ones. After we were identified by the lead car, we drove through with the same military honors.

To my surprise, this particular hangar was particularly large and long with doors only at one side. The far end of the hangar stopped at the ocean, with rails and ramps lining berthed submarines. It looked like a huge cave with the few submarines stationed there.

I asked no questions but only observed everything and tried my best to commit to memory every detail of this extremely high-security installation. The only comparison I could draw to this level of security was when I had visited the missile launching sites in Pinar del Rio with Canen. This security was much tighter than even that, and I couldn't help but wonder how much money this installation had cost to build.

I knew all these weapons and all this military equipment had been purchased from the Soviet Union at a very low cost and were here with the ambition to conquer the world in the name of Marxist ideology. But even at that discount, it must have cost the Castros a small fortune, though they shared that dream of global domination.

Che had been silent all this time, and he finally broke it to speak to me. "I see you are in awe of this installation. Impressive, eh?"

I nodded with a smile. "This is something else! I think it's even superior to San Cristobal."

Che nodded. "Bingo! You guessed right."

I looked at him in surprise.

He put his right hand on my shoulder and said, "This is our first nuclear submarine base here in Cuba. We will have several on the whole island with the support of the Soviet Union. We'll soon have another in Cienfuegos." He said this with the shine of greed and the lust for power in his eyes.

"A time will come when we'll run out of money," he continued. "We have too much to invest in order to fulfill our plans and dreams. That is the reason we have to extend ourselves—first into Central and South America. Then, once we've united the rest of the hemisphere with all of their resources, we can conquer our real enemy—the Yankee Imperialist."

I smiled and nodded, and he reciprocated, even more satisfied by my show of agreement.

He smiled cynically. "We have assured the victory in November of that bastard, John F. Kennedy. He'll think he's king of the world, but his reign will be very short-lived."

Entrances to the submarine base

The cars stopped at the ramp nearest the submarines, and we all got out. The naval officer in charge came up and saluted. He identified himself as Richard and told us the base CO would be with us in a few minutes.

We walked through a series of offices. The walls were lined with maps of the world, and naval personnel were all around, manning sonar, radar, and nautical communication stations.

Shortly after we arrived, a man dressed in a Commander's uniform entered. He was in a wheelchair, his body hunched over grotesquely, his legs atrophied from disuse. His teeth were rotten and stained from cigarette smoking. He had dark, greasy hair. He saluted us and addressed Che. "My friend, we were expecting you yesterday."

With a wide smile, Che shook the man's hand and replied, "I almost didn't make it. There was an attempt on my life on the road here, and I had to stop to attend to some business in Santa Clara." He pointed at me. "I owe my life to the Commandantico here. We had a very close shave, Nogueira."

From his wheelchair Commander Nogueira shot me a look that approached jealousy. "Very good—very opportune that he was in the car to save you."

Perhaps it was because Che kept his hand on my shoulder out of paternal affection during their conversation, but Nogueira reminded me of a little kid who was envious of his father showing favor to another son.

"You are very close to Che, are you, to save his life?" He wheeled his chair over to me to shake my hand. "Well, Commandantico. Why don't you save me, and serve me like a pair of legs? Come close to me, and I'll jump on your back. You can be my legs while I give you a tour of the submarines. I'm so skinny that I don't have any weight."

I had every intention of helping him. Che, however, squeezed my shoulder and held me back, smiling tightly. "Don't fuck around with my people Nogueira. You can have one of your guards or assistants do that for you. I want the Commandantico to stay close to me."

I later discovered that Nogueira had allowed his crippled condition to embitter him to the point that he had become the most vindictive of bullies.

"Come on, Che," Nogueira replied. "He's a young horse; let me break him in."

This time, the smile dropped from Che's face, and he said in a deadly serious tone, "I said no! Don't cross the line with this kid, OK?"

Nogueira looked apologetic and summoned one of his men over in resignation. He climbed onto the back of the man, and we walked down a metal ramp and into one of the submarines. It was huge. My God, I thought to myself, this craft is capable of destroying cities, if not even entire countries.

The submarine captain described the vessel as a killing machine, explaining the various mechanisms and the nuclear warheads mounted not only on ballistic missiles but also on wheeled torpedoes designed to attack land-based targets.

Che smiled, "With this kind of equipment, we are at the same level as the gringos. In case of a direct confrontation, we will be on a par with them. The only difference will be who has the cojones to shoot first."

We all smiled and some laughed at that.

You need more than cojones to do that, you moron, I thought. You need brains! In a nuclear confrontation, no one will be left alive to tell the tale.

I realized at that moment that Che was not a particularly smart man. He was a stupid, egotistical maniac like Fidel Castro. I remembered the very savvy words of my maternal grandfather: "You have to have more cojones to hold yourself back from hitting somebody than to throw the first punch. In any conflict, we know how it starts but never how it will end or what the consequences will be. A small aggression can sometimes end the life of the aggressor or the recipient. So why start it?"

I shook my head and smiled.

Che looked at me, taking my expression as

satisfaction and slapped me on the shoulder. "You like it, eh?"

I nodded in agreement.

After the tour, we went down the metal ramps towards some high-speed torpedo boats that were also recent deliveries from the USSR. They were very sophisticated, and they looked much like armored tanks in the water. We rode in them to a small island a short distance away from the base. They had improvised another installation there with a pair of wooden guard towers and barracks made of aluminum. It looked brand new. I thought it looked like a terrorist military camp, and as we walked in, I could see I was not mistaken. There were people from several different nations and ethnic backgrounds, and there was even an amphitheater. The camp was called Lenin Internationalist Proletariat Warriors. I thought this was the most ridiculous waste of money.

We spent several hours there and had a typical Cuban meal in the long mess. The logistical heart of the camp stood to one side—a long, camouflaged building. We went inside, and I could see many huge bulletin boards entirely covered with black tarps. The side of the tarp had fallen away over one of the bulletin boards, revealing the details of the planned assassination of the dictator of the Dominican Republic. His picture and name were written in large block letters at the bottom—Rafael Leónidas Trujillo Molina. The marks on the board included a series of cards with pictures of cars pinned to the board. In the middle of the diagram was a card with Molina's picture, and several marks leading to it. His picture bore a large X, and an arrow pointed towards his head. Another mark bore date of May 30, 1961—over a year in advance. Che was speaking with a man who appeared to be the leader of the group. Their conversation lasted for a long while. I drifted close to the board so that I could casually examine the details. I lifted the card with the dictator's photograph, trying to see how it was affixed to the board.

The leader saw me and came over. "Excuse me, this should be covered." He replaced the tarp.

"No, no, it's OK," I said. "I was just fixing the card."

"Hey, it's OK," Che said. "He's one of us."

The leader looked embarrassed. "I'm sorry—did you want to look again?"

"No, like I said, I was just fixing the card."

I didn't really need to see it again.

Mercenary soldiers training in terrorist tactics

All the men were dressed in camouflage uniforms and carried very sophisticated weaponry. No one, however, bore any military unit or rank insignia.

We stayed there until quite late at night. I took every opportunity to walk around and look for any shred of evidence or information that would give me an idea what plans they had for the sabotage of *La Coubre*. At the same time, I had to make sure I didn't get too far away from Che so I didn't catch his attention or make him suspicious of my prolonged absence.

When we left the camp, I concluded that my judgment upon our arrival had been correct. This was an international camp of assassins. Some were there for money, some for ideology, but their purpose was the same: to execute plans of assassination, methodically and precisely, no matter whether the target was a dictator or the head of state of a democratic nation. The sole purpose of these plots would be to take over and suck the wealth out of a nation or to impose on someone in power who would be at their service.

It was already past midnight when we returned. They took us up the coast along the island, but not back to the base. We tied up at a pier. After we said goodbye to the pilots of the torpedo boats, we went up the pier to the small barracks that were likewise separate from the naval base.

Four or five small rowboats were tied to the pier on the opposite side. I was glad they left us there, as it was closer to the terrorist camp, which would allow me greater access to return that night to look more closely at those boards. I thought I might get lucky and get the details of Che's plans for *La Coubre*.

I knew it was an immense risk if I got caught on that island with its high security, but I had set myself up with an excuse to return. I had "forgotten" my belt with my pistol, knife, and beret on a chair in the camp. It was a poor excuse, but if I were to be caught, it would be better to have a poor excuse than none at all.

I crossed my fingers after I went to bed and waited for everyone else to go to sleep. I prayed to God and His son, Jesus Christ, to give me enough courage to do what I intended to do. When I heard the regular breathing and snoring of the other men, I got dressed and quietly walked to the pier where I had seen the rowboats tied up. I looked up at the sky, searching for any help from God above and found it—the sky was dark with clouds, and in the distance I saw a flash of lightning. The clouds overhead were moving rapidly, covering the stars and the sliver of moon, casting an even deeper darkness over everything. Due to my own slight frame, I tried to pick the smallest boat. It, however, had no oars, so I jumped into the next larger boat that did.

Since we were so separated from the base and we were so far within a high security area, Che had decided not to post any guards. This made my task so much easier, and because we were closer to the island, I wouldn't have to row as far. I looked at my watch and noted the time as 2:30 a.m.

I started to row very slowly and purposefully, as the General and my uncle had instructed me. This way, I conserved my energy in case I needed it on my way back. It didn't take long to get to the island, but it still took longer than I had anticipated—my previous journey had been made in a much faster-moving craft, and so my concept of the distances and time to cover them involved was distorted. I had thought it would take only ten or twenty minutes; instead, it took me nearly an hour.

I found a small, hidden cove in which to conceal my boat. Guided by the lights of the camp, I made my way around the cove, concealing myself in the shadows along the edge. I took some of the branches and used them to cover the boat as best I could. I walked a short distance along the beach and found a small pond filled with stagnant water, rotten algae, and seaweed. I dug down into the goop and scooped up a handful of the black, smelly mess. I covered my face and neck with the noxious muck, not only to conceal my pale skin but to protect myself from the mosquitoes. I washed my hands in the water and started to make my way to the camp.

I walked at a very slow pace, carefully observing my surroundings and watching every step I took. I picked up a few rocks and filled my pockets, keeping a few small ones in my hands. Every time I noticed something abnormal on the ground, I would toss some rocks ahead on the off chance that the abnormality was a landmine or some other explosive perimeter defense. I would then walk up and retrieve the rocks. This method kept me safe, but it was also time-consuming. I knew from experience, however, that it had to be done, as camps such as this were commonly protected by booby traps. Apparently, in this case, they felt secure enough between the island setting and the location deep inside a restricted area that such protections were unnecessary.

When I got to the camp, everyone was asleep. Only two guards were on duty, each in a tower—one to my right and one to my left. I observed them for a while; the guard in the tower on the left was certainly asleep, as he didn't move for fifteen minutes. The one in the right tower, however, was moving around. He had lit a cigarette and continued his patrol. I moved towards the left, even though it was a longer route, as my cove and boat were nearer the right tower. I wasn't very happy with this turn of events, because if I had need for an emergency exit, I was going to have to cross nearly the entire camp to get back to the boat. I decided, however, that it was more important that my entry be undetected, as I might be able to avoid setting off any alarms or needing to make a hasty departure.

I circled the camp and penetrated their final defenses underneath the sleeping guard. Very carefully, I made my way towards the logistics barracks where the bulletin boards were. I explored the exterior, seeking a way to enter the building without making any noise and hoping to find an open window. I reached the back door, gently tried the knob, but discovered that it was locked. I continued my circle, and as I came around to the front, I saw a guard sitting by the door, a machine gun hanging around his neck. He was no surprise to me, because as I had come around the building, I could hear his snoring. What was a surprise, however, was that the front door was standing ajar, a beam of light from within thrusting out along the darkened ground. The gentle breeze was moving the door slightly, the hinges creaking from the motion.

Before I reached the guard, the breeze nearly shut the door. I froze, concerned that the sound of the door slamming shut would wake the guard. I backed around the corner into cover. I knelt on the ground and took off my boots. Carefully, quietly, I crept around the corner and saw that the guard was still sound asleep. I picked a branch up off the ground. Cautiously, I made my way a few inches behind him, past him, and inside the building.

The floor was made of aged wood, and I had to step very cautiously to minimize the squeak of the floorboards. I put the branch under the door and wedged it securely to make sure the door no longer swung in the breeze. I neither wanted the door to slam shut and lock me inside nor the sound of the slam to wake the guard up.

There were several single lamps hanging by their wires from the ceiling, but only one was lit. I checked the wire to ensure that it was secure. I folded up a piece of paper in case the bulb had grown hot and then took the instrument over by each board to light it as I lifted up the tarp on each one to examine what was underneath. To my surprise, I saw that not only General Trujillo had been condemned to death—with the full details and date—but also that Senator John F. Kennedy, Vice President Richard M. Nixon, and all other U.S. presidential candidates running that year were among the heads of state with detailed plans in miniature as to how the assassinations would be carried out. It was exactly as had been outlined in Che's portfolio—only here, it was expanded in scale and detailed more fully. I could also see that these plots were no longer in the planning stages—they were actively in progress, complete with financial details, the projected budgets and actual costs included, and the names of the individuals in charge of each plan. However, they were marked not by full names, but as initials: CJ, TD, JR, TA, ER, and so on.

I realized at that moment that what I was looking for was probably not there. This camp was a strategic headquarters for international assassins on a major scale, and what I was searching for was, to them, of minor importance—more of a domestic category with civilian casualties, diplomatic disputes, and other objectives.

I took my camera pen out of the campaign pocket of my pants and without losing a second started to photograph the bulletin boards and their contents.

I retrieved my belt and my olive green beret, but I stopped. What if someone else had noticed my belongings here? I wouldn't be able to explain how I had obtained them at that point. Not only that, if I were caught with that pen containing those pictures, I would be executed on the spot.

I decided to leave my pistol, knife, and beret there, and not take any unnecessary chances. I left the place, walking slowly to the door.

A loud noise made me duck under one of the tables. I waited in silence to see what had made it. After a short time, my anxiety disappeared, and I rose to slowly creep over to the small window by left side of the front door. The guard had leaned back in his seat against the aluminum wall to make himself more comfortable. I realized that his movement was probably what had made that noise.

Placing one foot purposefully after the other, I squeezed through the door. The wind had picked up, and it had started to sprinkle. The wind blew some mist into my face as I sneaked past the guard, and I halted, assuming that he had been hit as well. I froze immediately beside him, but he didn't wake up—he only brushed his face as if brushing away a fly.

He started to get comfortable in the chair once more, so I stepped down off the porch and stealthily made my way back around the corner where I had left my boots. I put them on and moved back towards the camp perimeter. I watched the one tower to make certain the guard was still asleep.

After watching for a few minutes and detecting no motion, I decided the time had come for me to leave that place, and I made my way past the tower and towards the cove where I had left the boat. I looked at my watch, and noted that it was 4:30 a.m. I pushed the boat into the water and began to row, this time, with more vigor and speed. I was afraid that someone might be awake by the time I got back, and so I weighed my exhaustion against the need to be back in those barracks and in my bed as soon as possible.

When I reached the pier forty-five minutes later and drenched in sweat, I tied the small boat next to the others. It started to rain harder, a light shower. I felt good about that, as it would explain to anyone who saw me why my clothes were so wet; it also was refreshing to feel that cool, clean water coming down after the steam bath my uniform had become.

When I reached the barracks, I was relieved to see that everyone was still asleep; no one was moving around. I took my boots off so that I wouldn't make any noise. With them in my hand, I went into the back where the showers were located. I stopped by my assigned bed where I had my travel bag and took out some underclothes. I then took a shower, and finally breathed deeply, resting my head against the wall, inclining my face up so that the hot water hit it. Finally, I felt my nerves had released the tension from my long night's adventure. I dried myself off and put on fresh clothes.

As I drew near my bed, one of the guards had woken and asked with a smile, "What? You couldn't sleep?"

"Not a wink all night," I replied. "I tried everything, from walking around the entire camp to taking a long, hot shower." I pointed outside. "I even tried to paddle around in one of those row boats. Tell the others to let me sleep, please?"

The guard said, "Don't worry about it, Little Commander. I will tell them not to bother you until you wake up by yourself."

I nodded my head. "Thank you."

"You're welcome. Rest well." He got up and went back to the showers.

I smiled, as I had covered myself completely. I fell into a deep sleep, though I don't know for how long.

Dr. Julio Antonio del Marmol

Chapter 2: A Deranged Commander's Psychosis

Several hours later, I felt something cold on my temple and an uncomfortable weight on my stomach by my waist. To my surprise, I had sitting on my body, practically on my waist, Commander Nogueira, with a revolver pressed against my head.

"What the hell?" I exclaimed, still half-asleep. "What are you doing?" I tried to move my arms but both hands were handcuffed against the bunk. "Where are Che and the others?"

He smiled cynically, flashing his rotten, cavity-filled teeth. "Surprise, surprise—I caught your hands in the cookie jar, you little spy piece of shit."

I looked around and saw that we were alone. He emptied the bullets from the revolver and placed them on my chest. He picked one up and put it into a chamber. He spun the cylinder and said, "You talk and you tell me the truth, or you will die here today, and I will feed you to the sharks. They'll probably enjoy your young, tender meat."

I looked at him incredulously. "What are you talking

about? Is this some kind of joke? You're playing with fire. You're crossing the line."

"No, this is no joke. I'm going to show you in a minute." He placed the revolver against my head and pulled the trigger. There was a click. He pulled it away and spun the cylinder again. I didn't even blink, as I hadn't expected that.

"You think you're going to intimidate me with that piece of shit revolver?" I spat. "You can stick it in your ass—if you still have a functional ass, you son of a bitch! I don't know what kind of game you're playing, but you're going to regret this!" I started to shake the handcuffs on the bed. "You let me go! When Fidel finds out what you're doing to me, you'll regret this for the rest of your life!"

I was trying to think fast and put together what might be behind this, but I realized that this was serious. I couldn't for the life of me determine what this guy might know that would make him do this. Perhaps Che had put him up to it. Had Che seen me come back in the middle of the night? Che certainly was capable of doing something like this as a means of intimidating me.

My thoughts and my struggling stopped as soon as he held up the pen.

"Where did you buy this sophisticated pen?" he asked sarcastically. "Don't tell me you bought it in Chinatown." He spun the revolver once more and placed it against my head.

I screamed this time. "You imbecile! That pen is a present from Fidel, just like my pistol! When I tell Fidel all this shit you're doing right now, you'll wind up in a nuthouse for the rest of your life, you stupid maniac!"

Nogueira laughed sadistically, spraying some of his saliva onto my lips. I tried to wipe the smelly saliva against the shoulder of my t-shirt. He pulled the trigger of the revolver, producing another click. This time I braced myself, as I knew now what he was going to do.

He spun the chamber again, and I was growing ever angrier. I could feel my blood rushing into my face and ears, and I felt like my head would explode from sheer rage. It was as if I had a high fever.

"This time, you're not going to be safe," he said, putting the pistol to my temple again. "Tell me—are you working for the CIA, the Counterrevolutionaries, the Jews, or the mafia? This is your last chance to save your ass!"

I looked him in the eyes and said, "If you don't kill me, you son of a bitch, when I get out of these handcuffs, you will need a dentist. I will take all of your rotten teeth out of your mouth with my bare hands!"

"Goodbye, Commandantico."

I knew he meant it. I could see how deranged he was in the pure malice of his smile. In a gesture of pure desperation, I doubled my legs, which were unrestrained and hit him in the back of the head with my knees. He lost his balance and rolled forward on my chest, so I twisted my body to dump him onto the floor. He landed heavily. The revolver hit the floor. The shock cause the hammer to fall, hitting the bullet that was this time in the chamber. The thunderous boom of the discharge echoed throughout the barracks.

I screamed at the top of my lungs, "I hope that bullet hit you in your balls, if you have any left, you crippled demon!"

I was enraged, but to my disappointment, I saw that he wasn't hit at all. He was crawling along the floor like a rattlesnake towards the revolver, which had landed only a few feet away. To add to my frustration, no matter how hard I tried, I could not squeeze my way out of the handcuffs. He had put them on so tight that, no matter which way I moved, I was in pain. By now, my wrists were growing raw.

I was overjoyed to see the front door of the barracks open, and I saw the silhouette of Silvano. He was surprised and confused by the scene of me restrained to the bed and Nogueira on the floor, slithering his way towards the gun.

"What the hell is going on here?" Silvano demanded of Nogueira. He didn't halt but continued walking towards us.

Nogueira stopped guiltily a couple of feet from the revolver. He hesitated for a few seconds, as if uncertain what he should do.

"Silvano, help me!" I screamed. "This crazy son of a bitch cuffed me to the bed. Look at this! He's been playing Russian roulette with that revolver against my head for the last half hour!"

Silvano was close to Nogueira by now. He looked at me, still confused by what he had walked in on. Clearly, he didn't want to be on Nogueira's bad side.

Nogueira reached out towards the revolver with his right arm. Silvano was a little distracted by watching me, so I screamed, "Don't let him get that revolver! That crazy, paranoid maniac can kill you and then claim he did it in self-defense against something you didn't—!"

I was interrupted by the scream of Nogueira as Silvano stomped very firmly on his hand, which had just grasped the weapon. Silvano looked at me, still with some fear in his eyes. He was searching my face for answers and expecting the worst from this action.

"Don't be afraid of him," I said reassuringly. "This crazy psychotic will kill you and me both if he gets that firearm in his hand. He's been accusing me for the last half hour of being spy for the CIA. He spun that chamber in his roulette game five times. Each time, he held the barrel to my temple and pulled the trigger. Get the keys to these handcuffs, and we'll restrain him until Che comes back and decides what to do with him."

As I spoke, Nogueira pulled a jack knife out of the right shirt pocket of his uniform with his left hand, opened the blade with his teeth and stabbed down on Silvano's boot. Silvano screamed in pain and lifted the foot off of Nogueira's hand. Nogueira grabbed the revolver, raised it and cocked the hammer back—completely forgetting that he had only loaded one chamber with a bullet. The others he had emptied out on my chest and were now scattered around the floor and wedged between the bed frame and mattress as a result of my sudden action.

Silvano froze as he saw the firearm pointed directly at him. Nogueira futilely pulled the trigger, resulting in a loud click.

Now realizing that I had been telling the truth, Silvano used his uninjured foot to kick Nogueira so hard in the mouth that I saw a tooth fly away. The crippled man rolled around the floor in pain, his still-open shirt pocket spilling out his lighter, cigarettes, the key, and my pen.

Silvano grabbed him by the neck and raised him into the air. He whirled and flung Nogueira into the wheelchair that was next to my bed. He stooped and pulled the knife out of his foot, the blade dripping blood, and angrily flung it across the room. He limped over to pick up the keys, hobbled over to the bed, and released me. As soon as I was free, I sprang like a cat over to Nogueira and began to strike him in the face and chest. The madman began to laugh hysterically in spite of my blows.

Silvano stopped me and calmed me down. "No—what are you doing? This man is crazy; he's not all together. He doesn't know what he's doing. Calm down—look at what he did to me," he added, pointing at his bloody foot.

I regained my composure and nodded. Silvano used the handcuffs to restrain Nogueira to his chair. Nogueira continued to laugh but abruptly stopped. He then began to weep loudly and asked both of us to forgive him. He claimed that he had just been joking and wanted to test me to see if I had the guts and machismo to actually save Che's life.

As he spoke, I discretely went over to pick up my pen and replace it in the pocket of my fatigues, hoping that Nogueira wouldn't bring it up again.

I was getting worried. It had been almost two hours since Che had gone and left Silvano behind to watch out for me—two very long hours. That pen was causing me all kinds of anxiety at this point. I contemplated throwing it into the ocean, but I knew that should anyone see me, the act would incriminate me even more. Besides, the information I had in it was too valuable. I thought about tucking it into my boot, but again, if for some reason I was to be searched, a concealed pen in my boot would only show that I was aware of its purpose and the information it contained.

I decided to chance everything and trust that Nogueira's clear insanity would cause the others to dismiss out of hand any accusations he might make towards me and that pen.

When Che finally returned with the others, we updated them as to what had happened. Nogueira started to cry once more, sobbing like an infant.

Che insulted him and called him a number of names. Che's vituperation indicated that this had happened before and that the previous incident had cost the life of Nogueira's assistant. Since there had been no witnesses, they swept the incident under the rug. Unfortunately for Nogueira, I was alive, and now Che had a witness.

"The Devil only knows how many men in your platoon you've done this to," Che screamed. "There have been a lot of mysterious deaths under your command. I will send you to Mazorra, the goddamn psychiatric hospital, you crazy sack of shit!" He raised his right arm in indignation and told the escorts, "Take this deranged psychopath out of my face and put him on the first plane back to Havana."

Che walked toward me as I rubbed my chafed wrists. "I'm very sorry that you had to go through this nasty and unnecessary ordeal. I assure you that this son of a bitch isn't going to see the light of the sun for a long time."

I nodded, pointed at the weapon, and said, "Five times this crazy son of a bitch pulled the trigger with that thing against my head. If I hadn't kicked him out of the bed, that bullet—" I pointed at the hole in the beam against the ceiling—"would be in my brain."

"I know," Che said conciliatorily, "I know. The most important thing is that you're alive and unharmed. Well, except for the scratches on your wrists—we can be thankful that's all you got."

He nodded towards the escort. "Take Silvano to the infirmary and get that foot checked out. We have to leave for the training camp. You two guys should stay here. I think you've earned a mini vacation to rest and recuperate from that terrible ordeal."

I replied, "That's not necessary."

"No," Che said, "you should unwind here. That stress you both just endured can fester and become a time bomb in the future. It's best if you stay here and relax and get the tension out of your system."

I nodded in acceptance. "OK. Would you please bring me some things I forgot in the camp? I left my pistol, knife, and beret there."

"Sure," Che said, "we'll bring them back for you."

They left, and a few minutes later we could hear the engines of the torpedo boat start up and roar as they left the pier.

A little while later, Silvano returned from the infirmary. We both lay in bed and talked for a while about the crazy ordeal we had just gone through. Finally, Silvano asked if I wanted to go get something to eat, as it was around lunch time and he was hungry. We got up and took a jeep to the base mess, stopping first at the laundry to drop off our dirty clothes and grab clean sets.

The food at the mess was horrible: white beans, rice, and a small piece of bread with a fig pastry that was far too sweet. In spite of our best attempts, we simply couldn't eat it.

"You know," Silvano said, "Che said we should relax. Instead of this sarcocho, let's go into town and eat a good steak or a fried chicken, Chinese food, whatever."

I grinned from ear to ear. "Now you're talking my language! You know I like good food, and this I wouldn't even call 'food' at all."

He leaned in and said sarcastically, "This is slave food." He pointed to the other soldiers in line. "I'm not a slave—are you?"

I smiled and said, "No, for sure."

We both stood up, took our trays, and dumped them in the garbage cans. We climbed into the jeep and drove into town.

Caibarién was a small coastal village that had beautiful 18th century colonial architecture and an active cultural life. The two-story buildings with balconies lined by iron railings and planters with bougainvillea and other beautiful flowers made one feel as if one had stepped back in time.

We drove through the narrow cobblestoned streets. We passed fruit vendors and other open air merchants and artisans—remnants of what was once so typically Cuban, in my mind. Some wares had beautiful designs of coral and sea shells, others of equally beautiful artwork.

As we drove, we enjoyed the scenery. We saw some beautiful Cuban ladies with sculptured bodies wearing tight pants showing off their voluptuous forms. They greeted us flirtatiously; it made Silvano very happy, thinking that he might perhaps get lucky with one of them. I thought he was going to break his neck, the way he kept looking at the women on either side.

We continued driving until we reached a restaurant with a sign outside bearing the name Los Cocoteros. At the bottom it read, "Typical International Food. Specialties in Argentinian, Spanish, French, and Cuban."

We parked the jeep in front and got out. As we entered, a very tall gentleman with skin bronzed by the sun received Silvano joyfully as a friend of long standing, asking after his health and inquiring where Che was. Silvano introduced him to me as Alberto.

"You've never been here? Welcome to the Los Cocoteros. We have the best food in town, if not the state." He beamed. "Maybe even in all of Cuba."

Silvano said, "*Afloja, chico, afloja*[1]." Alberto handed a menu to me and was about to hand one to Silvano. Silvano, however, refused it. "You know what I want. Un bistet de palomilla, the juicy steak with fries." He rubbed his stomach in anticipation.

Alberto brought a couple of large glasses of ice water. "You want it with white rice and black beans, or with congri?"

"With congri, please," Silvano replied.

Alberto asked, "Something to drink besides the water?"

---

[1] Relax, man, relax.

"Yes," Silvano said, "*Hatuey bien sudada*[2]."

Alberto smiled. He turned to me, "Young Commander, what would you like to eat?"

"I want the lobster enchilada with white rice and ripe fried plantains."

"And to drink?"

"*Jupiña, muy sudada*[3]." They both laughed at that, and Alberto went into the kitchen with a big smile on his face.

He returned soon after with our drinks, and while we waited for the food, we relaxed and watched the people moving back and forth on the sidewalks outside. There were several windows, some with an ocean view, others overlooking the traffic in the street outside. The chairs in which we reclined were typical Cuban chairs called tahuretes that were made of wood and covered at the bottom with cowhide that still had the hair. From the window where we were seated, we could see everything in the street, the small business vendors crossing by on the narrow sidewalks, selling flowers, vegetables, and seafood. We both sipped our drinks and enjoyed the panorama.

Silvano smiled and said, "We have to say thank you to Nogueira for this mini vacation." He winced as he raised his injured foot. "The most suffering in this whole thing is my foot." He shook his head and continued, "Well, I have to correct that. The one who suffered more is you. I don't even want to think about what it would be like to wake up in the morning with that crazy, maniac son of a

---

[2] A very sweaty Hatuey (a Cuban beer)
[3] A very sweaty pineapple soda

bitch on top of me, find myself tied by my hands to the bed, and then on top of that to have him play with that revolver next to my head."

I smiled sarcastically and nodded with my lips pursed. "Why don't we change the subject? That way, we won't spoil our delicious lunch."

"Very good idea. Thank you for the suggestion. I think the more you stir the shit, the worse it stinks."

We could hear music coming from somewhere—it sounded like a musical band with drums, flutes, and cymbals crashing. We couldn't see who was playing until they started to cross the street in front of us. We saw women crying and some men bearing a coffin on their shoulders. The women were dressed in black with veils and hats. It looked somewhat staged, almost like the wailing was forced. In the middle of this funeral procession walked the family of the deceased carrying floral arrangements on their shoulders by wooden frames. The mourning and screaming seemed to accompany the music. I later learned from my mother that a woman had been hired by the family to cry professionally, to demonstrate to the entire town the pain the family was enduring.

The funeral procession passed slowly in front of our window just as the food arrived and Alberto started to serve us. As he noticed the procession, he crossed himself and said, "*Solabaya por mi casa nunca ballas*[4]."

Silvano looked at him, smiled, and shook his head

---

[4] Death, don't come by my house.

as if making fun of his friend's superstitious remark. Once Alberto left, Silvano said, still chewing his mouthful of food, "Superstitious and ignorant people. There is no Paradise, no Hell. Everything starts right here and ends right here, in one way or the other."

I smiled, shook my head barely perceptibly, and started to eat my lobster. He interpreted this as an agreement of his belief.

"You are very young, but according to Che, you have great intelligence, very mature politics, and ideologically solid roots. You have solid convictions like no one else your age."

I smiled again as I ate my lobster enchilada and thought that this moron could think whatever he wanted. He didn't even know what convictions were, let alone what mine were.

I noticed an elegantly-dressed man across the street, which was unusual in a provincial town such as this. He wore a panama hat with a green bandana. He touched his hat, as if he were sending a signal to someone.

I looked at Silvano; he also touched his forehead, as if he were likewise sending a signal. I couldn't be sure if the man outside could see Silvano, as we were sitting in a half-light, or if Silvano did that instinctively, but as soon as he noticed me looking at him, he jerked his hand away. He attempted to dissemble but rushed his way through the last of his steak.

"Oh," he said suddenly, "I forgot that I promised Che that I would get a box of Monte Cristo cigars for a friend of his. This man has done great work for him, and he wants to reward him with a very nice gift. Do you mind, after you finish your meal, if you could go around and kill some time? I need at least a couple of hours." He winked at me. "I want to see if I can get lucky, even if it costs me a few pesos. I might have enough at least for an hour."

I raised my right arm and said, "Don't worry—go. Take all the time you want. I might go and see if I can find a souvenir of this little town and bring it to a good friend of mine."

He smiled mischievously. "A good friend of yours, or a girlfriend?"

"Well, a little more than a girlfriend, you know. We already did it."

"Oooh, boy! You don't waste any time! That's why you're such a happy guy. And a lot luckier than me, because I have to pay for it. I don't have any time for relationships or sentiment. With all the work the Revolution is dumping on my shoulders, I don't even have time to shave."

He rubbed his hand over the stubble on his face. He looked at his watch. "We'll meet back here in two hours, OK? That way, we're on the same page." He put the keys to the jeep on the table and said, "You take it."

"No, no—you take it. I can walk."

"I'll need it less," he insisted. "I'll be lying in bed. Go around the town, maybe you'll get lucky and get another girlfriend here in Caibarién."

"No, I've got enough with the one I have."

He smiled and stood up. "With that uniform and those stars on your shoulders, you watch out. The women will jump you, especially in this town. I don't know if you've heard, but these provincial girls are more promiscuous and hot than even those in the capital—they just keep it a little more hush-hush out here."

"Sir—I think you're forgetting where I come from. I'm from the provinces, in Pinar del Rio. I know how the provincial girls are!"

He saluted me. "I'm sorry, Commander." He smiled and walked away. I looked over by the door and saw him take care of the bill, point at my table, and hand Alberto some money.

I finished my lobster and got the dessert that Silvano missed because of his rush. I watched him out the window. Once he left my immediate field of view, I picked up my dessert and, still eating it, I followed him from window to window through the empty restaurant, watching him. I knew I was well-concealed, since I was not in a lit area, and they were out in the tropical midday sun. I wanted to see what he was up to.

He approached the man in the Panama hat. Once they felt that they were in a secure place where no one could watch them, they began to talk. The man in the hat appeared very agitated.

I watched them talk for a few minutes until they walked away and I lost them in the crowd. I went back to my table and finished my dessert. Alberto came over to me and said, "Something else you need, Young Commander?"

"No, everything is wonderful, thank you very much. By the way, Silvano give you a good tip? You did a great job, and you gave us very good service."

He smiled at my words with pleasure. "No, no, you don't have to give me anything. Silvano was very generous. Thank you for asking me, anyway."

"No problem. I always say that you should take care of the people serving you properly. That way, they don't spit in your food."

He smiled and chuckled. "No, we don't do those things here."

"I'm just joking with you."

"I know."

I said goodbye to Alberto and left the restaurant. When I came out onto the sidewalk, I could see an elderly blind Asian lady begging for coins next to the jeep. I put both of my hands in my pockets in search of change. I found a little in each and put them together to form a small handful. I walked over and dropped the coins in the aluminum cup. Instead of her saying thank you, she surprised me by saying in a strangely familiar voice, "Julio Antonio—grab my arm and take me with you as if you were going to give me a ride someplace."

Dr. Julio Antonio del Marmol

Chapter 3: Chandee, the Courier of Desperation

I was struck mute and stood there looking at the old lady, wondering how she even knew my name. She looked at me for a moment and then realized my confusion. "Dummy," she whispered quickly, "it's Chandee, Yaneba's friend. Your uncle sent me. He needed a familiar face. This is a life or death emergency, so don't just stand there looking unnatural, like you've seen a ghost."

"Very well," I said out loud, immediately assuming my role. "Don't worry, my lady—I'll take you home at once."

As we walked to the jeep, I muttered through my closed lips, "Why are you calling me dummy when your own mother wouldn't recognize you? I hardly even know you. What are you doing here?"

She just nodded and smiled. She also muttered through her lips, "You never know who may be watching." She held on to my arm with one hand and carried her cane in the other.

She was very good at this act. She didn't even raise her leg to step into the jeep.

"My lady, you have very nice legs," I said impishly as I helped her in. "They don't really go with your body."

She maintained her composure and didn't even crack so much as a smile. Once she was inside the jeep, I arranged her for the trip, and she murmured, "As we say: pretend, pretend—that way, you keep your genitals in the same place."

I smiled, and got in on the other side. I started up the jeep and drove off. "I didn't know you were a comedienne, too."

She gave me directions as we drove, and I joked, "I thought you were blind."

She repeated, "Pretend, pretend. . . ."

We got to the main highway, Carretera Central, which traversed the entire island, connecting the Occidental with the Oriental sides. We continued to drive until she told me to turn off onto a disused, dusty road. We drove a few miles along this road until we arrived at a cabin near the ocean. There was a turquoise and white 1957 Ford Fairlane parked outside.

Dr. Julio Antonio del Marmol

Mr. Xiang's car

She took off her glasses once we were out of the jeep and smiled. "It's a very great pleasure to see you again."

I smiled. "What the devil are you doing here, and how did you know where to find me? And how do you know my uncle?"

Chandee placed her arm over my shoulder. "Calm down—slow down. I will answer all your questions. We've got two hours."

I was flabbergasted. How did she know about my conversation with Silvano? "Let's go inside the house, and I'll explain to you in luxurious detail."

I was still shocked but followed her into the cabin with a mountain of doubts screaming in my brain. My instincts were on high alert, only trusting entirely in two facts: that I knew her and that she was a good friend of Yaneba's.

Yet I still was assuming the worst. I tried to be patient.

Once inside, she closed the door behind us and gestured for me to sit down. She began to remove some of her costume so that I could better recognize her. She went to a small kitchen and started to fry some eggs in an old skillet on the propane range.

"I've brought you two new pens in case yours are full. I can take them back to your uncle and the General. By the way, my father and your uncle are very old friends. They worked together for the same cause a very long time before you and I were born. They sent me because I'm a familiar face. I'm only a messenger. I'm in training. But my dream is to someday be like you—a great spy and freedom fighter."

I shook my head. "There's not too much glamour in that. I've nearly gotten killed twice this week already. But if that is your wish, be my guest. Carry with you a bag of diapers."

She shook her head. "You're a typical man. You think that because you've got a couple of little balls behind your penis, you can handle more. Mine are bigger and inside my stomach—no one can castrate me. Yours are on display for everyone to see. But if you don't like me, it's fine. Let's get to the important thing so that I can get out of here as soon as possible."

I saluted her. "Yes sir, Commander." I patted my epaulette. "I'm forgetting who the Commander here is."

"The important thing here is that we've been penetrated. Your uncle, the General, and everyone believes that the MQ-1 has someone inside our organization. They're still not sure who he is. That's the reason they've immediately changed all of the protocol. Only when this informant is identified and killed will either your uncle or the General be able to talk to you directly again."

She put the eggs on the plate along with some Cuban crackers and came to sit down by me.

"That is great," I said sarcastically.

"I don't offer you this junk, because I know you've had a great lobster enchilada lunch." She elbowed me. "Lucky you."

Then she looked at me seriously. "They've given me strict orders to tell you that for your own security you cannot get close to either one of them. The mission of the agent who's penetrated our group is to either detain or exterminate you. Immediately. 'The Cuban Lightning' has caused too much damage, and they've put you on the highest level of priority. Whatever it costs."

She paused, put an egg on one of the crackers, and ate it.

I had listened to her in silence, confused and not entirely convinced by her story. She was referring to the code name Cuban intelligence had given the spy who had been wreaking havoc on their operations. She was implying—correctly—that I was the Lightning.

There was doubt in my mind that Che or someone else had sent her to test me. I scrutinized her carefully, and she looked at me as she finished chewing. "You don't believe anything that I'm telling you. They've trained you too well, if you don't even believe your own shadow."

"Why do you think I'm still alive and undetected?"

"Go ahead—ask me anything you need to know to convince yourself that what I'm telling you is the truth."

"My first question is, what the hell were you doing in Pinar del Rio with Yaneba during the raping incident with the soldiers?"

"That's an easy one. You should start with the hardest. It's very simple. My father and your uncle took me to Yaneba's house, because they intended to introduce me to you at your sister's wedding. They wanted to have a courier on standby in case of an emergency, like today. I almost lost my virginity to those pigs in the process of meeting you. My father and Josue, Yaneba's father, not only have been friends for years, but they went to the university together.

"Josue doesn't want anything to do with what we're doing, unfortunately. He's put it into his head that by running, hiding, and leaving Cuba to live in another country, he can put all of this behind him, keep his family safe, and put his life back in order. Yaneba, of course, thinks completely differently." She shrugged. "But what can she do? She's too young, and they are her parents. She has to follow them, wherever they're going."

She took two pens out of a money belt she had concealed around her waist. I immediately recognized them as the same type of multi-use pens I had. She removed her wig and put it on the table. She untied her beautiful long black tresses. As she did this, she became more and more recognizable.

She held the pens out to me and asked, "Do you have anything to send to your uncle or the General?"

I was a little more relaxed, but still not entirely trusting her. "I'm going to ask a final question before I answer that. Be careful how you answer." I put my hand on my pistol and stepped back. "What day was I born on?"

She smiled. "The day that your mother almost died."

This time my smile was genuine and broad as she gave the correct response to the code my uncle and I had worked out. I relaxed and took my hand off of my pistol. I took one of the *taburete*[5] and sat down in front of her. I took the pen I had out of my pocket and handed it to her.

"When you give this to my uncle and the General, tell them that there's nothing in here yet about that ship, *La Coubre*. I don't think I'm going to find more on that here—but what's in here is unexpected and much bigger: detailed corroboration of many of the assassination plans we already have of international leaders, including the North American presidential candidates, Senator John F. Kennedy and Vice President Richard M. Nixon. It's no longer in the planning stages but is actually in process. Exactly as our information and documents indicate, I've already confirmed and met two of the doubles who will execute this plan. The third one is the last piece in the puzzle—I just haven't met him yet. It should be pretty soon, I expect."

"I will inform them exactly what you've told me. But, please—be very careful. Silvano is not a typical assistant to Che. He is a very dangerous man—even Che doesn't know who he really is. He is a spy for Fidel and is the one tapping all Che's movements and informing Fidel. On top of that, he is the chief of the MQ-1."

The MQ-1 had been created by Fidel as a special elite unit of assassins to operate all over the world. Their

---

[5] Stool

agents track down Cuban dissidents on foreign soil and execute them so as to make it look like an accident to avoid international incident. Their target and specialty is to destroy anyone who creates any embarrassment or problem for the Cuban government.

"The mark for their targets is placed by Silvano," Chandee continued. "That is the reason your uncle and the General are worried sick. This man is ten times, if not a hundred times, more dangerous than Che is. He keeps Fidel updated on everything Che does, including what he's trying to keep hidden from Fidel. Fidel keeps Silvano on a short leash, using him as a guard dog on Che's ass."

She went to the refrigerator in the kitchen and took out a Materba soda pop. She opened the bottle and took a long drink.

"I knew Silvano was more than Che's assistant," I replied. "I'd been wondering who gave him the power to dress out of military uniform. But I never imagined he was so highly placed and dangerous." I smiled and said, "God works in mysterious ways. The crazy Commander Nogueira gave me a huge scare, and then he stabbed Silvano in the foot. That's the reason he's limping—it's God's punishment for Silvano's murders and felonies."

"What-what-what-what?" Chandee asked. "What are you talking about?"

I told her the details of the incident. She was shocked even as she seemed impressed by how I had handled it.

"Thank God the guy is completely deranged," I said.

Dr. Julio Antonio del Marmol

"Not only is his body paralyzed, I think his brain is, too. I was worried sick until Che showed up." I picked up one of the pens. "He mentioned the pen, and if he had told Che about it and it had been opened up, I wouldn't be talking to you now. It was a very close call."

She bit her lip and shook her head. "Just to be close to these people is dangerous. If one isn't crazy, he's a murderer or a professional assassin. But it looks like everyone has some mental sickness."

I smiled. "You don't even know how true that is. All of these people are not all together."

She looked at me gravely. "You know what? I have a deep admiration for you and what you're doing right now. You're very young. I don't see any adult men that could go through what you've been going through and not crack, to have the courage to let a crazy maniac shoot a revolver at you five times without giving up the game. I cannot conceive how you can wake up every day, surrounded by your worst enemies, and still look like a normal person and not lose your smile or your serenity."

I shook my head in resignation. "I have to be a great actor and stay exceptionally calm. Every occasion could be my last act or the end of my life."

She nodded her head with a sad expression.

"I know you've already put to rest my small doubts, including knowing the personal code that my uncle and I have between us," I said. "But I still have a small curiosity."

She smiled and said, "Well, it's good for you to feel relaxed and to know I'm your friend who will be there whenever you need me. God only knows when we'll discover this double agent infiltrating us. Until then, however, I will be your only contact with the external world. Why don't you go ahead and ask your final question and satisfy your curiosity?"

I looked at her carefully to note in detail her reactions. I fixed my shirt a little bit and said, "How did you know Silvano and I had agreed to meet in two hours? The restaurant was completely empty when we discussed that."

She smiled and said, "You haven't guessed?"

"No! Don't tell me it's Alberto?"

"Bingo! He is one of us. That place is one of Che and Silvano's favorites—they've got Argentinian food. I had been waiting for days for you to arrive and then waiting for the opportunity to communicate with you. And voila! My luck couldn't have been better, as if I had planned it myself."

"Now it makes sense to me," I said thoughtfully. "The contact who spoke with Silvano had been waiting for Silvano the same way you've been waiting for me, to hear the details of Che's trip. Fidel is probably anxious to hear about the meeting with the man in charge of the operation to kill whoever becomes the U.S. president. I still wonder why Silvano didn't want me to know that he was meeting with that man. He created all this confusion with his abrupt departure, his story about prostitutes, and so on—doesn't he trust me? I'm going to have to walk on ice around him from now on."

Chandee shook her head. "Classic—very classic from these people. He could create any excuse at all; why did it have to be sex with prostitutes? What a great example to a young man like you."

"You're forgetting, Chandee. Most of these people are low-lives without any class at all. If I had to pay a woman to have sex with her, I would cut this off," I said, pointing to my groin. "Sex is a combination of spirituality, harmony, and beauty. It's like a musical composition: to enjoy it at maximum pleasure, it has to be original and clean, with the essence of order which creates an ecstasy of pure intoxication. Sex with a prostitute has none of those ingredients."

"Whoo!" Chandee exclaimed in surprise. "That is the most beautiful thing I've ever heard in my life. On top of being a brave gentleman, you are a romantic poet. You are very sweet. That is the reason Yaneba is crazy about you." She stroked my face with a hand in admiration and affection.

I blushed a little at her compliments.

"Ho, ho! I got your color up," she teased. "You don't take compliments well, eh? You are something special, because you are also modest. What other good qualities do you have that I don't know about?"

This time I smiled. "Ah, ah, ah! You're not going to get me to blush again. The first time, you caught me by surprise, but now I know it's coming. I'm not going to let you do that again."

"No, that's not my intention, I swear. But you are very sharp." She patted me on my shoulder. "You prepare for everything, don't you?"

I pointed at my watch. "The conversation is beautiful and very pleasant, but I think we're running out of time."

She pouted jokingly. We stood up and she gave me a strong hug, saying in my ear, "Take care of yourself.

You're becoming the hope of many young men and women in this country."

"Thank you, but you're not going to get me to blush again. By the way, it's good that nobody knows who I am and I keep myself incognito. If by any chance I get killed in a fight, somebody else can assume my identity, and the Cuban Lightning can continue his legacy."

She pushed me away a little and placed a finger on my lips. "Shhh, please! Don't say that, not even as a joke."

"I'm not joking at all."

Her eyes grew misty. She drew near and surprised me with an unexpected kiss on the lips. She stepped back, and this time she was the one to blush. I didn't say a word so as not to embarrass her but stroked her face in a similar manner as she had stroked mine and said, "Don't worry, I know you mean love and friendship. I'll see you soon."

I went back out to my jeep, got in, and drove back to the main highway. When I arrived at the restaurant, I saw Silvano was already back and sitting at the same table. He had beside him an extravagantly decorated box of Monte Cristos—it looked specially designed and crafted for affluent foreign customers.

I walked in and said, "Wow! I've never seen such a fancy cigar box."

Silvano smiled and said, "Yes, it cost me a pretty penny. I found it in a store that specializes in exporting goods."

"Well, I stopped in a small store, and look at what I

found: two small pictures of Caibaríen carved in cedar wood, decorated with marine kelp and seashells. I bought two—one for my mother, and the other for Yaneba."

Silvano loved the pictures so much that he made me take him back to the place where I had bought them so he could get one for himself. When we returned to the naval base, we found that Che and the others had already returned. They had taken showers, and I could see my pistol, knife, and beret lying on my bed. I decided to take a shower myself.

Afterward, we went to the mess for dinner. Once we were finished, Che told me he needed to speak to me in private.

We walked out on to the pier. He placed his hand on my shoulder and lit one of his cigars. "I need to ask you a big favor." We crossed over by the row boats.

He inhaled on the cigar deeply and said in a dramatic voice, "I need you to go back with Silvano to Havana. I need you to corroborate what happened here today. I don't want this crazy idiot to fill Fidel's head with shit about suspicions that you are a spy or some other crap about Silvano to justify his irrational attitude. I've already told Fidel and Raul several times that this man is unreliable, psychotic, paranoid, and dangerous, and I suspect many of the people who've died under his command were killed by his hand.

"But Nogueira is a very good friend of Raul. They were very close in the fight in the mountains, and when he got shot in the back and paralyzed, Raul worked very hard to get him this position."

He threw his hands in the air. "Who knows what else

has gone on between those two? You know how these things are—Raul is Fidel's brother, so Raul can make mistakes and never have a problem. But if one of us does something, then he'll scream and cuss at us as if he is the only one who is perfect." Che grew more agitated and angered as he went on. "You understand?"

"I understand you perfectly, loud and clear."

"Fidel is very fond of you, and I know he trusts you very much. It will make a big difference if you go with Silvano and tell Fidel in detail what happened here. Especially when he sees Silvano's wounded foot."

Of course, I couldn't tell Che that I knew Silvano would have no problem convincing Fidel. I felt a great deal of joy, however, to return to Havana, since I knew Che had been planning to stay for two or three weeks in Caibarién. There was not much more I could accomplish in this small town. Perhaps the answer I was looking for regarding *La Coubre* would be found in Fidel's offices.

I rubbed my face and said, "When did you want me to go back?"

"Tomorrow morning, very early. Nogueira is already there, and I called Fidel on the phone this afternoon. I told him that you and Silvano would be there tomorrow to sign the statement so they can put this crazy moron in the psychiatric hospital. He told me he wanted to talk especially to you."

"No problem. We'll leave early in the morning. Just tell Silvano and arrange everything."

"Thank you very much."

"No reason at all to thank me," I said. "It is a great pleasure. No one suffered more in this than I did, and I will tell Fidel in every detail what that son of a bitch did to me."

I wanted to get out of there because I couldn't stand the smell of that cigar. "If you don't need me for anything else, I'm going to go to bed now so we can get up very early. If you'll excuse me. . . ."

"Yes, yes—go now. I will see you when I get back to Havana in a few weeks."

"I hope you accomplish everything you need to do here. Have a good evening."

With a wave, I headed back towards the barracks. I had a huge smile on my face, and I breathed a deep sigh of relief. Everything had been resolved in my favor without any major complications.

I was ready to depart at 4:30 the next morning. It was still dark when Silvano and I left the base for Havana. Several hours later, we arrived in the capitol, and we went straight to Fidel's office. They informed us that Fidel was in the luxury beach resort of Varadero attending a meeting of foreign dignitaries and investors, but he would return the following evening. He had left instructions that he wanted to meet with us at 8:00 the next evening.

We had only had a couple of sandwiches on the road, and I was hungry. However, when Silvano asked if I wanted to have dinner with him, I refused, stating that I wanted to visit some family and friends in the city.

We returned to Che's office. Silvano told me to take the jeep with me and that he would take one of the new Russian models, a car called the Volga. They were available only to the top executives and those in charge of the bank bureaucracies. We agreed to meet the next evening at 7:00 in Che's office and then go together to the meeting with Fidel.

After we parted, I drove to the house of one of my uncles, who was an attorney. He had lost his job after his law firm had been nationalized. Since he never performed the "voluntary" work that was required of all employees of nationalized businesses in Cuba, they demoted him from a legal department manager to a courier. He was a little older and had some money to get by, so he gave his resignation and told them what they could do with that job.

I had called when I got into town, and he invited me to dinner. They were waiting for me when I arrived in Havana. The traffic in the capitol was beginning to disappear due to the number of people leaving the country. The streets were emptier each time I visited. Even though the Castros had not officially declared themselves as communists, those who were politically savvy knew which way this was going and so were leaving and taking their money with them.

My uncle lived on Avenue Carlos III, and I drove along slowly, looking for their house. The undeniable reality of what was happening was visible along these roads, as I could see business after business closed up, and fewer and fewer trucks moving merchandise and goods around the capitol. The beautiful Havana was dying; it was like a coma patient, sustained only by IV tubes. That horrible traffic that had irritated us for so many years now seemed beautiful, a symbol of prosperity and plenty under the capitalist democracy that had existed in that lovely Cuban capitol.

I shook my head in discontent as I drove along and asked myself how much resentment must the Castros have in their hearts against that established society, when everything they were doing was slowly and inevitably destroying that previous social structure. It had cost so much blood, going back to the 18th century, when my great-grandfather fought with so many others to free Cuba from Spanish colonial authority.

Evidently, the Castros were mediocre individuals, lazy bandits. They didn't start that beautiful Revolution, supported by 90% of the population, to remove the Dictator. They were instead conniving to establish arbitrary laws and take away all the wealth from the existing inhabitants, labeling those who had accumulated wealth as "fat cats" and "bad people." They enslaved that class of people and slept in the silk linen sheets of those who had worked all their lives to obtain them.

I thought of all this and realized that I had passed the 18th century Castillo del Principe. The Revolution had converted this building into the biggest political prison in Cuba, with men like Huber Matos imprisoned for twenty years and even more unfortunate men getting sentences of up to fifty years, all on fabricated charges, simply because they disagreed with the government.

My uncle's house was only a couple of blocks further. I parked the jeep out front and looked at the two great lion statues seated on top of columns on either side of the gate on the front porch. I smiled at those symbols of the union of the two prominent families in Cuba: the Leones and the Marmols. The Leones were the family of my Aunt

Violeta, who had married my Uncle Francisco, or Pancho, as we lovingly called him.

I looked at that beautiful colonial mansion and thought about how much work and history had gone into its construction. The residence wasn't simply a material thing; it was also a representation of honesty, decency, and cooperation between those two families, built and maintained through respect and the prestige and honor of their last names.

Today, the new dictator had the audacity to insult them and call them the maggots of society. I shook my head once more as I thought about the injustice of it all, how much indecency and jealousy was shown in such sentiments.

I rang the bell outside the huge double gates. Aunt Violeta opened the door, a huge smile on her face. "Julio Antonio, how good to see you!" She was in her forties with long black hair beginning to grow gray. She was pleasant-looking with white skin and perfect teeth. Her smile reflected her beautiful personality.

She gave me a hug and a kiss on each cheek as I came in. She held me out and looked me up and down. "My God, you're becoming a man in front of our very eyes! How long has it been since we've seen each other?"

My balding uncle came up behind her, smiling. He pushed her gently to one side, impatient to see me, as well. "At least two or three years, Violeta," he answered for me. "With all of this convulsion surrounding the Revolution—but for God's sake, stand back and let him come in! We'll have all the time in the world to talk about details inside the house. Thank God we still have that! I don't know how long that will be. One of these days, the Revolution and the Castros will accuse us of being thieves or something, and we might find ourselves in our old age sleeping in the central park, covered with newspapers."

Violeta stepped away a little and turned to him to slap him in the chest. "Why don't you keep your mouth shut? Don't say those kinds of things. We've never stolen from anyone, neither your family nor mine." In fact, they had given thousands, if not millions, to the poor, and their family had founded the first free infant clinic in Havana for the needy.

My uncle smiled as we walked into the house. He closed the door and pointed to the prison. "Go over there and ask those guys spending twenty, thirty, or fifty years in there, and ask them if they ever stole anything or what they had done wrong, and see what they have to say!"

My aunt looked at him in shocked anger, tapped her head and gesticulated in astonishment as she indicated me in my uniform. "What are you saying!? Look at your nephew! He's dressed as a military officer—look at his gun! Do you want him to come back and visit us again, or do you want him to turn around and not even have dinner with us?"

My uncle lowered his head in partial repentance. "I'm sorry—but you know how we Marmols can't keep our mouths shut when we see injustice. We don't always realize that it could be offensive to others."

We walked through the long salon into the back of the house and sat down in the dining room. My aunt already had set out a couple of jars of orange juice and lemonade. "What would you like, Julio Antonio? We have these, or I can open a can of tomato juice."

"No, no," I replied. "This is fine."

She had a bucket of ice on the table, put some cubes in it, and filled it with lemonade.

"Thank you," I said as I accepted the glass.

"What nice manners! Your mom and dad did a great job in raising you." She asked my uncle, "That's the second time he's said thank you. Isn't that nice?"

My uncle nodded and grunted assent.

I took my beret off and placed it on the table next to me. "It's a great joy and sadness at the same time to see you tonight," I said. "Joy, because I love you and haven't seen you for a long time. Sadness, because we've spent such great times together, and things have changed so much in only a few years. I really, from my heart, was not even expecting to have dinner with you tonight. I appreciate very much the opportunity to share this with you. I have such great memories of both of you from when I was a little boy, before I could even speak. You were always so generous with me and with all my brothers and sisters. Whenever you visited, you would shower us with toys and gifts, and whenever you left, we always wanted to see you back right away."

Violeta grinned. "You probably don't remember, but when you were three or four years old, as we were leaving your house, you said, 'Take them, wind from the storm!'"

"No, I don't remember, but I've heard that so many

times in my house that it seems I do." We all smiled. "Remember that incident when, just after I could speak, I said, 'Go with the wind of the storm and don't come back.' It was probably something I heard from some adults, and repeated it without even knowing what it meant.'"

She laughed and said, "I knelt down after you said that and said, 'You couldn't mean that to me, after all the toys I've brought you? You don't mean Violeta, do you, my lovely Julio Antonio—you meant Pancho, didn't you?' And you looked at the sky, and then at your parents—who looked scared at what you were going to say—and you said, 'And Violeta, too!'"

We all laughed.

I said, "My parents never allowed me around visitors after that. Anytime we had someone important come over, they made sure I was sent to visit a friend or family member elsewhere. They never knew what I was going to say next!" We all laughed. "That's why you have to be very careful about what you say in front of little kids. They're like little sponges, and they pick up both the good and the bad. I don't remember where I'd heard that, but I'm sure I heard them say that about someone else, and I thought it was something someone says to everybody!"

My uncle replied sarcastically, "Tell that to the leaders of this Revolution."

My aunt looked at him reproachfully. "Pancho!"

He looked at her and nodded sadly. He raised his arm and was about to apologize, but I interrupted him. "You don't have to apologize for speaking the truth. Remember what our great patriot, José Martí, said: the word is created to speak the truth, not to cover it up."

The looked at me in astonishment. Neither one of them had expected to hear that from me, dressed as I was in my uniform. They hadn't seen me since the beginning of the Revolution, and here I was with a .38 at my side and having been seen on television several times with Fidel and other government leaders.

Pancho smiled broadly at my statement, but still with caution in his voice he asked, "How is your father? Does his still have his business, or has the government taken it away from him yet?"

I smiled. "He is very well, health wise; but he is completely blind and brainwashed by this Revolution and its leaders. He's completely clueless as to what this government wants to do with Cuba. Eventually, he will lose everything he's been working for all his life. I feel really sorry for Papi, because in the end the Revolution he's worked to create and support will steal the fruit of his work and sacrifice."

I sadly took a sip of my lemonade. I looked at them, and saw they were looking at me like they were seeing a ghost. I was being completely open and sincere with them, but the psychological terror that had been created by the government in only a couple of years caused them to look at me in fear and mistrust. That bothered me, because they had known me ever since I had been born. Evidently, the more I showed my feelings, the more withdrawn they were going to be. They were probably thinking of the many stories we had heard of children accusing their parents of disloyalty to the Revolution and getting the parents imprisoned for long terms.

I felt terrible, watching their confusion and distrust of me. For that reason, I continued to make an effort to convince them that I was not their enemy and meant no harm to them. I leaned back in my chair, got comfortable, and said, "On the trip back from Caibarién with Che a few days ago, we went through a huge ordeal in which I almost lost my life. Just by instinct, I saw it coming before they did, and I pushed Che down, saving his life. If I hadn't done that, Che would be dead now. For the first time in my life, I question whether I had done the correct thing or not. It might have been better had I not saved his life and let him be killed for all the horrible things he's been doing in Cuba. I have to wonder if I'm letting myself get to be a bad person, too, and let my hate and resentment control me to the point where I become one of them."

My aunt pushed her chair back and stood up. With tears in her eyes, she put her arms around me and gave me a tender hug. "No, no! Never should you say that! You are one of us, and we are all good people—men and women with dignity and full of love and compassion, not only for our family, but for everyone. We are on the side of the good and beautiful in this world. Never let yourself have even the smallest doubt that what you did was right. You did the Christian thing—you don't let him or anyone die if you can prevent it. Don't worry, Che will find his destiny. Remember my words very well—his death will be a violent one, exactly like his character and personality. Violence breeds violence. If that happens after I leave this world, you remember this for the rest of your life. The Bible says it very plainly: 'Those who live by the sword die by the sword.'"

I nodded and rubbed my forehead with my fingers. "I cannot forget the faces of those three men and that woman who died in the failed attempt to kill him. Those poor people did what they thought was best to get rid of this horrible guy, and they met a horrible death."

My aunt hugged me again, this time harder. "My poor boy, Julio Antonio. What a horrible way to go through adolescence. You should be enjoying music and being with your friends at parties. And you have to go through all these horrible and sad experiences. God must have a very important reason to guide you along this road, to make you stronger physically and spiritually. He might be preparing you for something huge and sublime. But we should not talk about any more sad things. If you're hungry, I'll serve dinner."

I rubbed my stomach. "Hungry? I'm starving! I've only eaten a sandwich all day!"

She smiled and started to serve the food. I said in a voice of very strong conviction, "I cannot tell you very much about what I'm doing or what I'm involved in, for your security and mine. I've learned that what you don't know, no one can force you to talk about, even if your life depends on it. But I can guarantee you one thing: on the honor I've inherited from you and keep within, I'm very proud of myself and all our family. I don't want to leave any doubts in your minds what I feel in my heart. I don't want to hate anyone, because it's not good for the spirit."

My uncle nodded. I leaned back so that my aunt could put down a plate of food in front of me. "I want to make very clear that I believe in Jesus Christ, I don't like what this government is doing to Cuba, and I will do everything in my power to bring these people down."

They both looked at me in frightened astonishment. My aunt tried to change the topic. "I hope you like the chicken fricassee I made."

"If it tastes like it smells, it must be delicious. But to continue my point," I pointed at my chest, "this uniform might be the first experience of hatred I've had in my life. What this uniform represents is completely contrary to what I believe in. I still have it on because it's convenient to the work I've been doing, and only because of that do I still wear it. I have a strong, unbearable desire to rip it off all the time, throw it on the floor, stomp on it, set it on fire, and watch it burn to ashes. I believe that day might be the happiest day of my life." My expression was sad, and my eyes had grown misty. I bit my lip.

Pancho slowly shook his head in amazed compassion. "I never imagined even in my wildest dreams the tremendous pain and the cross you carry on your shoulders, dragging it with you even when you don't want it. I'm sorry—I have to apologize to you, because I might have doubted you in some moments. There's no denying that you are a Marmol, with the greatest integrity. No doubt, you have in your veins your great-grandfather's blood, and your father made no mistake when he decided among all three of his boys to choose you to bear the name Donato, even though they call you Julio Antonio. Look at your birth certificate."

"I know," I said.

"Your father saw your spirit, even before you could speak or crawl. That is why he gave you that name."

My aunt stood up and hugged me again compassionately. "My boy, my boy—how much pain you must have to bear! Remember we are here for you, any time you need us. Jesus has been with you and kept you safe and sound, and has given you the energy to continue doing whatever you've been doing—which I do not want to know. But I know that whatever it is, it is good not just for yourself, but for everyone, because there's not a single bad hair on your body. Your spirit is pure and clean as the water in a mountain creek."

To hear this from them after their doubts of me, I completely broke down. They finally understood who I was, and two tears rolled down my cheeks. She saw that and wiped one tear away. "Go to the bathroom and wash your face with cold water. That will take all these bad things out of your head. Talk to Jesus for a few seconds in the bathroom. You will get back your tranquility. You are completely secure here. We love you so much, and you won't have to fear any evil. Nobody can touch you here."

I nodded, pushed back my chair, and prepared to go into the bathroom. Before I left, I said, "Thank you, very much." She took my hand and gave it a squeeze, and then I left.

I washed my face with cold, clean water. I breathed deeply and closed my eyes. I massaged my temples and tried to calm down. Evidently, all the tension from that trip, including the assassination attempt on the highway, Che's plans, Nogueira, and Silvano's spying for Fidel had taken a toll on my system, and I had become emotional. But I remembered my training from my uncle and the General and knew that emotion was a luxury we cannot afford in our line of work. If we allow emotion to take control of us, we would become vulnerable and die.

I raised both arms, closed my eyes, laid my head back, and tried to release all the tension. I left the bathroom and came back to the table with a smile on my face. "This was a remedy I didn't have any knowledge of before. From now on, whenever I'm dealing with tension, I'll remember my Aunt Violeta and the love with which she suggested it to me. I feel a lot better."

Violeta smiled at my compliment. She patted my chair. "Come on—the food is going to get cold. Let's eat."

After we finished dinner, we went into the living room. They had a large wall unit with a television and a stereo. My uncle said, "Let's see if we're lucky tonight and there's something to see on TV that's not Castro talking." He waved his finger in the air in a mockery of Fidel's customary gestures.

He turned the TV on and sure enough, one of the famous anchormen, German Pinelli, was giving an interview with Che. My uncle changed to the other channel, which showed a speech by Fidel in the Plaza de la Revolución. He turned off the TV and looked at me in irritation. "These guys—even when you don't order the soup, they serve you the soup. And you'll find them in the soup! Well, let's listen to some Classical music. It will be good to relax to after dinner."

He pulled out a record of a selection of Chopin's music and put it on the stereo. The Revolutionary Étude was the first thing to play. My uncle smiled at me. "Oh, my

God! We even have the Revolution with Chopin!"

I smiled. "At least Chopin has merit—he had musical talent!"

He smiled and said with mock seriousness, "We are very much in agreement!"

I asked my aunt if I could use their phone.

"Of course. Come into the library where you'll have more privacy."

I sat in a very comfortable chair in the library and dialed the number for the Pan American Pier. It wasn't that late, and I was hoping to find Lazaro in the union office. Somebody with a very deep voice answered. "Union Stevedores of the Port—can I help you?" He sounded like a mafioso.

"Compañero, I'm looking for Lazaro Zardiñas."

"Yes, who wants him?"

"Commander Julio Antonio del Marmol," I said in a very firm voice.

His voice changed immediately from a harsh tone to a very friendly one. "Oh! Of course, Commandante. Can you wait for a few minutes? He's taking a group of volunteers to the boat *La Coubre*, because they're unloading a very important cargo from the ship. I can get you on a radio with him."

"It's no problem—I will wait."

I could hear the sound of the receiver being put down on the table and the sound of him speaking with Lazaro on the radio.

"*Jefe*[6], I have the Commander Julio Antonio del

---

[6] Boss or chief

Marmol on the phone for you."

"Tell him to hold on," I heard Lazaro say over the radio. "I'll be in the office in five minutes."

The voice of the mafioso was still accommodating. "Commandante, it will only take about five minutes, eh? Do you want to wait or call back?"

"No, I'll wait."

"Don't hang up, OK? I'm going to put the phone down."

"OK," I replied. I shook my head and smiled cynically at the man's volte-face. I was a little irritated by the sudden friendliness of the guy. It was clear that this guy was one of the communists Lazaro used to keep control of the piers.

Finally, Lazaro came on the line. "Hello? Hello? This is Lazaro."

"It's the Commandantico. How are you?"

"Very well, thank you. Where are you?"

"I'm here in Havana. I'm in the house of some family in Carlos III. I just came back from a trip to Santa Clara with Che, and then I have a meeting tomorrow night with Fidel, but I wanted to take the occasion to stop by and say hello to you and Daniel."

"Oh, that will give us great pleasure. Where are you staying tonight?"

"I don't know yet—the night is still young."

I could hear his smile in his voice. "You should come and stay with us tonight. Daniel will be very happy to see you. He's been really distant and sad, and I think it's because he's missing his mother and grandmother. I won't be back until very late, because I'm waiting for another group of volunteers that won't arrive for several hours."

"Thank you for the invitation. Very well, I will tell my family that I will stay with you guys, and they shouldn't wait for me tonight here."

"You have the directions?"

"Yes. Daniel's mother gave them to me."

"Well, I may get home late, so if I don't see you tonight, I'll see you in the morning before I return to work. It's a huge surprise you'll be giving to Daniel, and he needs to see a friendly face. Thank you for remembering us."

"Very well. I will leave at this moment."

"OK. You have a good night, and please tell Daniel to take his medication before he goes to sleep."

"Is he sick?" I asked in concern.

"No, he's not been able to sleep lately. I took him to the doctor, who said he has anxiety, probably due to separation from his mother."

We said goodbye and I hung up, happy that I had established contact with them. After all, nothing had happened yet; perhaps I was still in time to save the lives of my friend and his father, or perhaps even find a way of preventing their deaths without blowing my cover. With a smile on my face, I left the library and went to join my aunt and uncle as they sat in reclining chairs, listening to Chopin and drinking some Cuban espresso.

My aunt said, "You want to have some coffee, my nephew? I don't know who you were talking to, but I see that you're very happy. It must be a good friend that can so change your mood tonight."

I smiled and said, "Well, I spoke with the father of a friend of mine, the one who used to be my chauffeur in Pinar del Rio. But he moved down here, and I haven't seen him in a long time. They invited me to stay the night with them, as it's been such a long time since I've seen him. It'll be a great pleasure to see him tonight, since he wasn't just my chauffeur, he was also my best friend."

"Well, it's a pity you're not staying with us tonight, but perhaps tomorrow you can stay here. That will make you feel very good. To talk to an old friend will dissipate your emotions. By the way, are you going to have a coffee before you leave?"

"No, thank you—if I take a coffee now, I don't think I'll sleep all night. Even though it's strange for a Cuban to say no to a coffee."

"Unfortunately," my aunt said, "I'm hooked on the caffeine. Even though my doctor says I should stop drinking it, I can't. Don't let it happen to you."

I smiled. "I cannot give myself the luxury to have any kind of dependency. What if I one day end up on a desert island? Then I'll have to worry more about my need for a coffee or something other than food and water. That would make my survival a lot simpler, don't you think?"

She smiled. "I never thought of that, but maybe you're right."

After we hugged each other, both of them accompanied me out to the front porch where we said our goodbyes, but not before my aunt told me several times to be careful and not to do anything that would cause me problems. I smiled and thought, If she only knew.

The Havana Conspiracies

Chapter 4: *La Coubre*, the Deadly Trap

The mansion given to Daniel's father, Lazaro

I drove to the address where Daniel lived in the beautiful seaside area of Miramar. This was a very wealthy area where the majority of the rich people lived, and Daniel and Lazaro lived on 9th Avenue. I crossed the city by the Malecon to find the number. When I got to the house, I parked the jeep in the street and walked to the massive gate, beyond which lay vast gardens. I pushed the intercom button. The lovely tone of the bell echoed throughout the place, and I thought the music very nice.

A few seconds later, Daniel's voice asked, "Who is there?" through the intercom.

I pressed the button to speak. "Your Commandante, Julio Antonio del Marmol."

"Oh, my God!" he laughed. "I cannot believe it!" The buzzer on the gate sounded. "Push on the gate really hard, because the automatic motor is broken."

I pressed the button and replied, "Don't worry about it."

I pushed on the large gate and walked into that extraordinary garden filled with coconut trees, exotic flowers, bougainvillea, jasmine, and tropical fruit. The scent brought to mind the memory of my sister's wedding and the beautiful moment of my first experience with Yaneba in the jasmine gardens.

I walked onto the sidewalk made of different colored flagstones and past a neglected water fountain. In the reflection of the flood lights in the ground, I saw Daniel coming towards me in silhouette.

"What a surprise you've given to me!" he exclaimed.

I smiled and we hugged in sincere friendship and affection. I looked over his shoulder at the opulence of the slightly neglected gardens. They had maintained their majesty and grandeur. There were Romanesque statues of Julius Caesar, Marc Anthony, and Cleopatra. I smiled once more after we separated and looked around at the ostentation surrounding us.

Daniel put his arm over my shoulder. "I believe Jesus Christ sent you to us tonight."

"Really?" I answered.

"No, believe it—I'm very sure."

Chills ran through my body. They started in my feet and climbed through my body up to my head. I shook my head slightly.

"Are you OK?" Daniel asked in a worried tone.

"Yeah," I replied untruthfully. As soon as the chills faded, a migraine headache took their place.

The nervous tension and stress of being forced to suppress the impending danger from him for so long while trying to find a solution to warn or protect him—all of these emotions were hitting me at once, and my brain had overloaded from the sheer volume. I took a deep breath, rubbed my forehead with my fingers, and tried to tell myself to relax.

"Are you sure you're OK?"

"Well, in truth, I just got a very strong, very sudden headache. Do you have any aspirin in the house? If you do, I would really appreciate it."

"Of course! I'll get you a couple at once," he said in a soothing tone. "I know you too well—there's something wrong with you. Come on, let's go inside."

We went into his house, and he refused to take his arm from my shoulder. I was awed by the magnificence of the place and the sheer luxury of the decor.

"What would you like to drink with the aspirins?"

"Whatever you have," I answered.

He smiled. "We have everything. I'm not joking—

whatever you want. They bring it to us twice a week—everything from freshly made yogurt to the most expensive champagne." He shrugged. "You can ask for whatever, but we have it. I don't mean to brag, but that's the way my father lives. Sometimes I kind of feel guilty living so extravagantly, knowing so many don't have even the most elemental necessities to live, two years after the Revolution."

"If you have it, enjoy it, brother, and thank God for it. We cannot fix the whole world at once. I will make it easy for you—just a glass of fresh orange juice will be great."

He said with a big grin, "That is the easiest thing you could ask."

We had already entered a salon, somewhere between a large living room and a foyer, with a huge chandelier and medieval suits of full plate armor against the walls. He pointed to a beautiful, serpentine-shaped sofa in the middle of the room that took up almost half of the salon. "Sit down, get comfortable, and I'll come right back with your orange juice."

Dr. Julio Antonio del Marmol

The foyer of Lazaro's house

A fit of dizziness hit me suddenly. I felt like I did during my hangover the day after my sister's wedding—and yet I hadn't even smelled alcohol, let alone drunk any. I sat down on the vast sofa, leaned back, and massaged my pounding temples with my fingers. It made me feel a little better, and I heard from the kitchen a high-pitched buzzing noise, like a blender. Daniel came back with a huge jar of fresh-squeezed orange juice with foam all along the rim. He also had two glasses of ice.

"We have some orange trees in the back yard. We have an electronic orange juice extractor—it took me only a few seconds to squeeze ten oranges."

"Ah-ha! You'd better be careful, or you'll convert yourself before my eyes into a little bourgeois, like Che and Fidel say."

He made a face and grunted in response to that line of rubbish. "That is what they feed the masses in order to keep them from aspiring to better," he said, as he put the glasses down on a glass table that followed the curves of the sofa. "If you think this is luxurious and exuberant, you should see how the ministers and high officials in the Revolution live! I go with my father to almost all of their parties and dinners, and I can tell you that this is an outhouse compared with what they have."

He poured two glasses of juice as he spoke and handed one to me. He picked up his own glass and sat down next to me. The juice was the best I had ever tasted. He handed me my aspirin and made a face as I started to chew it.

"One of my uncles is a doctor," I explained, "and he says that the aspirin enters your bloodstream quicker if you chew it before you send it down to your stomach. It helps your stomach out, and it takes care of your pain quicker."

Daniel grimaced nauseously. "I couldn't do that! I think I would rather put up with the pain! How in the hell can you do that without vomiting?"

"Like everything in life, you get used to it, good or bad." I took a couple of sips to swallow the pieces of aspirin in my mouth, and then finished my glass. Daniel grabbed the jar and poured me another glass. "Thank you very much," I said.

"I hope I can do more for you than give you an orange juice. You've done so much good for me. I could be a servant for the rest of your life without pay."

"Come on, knock it off! You don't owe me

anything—remember, we're friends."

"Friends owe gratitude to each other."

"Well, that's true. You've got a point there."

He reached into his pocket and took out a small navy blue pouch. He loosened the drawstring and took out a couple of small, golden figures of Buddha sitting with an apple-like fruit in one hand and a full sack on his shoulder. After he showed me the figurines, he handed the pouch to me and said in a sad voice, "When you get back to Pinar del Rio, I want to ask you, please give this to my mother and grandmother. Tell them not to be separated from it. I was told that it will protect them from all danger and give them luck and plenty."

I looked at him in surprise. I knew he believed in certain things, but I had no idea he was so devout. His eyes were moist with emotion. He appeared to have his own turmoil.

"Are you OK?" I asked this time. "Is anything wrong? You know you can tell me anything and I won't repeat a single word to anyone, not even your mother or grandmother."

He nodded and rubbed his eyes, trying to hide his tears. "The truth is, I'm not very happy here. I feel out of place, like a fish out of water."

I didn't take that very seriously. "Of course," I said with a smile. "Your father told me that you're probably homesick and missing your mom and grandmom. It's nothing to be ashamed of; it's your first separation, and it's completely normal."

He looked at me skeptically. "My father told you that?"

"Yes."

The Havana Conspiracies

"He didn't say anything else?"

"No. What else would he tell me?" I asked in surprise.

He scratched his head unhappily. "Well, we had a huge argument, my father and I, last week. Since then, we haven't been talking to each other directly. When I need to tell him something, I leave him a note—even at work, I leave him a note on his desk. I don't even want to look at his face."

I was surprised to hear this and shook my head. "Is it that serious? What happened?"

He nodded and took another sip of his juice. "The whole thing is just because of a stupid letter that I wasn't supposed to open. It was addressed to him, and I opened it by mistake, because the writing on the envelope looked like my mother's. It wasn't my intention to open his letter."

I took another sip of my orange juice. Combined with the aspirins, it was having an effect, as the intensity of my migraine was diminishing. "That's not very logical. Why would he get so upset because you mistakenly opened a letter?" I smiled encouragingly. "Was there something important in it that would make him react in that crazy way? You're not a stranger—you're his son. I assume you apologized, and he would then see it was an innocent mistake."

He threw his right arm up in disgust. "Apologized? Not only once, but many times. It wasn't sufficient, and with his words he disrespected me. He said I must be stupid to not be able to distinguish what is addressed to me and what is addressed to him. That really bothered me, because he had absolutely no right to offend me or disrespect me."

I leaned back in the sofa and stroked my chin with index finger and thumb, trying to figure out what was going on.

He looked at me and said, "The stupid letter said nothing in writing—it was only a map and traces with crosses in different places."

That caught my attention, and I leaned back and looked at him. I laced my fingers behind my head as I leaned back. I thought, What the hell can that signify and be of such importance that Lazaro didn't want Daniel to see? And cause him to lose control so much as to be disrespectful to Daniel, who has excellent manners. He was so verbally violent with his son, and there must be something that created this conflict.

I stood up and said, "Can I please use your restroom? I think I drank too much orange juice."

"Sure—to your right by the entry."

"Very well. I'll return right away."

I went through the living room to the hallway and the huge foyer in the direction of the bathroom. When I left the bathroom, I noticed something against the wall by the table near the door. The table was under a vast mirror with an antique frame near one of the suits of armor. The armor was so distinctive that, upon my entrance earlier, I had failed to notice the very expensively decorated box of Monte Cristos that Silvano had purchased in Caibarién. Next to it was a small gift box with an envelope which bore a large X in the center and four smaller Xs at the corners. There was no writing, just those marks.

I picked up the little box and as it moved, I could feel

something rolling around. I put it to my ear, and could hear something sliding around inside. My brow furrowed in puzzlement. I picked up the box of cigars and examined it carefully. I could see nothing unusual; it could have been from someplace other than Caibarién, but it was still such a coincidence. I left everything as I found it and went back to Daniel.

As I sat down next to him, Daniel said, "You know, it was a Hindu lady who gave me those little Buddhas in Old Havana, close to the pier where we work. This lady is supposed to be the best fortuneteller in all of Havana. What do you think she told me?"

I shook my head and kept my silence.

He continued with a nervous smile and a look of fear or worry, "She told me exactly what my grandmother had told my father at dinner that night, remember? Before we came to the capitol? You remember?"

"Claro, chico! Who can forget that day?"

"Well, this time, this lady said something a little more personal to me." He bit his lower lip. "She told me that Death is around me and to get the hell out of here immediately."

I got those chills once more. Fortunately, when they left me this time, they didn't leave me with that terrible headache. I looked at him seriously. "Do you believe it?"

"I don't know if I believe it or not."

"What are you going to do?"

He leaned back and laid his head on the back of the sofa. "Nothing. What can I do? If I tell this to my father, he'll laugh at me and say that it's a stupid excuse that I created to go back under the skirts of my mother and grandmother. He'll also rub my face in everything he's been doing for me, including recommending me in the union to be in charge of the personnel in one of the ships. It would embarrass him in front of all his union workers who entrusted me with that responsibility. He'll use every emotional weapon to make me feel so bad and guilty, calling me irresponsible and ungrateful. He'll probably never talk to me again. Even though he's a nice man, educated and polite, he can be a stubborn jerk."

He shook his head and said in resignation, "There's nothing I can do except to continue to get up at five a.m. to present myself for work on the pier at six a.m. each day as if nothing has happened." He slapped his forehead lightly. "I should have listened to my mother when she said I was rushing into this and shouldn't make such decisions in haste. I should have thought more carefully; but, being his son, I was stubborn, and I didn't pay attention to her. Now I'm caught in the alley with no way out. To be completely honest with you, I want to go back to Pinar del Rio, but I can't do it without humiliation from my father."

I had been listening quietly as he unburdened himself to me. I had a tremendous itch to tell him everything I knew, but I remembered the words of my uncle and the General and kept my silence. I realized that sometimes when one tries to do good for one person, it can cause devastation to others.

Daniel stood up and shook his shirt as if he were overheated. "Why don't we go out into the gardens for some fresh air? I don't know if it's just my emotions, but

I'm getting very hot in here. I can't even breathe."

"Why not? Let's go out and walk. The breeze should be very refreshing out there."

We walked through the foyer towards the door. As we passed by the table with the two boxes, I picked up the smaller box. "Is it your father's birthday?"

He shook his head. "No. That is a little present. People know him and friends try to kiss his ass to get some favor from him. He is the one who controls everything that comes into Cuba. Those presents arrived just a few minutes before you got here. A strange mustached man that looked more like a bodybuilder and a G-2 agent than anything else delivered them."

It rang like a bell in my ears. "What?" I stopped with the box in my hand and looked in his eyes seriously. "The man who brought this present just before I got here—mustached, tall, muscular—by any chance, was he dressed in black pants and a black shirt with green palm trees on it? Silk, like foreigners wear?" He nodded silently in surprise.

"How in the hell did you know?"

I was completely paralyzed. I already had my doubts with the box of cigars. But he had just described Silvano. Everything was corroborated. My chills returned even stronger as I saw the clear answer I had been looking all over the island for, right in front of my eyes. This was something I had not been expecting. Without even knowing it, from the minute I had walked into that house, I had that strange feeling.

I didn't reply to his question, but grabbed the letter.

I took it to a lamp and put it up to the light, observing it carefully. Daniel followed me in confusion, repeating his question. "How in the hell did you know how he was dressed?"

I looked at him in silence. I raised the envelope high. "Maybe your answer lies in this envelope, as well as the answer I've been anxiously looking for these past several weeks."

He looked at me in blank incomprehension.

"This individual—have you seen him before?"

"Yes, many times. He comes to the house frequently and leaves stuff for my father. Occasionally, I see him in my father's office in private conversation with him." This time, he couldn't stand it anymore. "What is going on here? Are you going to tell me, or what? When I told you about this guy, your face changed colors like you'd seen a ghost."

"Yes, you are completely right. More than a ghost—a demon! Don't ask me details, but maybe we have in our hand a way to change destiny. I can tell you one thing: the individual who delivered this package to you today is not a good man. His name is Silvano. He's not only the most dangerous man in Cuba, but possibly the most dangerous man on the continent. He's an assassin."

Daniel was completely confused and rubbed his forehead with his fingers. "What the hell does an assassin have to do with my father?"

I raised the letter. "Maybe in here, we can have the answer to your question, as well as to mine."

He raised the index finger of his right hand and moved it back and forth in negation. "Please, no! I don't want any more problems with my father. This one, he would never forgive me for!"

"I smiled largely. "Not if he never finds out that we opened that letter or those packages."

He clapped a hand to his head. "Oh, no! You want to open the packages, too? How are you going to do that? How is he never going to notice?" he asked in anguish. "No, please—no!"

"Daniel! Do you trust me?" I asked him sternly.

"Yes, I trust you with my life, but what has that to do with this? It's going to be obvious these were opened. What will I tell him? That you opened them?"

"Daniel—look at me!" I met his eyes. "I give you my word of honor that he'll never find out that those packages have been opened. I guarantee you that."

He breathed deeply. "How are you going to do that?"

"Don't worry. Just do as I tell you, and he'll never find out."

He finally shook his head and said in resignation, "OK—what do you want me to do?"

"Go into the kitchen and put a large pot of water on to boil. Get me some transparent adhesive tape, as well. I also need a razor blade."

"My father has everything in his office. I'll go and get them for you."

He left to get the items I had requested. I stayed there, trying to remember all of the details of the schematics I had seen in Che's portfolio. Even the smallest detail would help me discover what I would find when I opened these things. A few minutes later,

Daniel returned with the items and reported that the water was already being heated.

"Very well, thank you. What time does your father normally return home?"

"Never before ten p.m., sometimes not before ten-thirty."

I looked at my watch. "Good. It's eight now, so we have to finish things in one hour. Even sooner, in case he decides to come home early to say hello to me in person."

Daniel swallowed hard. I understood his worry and hesitation, so I put one hand on his shoulder. "Don't worry—I'm a professional, and it won't take me too much time. I've been taught properly, and I promise you that it will be done well, and he won't even dream that we've opened anything."

He relaxed a little, and we went into the kitchen. I held the envelope in the steam, not too close, until it opened by itself without any problem. It had inside a single sheet of white paper which read, "March 4. Your gift. Little package. Big present. Power, wealth, and internationalist. The door is open. All you have to do is push it. Be ready."

I read it a few times to memorize everything, and then we carefully resealed the envelope. I put it against the heat of a light bulb to dry it.

I cut the seal on the Monte Cristo box carefully. I examined each cigar, one by one, but found nothing. Finally, I opened the small box—the same pictures of Caibarién that I had bought for Yaneba and my mother lay within. One of the small shells, however, had come loose, and fell onto the sofa when we opened the box. It was that which I had heard sliding around inside. This caught my attention, since the artisan's work was so excellent that it was unlikely something like this would happen, unless Silvano had dropped it.

It was still strange to me—why, if he had liked it so much, would he give it to Lazaro, unless it were some kind of code? Perhaps it meant something that was coming from Caibarién. I couldn't figure it out, but I wanted to concentrate on the most important thing: this completely corroborated beyond any doubt that Silvano and Che were behind the whole operation, and I saw before me Mister X as Daniel's father. The puzzle was almost complete.

I very meticulously used the tape double-sided to reseal the boxes so well that not even an expert would be able to tell they had been opened.

Daniel watched me as I did all of this. When I finished, he asked, "Where did you learn to do this so professionally?"

I smiled. "Remember what I told you before—I cannot tell you any details. But, as you can see, everything is exactly as they were before we took them. But I only did this for your comfort. I've learned that the average person, in his anxiety to see what's in a present, will rip it open quickly. It won't even cross his mind that someone's already opened it. And after he opens it, there is no way to tell if it's been previously unsealed. All that he's looking for is what joy the contents will bring and so will throw the wrappings away without a second thought.

"The other reason I did this so carefully," I continued, "is because I don't know who your father is yet. Forgive me—I know he's your father, but everything indicates that your father is either a spy or a useful fool that very powerful entities within the government or professional spies have been using to achieve their morbid purposes. He probably doesn't even know the magnitude of what he's been doing. That is the best scenario."

We returned everything exactly as we had found them, went back into the living room, and sat down.

"Daniel—this is very important. Concentrate. When you opened that letter that got your father so upset, and you saw that plan that had some crosses, or were they perhaps Xs?"

Daniel thought for a while and closed his eyes. "Oh, my God! Yes! They were Xs—I remember wondering why these people were playing tic-tac-toe."

"Oh, my God!" I raised my hand to my mouth and pretended that I had just solved the puzzle. It was only partly feigned. I could not tell him plainly that I had previous knowledge of the plan to sabotage *La Coubre*, which is why I could use this splendid opportunity to protect my friend once more from the danger he was incurring. I had no doubts now that his father was Mister X and the day that had been designated for the operation was March 4—two days away.

I said, "These individuals might have involved your father in something terrible. But you have to promise me that whatever I tell you will not be repeated to anyone, not even your father."

He raised his hand solemnly. "You know me very well. I give you my word that I will repeat nothing to anyone."

"I have complete trust in you. I believe that these

people will try to sabotage and blow up the ship *La Coubre* where you and your father work unloading those weapons. I don't know the reason why. But I believe those Xs mark the precise locations where the controlled explosions will be set. That envelope we just opened with the same schematic and the date of March fourth shows that it's set for the day after tomorrow. Your father got so mad at you because he didn't want you to see where those explosives were going to be placed. It will probably be the route that will get you, him, and the rest of the people to safety before they blow up the ship or whatever it is they have planned."

Daniel's skin changed from black to ashen. He remained silent for a few seconds. Then he half-smiled and shook his head in disbelief. "No, no—I cannot believe that my father, a man so educated and intelligent, could be involved in such an outrageous, sinister, and absurd scheme, not only putting both his life and mine at risk, but also those of his whole crew and friends. I know he's a communist and an atheist, but I cannot believe he's such a degenerate and such an unscrupulous assassin, too!"

I looked at him gravely. "I want you to remember that old saying we have here in Cuba: the adulterous woman is known as such by everyone in town, but the last one to know is her husband. Unfortunately, that is the way it is. The closest ones are the last to know. I want to give you some advice, not as a friend, but as a brother. I love you and hold you in high consideration. I don't have to meet with Fidel until tomorrow evening. Why don't you write a note to your father, as you have been doing for weeks, and tell him that you decided to come back to Pinar del Rio with me for a few days? Let him find somebody to replace you. To hell with it—it's just for a few days." I raised my arm and pointed at my chest. "I will take you in the jeep. After all, it's only two and a half hours. I will be back tomorrow before my meeting. You take a mini vacation there with your mom and grandmom. If nothing happens, then great—it's nothing but overreaction on my part and false predictions from your Hindu lady and your grandmother."

We both raised our hands like in church as if to say a hallelujah. He shook his head. "You don't know my father. I'm in charge of the early shift, and I'm the one who has to write all of the hours of entry and exit of every worker there, from six a.m. to three p.m., and I also arrange the payroll. If I disappear even for one day, it will be a major disaster." He rubbed his forehead with his fingers. "I don't think he'll ever talk to me again."

"Fine," I interrupted him, "he doesn't talk to you. At least you'll be alive and not in pieces!" I was growing emotional. "In that ship are enough explosives to destroy half of Havana. Imagine what it will be like if you're inside it?"

"I appreciate your concern," he said, "but what if that never happens? Can you imagine my embarrassment?"

I shook my head this time. "My grandfather has been living all his life in Guane by the Cuyaguateje River. He taught me that when you hear heavy rain approaching, you move your livestock to higher ground. If nothing happens, all you lose is a little work and time. But if the river floods, you lose your animals and possibly your life trying to save them."

I paused and looked him in the eyes. "For God's sake, Daniel, what do I have to do to get you out of here? Will you please trust me and go, at least for a few days? Nothing is more precious than your life. Don't play unnecessary games with it. If you lose that game, I'll be devastated, my friend."

He looked me in the eyes. "Do you know something I don't know? I know you too well. What is it? Please."

I closed my eyes and shook my head. I raised my left hand to my mouth and squeezed my lips together. I nodded this time, and said, "Maybe, my friend. Maybe. But remember what I said when we began this conversation. I cannot give you details. Please don't ask me anymore."

The voice of Lazaro boomed as he entered the foyer. "Well, well—if you don't give me details, that prevents us understanding, and we can't have a good time."

Daniel and I looked at each other as if we had seen a ghost. I looked at my watch, and saw that it was only nine o'clock.

Lazaro walked over to us with the envelope and the two boxes in his left hand, while his right hand held his portfolio. We had no idea how long he had been there listening to our conversation. We remained frozen and mute, anticipating an explosion and confrontation.

Instead, however, he came to the sofa, dropping his portfolio on the center table, and sat down near us. Exactly as I had predicted to Daniel, he tore open the cover of the small box and tossed the wrappings into the trash can next to the sofa. The small seashell that was loose fell once more onto the sofa. He picked it up and tried to put it back in its place. As soon as he realized it wasn't going to stay in place on its own, he carefully placed it on the table to glue in later on.

Daniel and I looked at each other as Lazaro said with a smile, "What—the cat got your tongues? I'm sorry if I interrupted your conversation. I only heard you say to Daniel that you couldn't give any details. What, is it maybe a state secret?"

I smiled and nodded. "Military protocol. I'm following a superior's orders. That is the reason Che told me not to comment to anybody until I talk to Fidel at eight o'clock tomorrow evening. Even though I have absolute trust in Daniel, I never break discipline and disobey a superior's order."

Lazaro opened the letter, and I kept my eyes on him like a hawk. He smiled, full of satisfaction, after he read the letter. He opened his portfolio, and placed only the letter inside. The little picture from Caibarién he replaced inside its box. Again, it occurred to me that it might be some kind of code between Silvano, Che, and Lazaro.

He raised his head and said, "I'm very proud that Daniel is your friend and confidante. I want to tell you that, because I believe he can learn a lot from the values you possess. Loyalty and trust cannot be bought by anything in this world, and in the end, that loyalty and trust brings to us a lot closer to the biggest treasure anyone can ever give to us."

I nodded. "I think we all can learn from each other. Maybe I have a couple of things to learn from Daniel, like patience and humility. If somebody unfairly accuses me of something or pushes me too far, I react violently, including my father and any member of my family. I consider it disrespectful and disgraceful and I don't tolerate injustice and abuse. I don't care where it comes from.

"Loyalty: we have to be very careful to whom we give it," I added seriously. "Just yesterday we found out that we had given loyalty to a paranoid schizophrenic that used that power of loyalty and trust to take innocent lives that had been serving him." I shook my finger. "That is why we have to be very careful as to whom we trust."

He looked at me and opened his eyes wide in surprise. Maybe he understood something of what I was trying to tell him, and was a little worried about his own judgment. My convictions and the facts I was presenting were clear. He raised his hand in placation. "I know you cannot give details, but this individual really took the lives of people?"

"Yes, and with only the purpose being his personal satisfaction. But that is all I can tell you."

Lazaro shook his head in amazed disbelief. Daniel smiled in agreement mingled with a little sarcasm. He stood up and said, "Well, this conversation is really great, and I'd love to be with you guys longer, but I have to be the six o'clock charm at my job tomorrow. I'm sorry. But you guys can continue to talk." He pointed to his father. "My father is the boss," he added with a little sarcasm. "He can stay up late and come in whenever he wants."

Lazaro forced a smile, not liking his son's tone. "Don't forget to take your medicine before you go to bed."

Daniel didn't say anything but only nodded his head. To me, he said, "Tomorrow, after you finish your meeting, if you have some extra time, come back here. Maybe we can go and get an ice cream or something to drink, and maybe you can elaborate more."

"Very well." I rose and we embraced.

"My father will show you the guest room. I'm sure you'll be delighted with it."

I nodded, and he went in towards his own quarters. I watched him walk into the interior of his house, and a heavy weight settled on my heart as I thought that it might be the last time I see him alive. Involuntarily, I shuddered slightly.

"Is something wrong?" Lazaro asked.

"No. I was just thinking how quickly life passes through and involves us in daily responsibilities to the point that it deprives us of the pleasure of enjoying even the best moments with our friends and families."

With an expression of resignation, I continued, "That is the reason kids rush to become adults. This is the sad compensation we get at the end of the day."

I put both hands on my face and slid them from forehead to chin in frustration. I didn't want to cross the line of what I could say, I certainly didn't want to involve anyone or blow my cover, and I had done everything possible to save the life of my friend. I didn't feel like I had accomplished that, but hopefully I had at least planted the seed of doubt in his mind with my information. It was his turn now to digest it and make an intelligent decision. It was up to God's divine power to protect him from the imminent danger to which he was going to expose himself. From his perspective, there was plenty of room for doubt; perhaps he thought my fears were completely unfounded.

Lazaro was watching me and noticed my eyes slightly moist and red. "I understand exactly what you're saying. The saddest part in the whole thing is that, unfortunately, when we realize what is going on, it is too late. We cannot go back." His expression grew sad. "Unfortunately, life is a one-way ticket with no return."

I nodded once more. I thought that he might have just provided me the opportunity that I had been waiting for, and I decided to take it. "Well, everything we've been talking about and saying is very sad. But, Lazaro, that is one of the most important reasons that we consider every step we make in life. Even minor things we decide to get involved in have to be carefully assessed. It doesn't matter who tells us to jump from the masthead to the deck without protection and reassures us that we will be uninjured; if it doesn't make sense to you, don't do it."

I stopped and removed my beret. I put it on top of the table and scratched my hair. A little sarcastically, I continued, "We cannot be ignorant or blind because someone we consider superior or omnipotent tells us to jump, when we know that if we jump, we'll be smashed to pieces when we hit that hard deck." I rested my index finger against my temple. "Common sense, only—we don't have to be educated, we don't have to be intelligent, to realize that the person pushing us to that act might have an ulterior motive—a vendetta or merely personal satisfaction. Like the commander we have in jail today for murder."

Lazaro opened his eyes wide in astonishment. "What the devil? The individual you were talking about before is a commander?"

I nodded. "Yes. A commander is another human being. What is the difference?" I grew grave. "I expect this will stay only between us. This is completely confidential and classified."

He looked at me in surprise, and this time, I saw a little fear in his eyes. I knew that I was slightly crossing the line—deliberately. But I was doing so with the sole purpose of scaring him. After I saw his expression, I felt I had accomplished it.

He had been leaning back in the sofa. He now shifted forward and cradled his mouth in his left hand. He remained silent in thought. I observed him carefully, scrutinizing every movement in his face without saying a word, waiting for his reaction. After a few seconds of silence, he said, "You know something I don't know? Are you trying to tell me something?"

I held his gaze silently.

"You do know," he said in a slightly condescending tone, "that no matter how terrible it is, any information you want to share with me will never be repeated anywhere." He breathed deeply in his increasing discomfort and impatience. "I know you are very young, but I also know that the leaders of this Revolution don't keep you around because you're a cute kid. It's because of your capabilities to distinguish between who is your friend and who is your enemy." He forced a smile and moved closer to me. He patted my leg. "Daniel and I are your true friends. Do you know that?"

I nodded. "I know and am completely convinced that Daniel is my best friend. He would never betray me. He's already shown me in the past. But you—as I told you the night when we spoke over the phone, our friendship is very young. Only time can make it better or worse. We have to be patient and not rush trust. I'm sorry, but survival instinct tells me to be cautious and never cross that line. There's an old saying: If you have any doubts in your mind, the logical thing to do is to stop."

He leaned back in the sofa and laced his fingers across his chest, rubbing his thumbs together. He shook his head slowly and looked around as if he were thinking very precisely what he wanted to tell me. His respiration was growing more agitated and nervous, and on his forehead and just below his lower lip were small beads of perspiration. Apparently, my conversation was having an impact, and he was carefully considering what his next move was going to be.

I didn't know his role in the plan to blow up the ship; I likewise didn't know what those people had promised him for his important collaboration in the sabotage. I was trying my best to figure it out as he continued in silence. He was avoiding my eyes, and continued to look around. I was thinking about how much I would give to know what was crossing his mind and the exact time the explosion would take place. I was still optimistic in my heart that a possibility would open up to stop that horrendous crime.

Finally, he leaned forward once more and said, "Maybe in a figurative way, without compromising each other, we can talk and reach an intelligent conclusion to put both our minds at ease."

I gestured with my hand for him to continue and nodded encouragingly.

He said nothing further, though.

"This is precisely what I've been doing all this time after Daniel left to go to sleep," I said. "Now it's your turn. Go ahead. What do you have to say? I'm all ears."

He hesitated in confusion. I had taken him by surprise, because he had wanted me to continue talking. I had already said all I was going to say. He looked at me gravely and swallowed hard. "You really are thirteen years old?"

"Yes. Why?"

He scratched his ear nervously. He obviously didn't know how to begin. He shook his head. "I don't know. When I'm talking with you, sometimes I get the impression I'm talking to man of at least sixty."

I smiled, remembering how my family always referred to me. "That is not the first time I've heard that."

"Well," he continued, gesturing at the room around him, "you see all this? As you understand, all of this didn't come out of nothing. Believe me, I'm no angel. I have a few regrets in my life that I'd rather not even think about. As you rise in success, certain forces demand more and more from you. It's like being a fly caught in a spider web at that point. If you want to maintain what you've achieved and not return to poverty, you wind up realizing that you've become a slave—to all of this." He gestured around once more.

"Those continual demands begin to strangle you," he continued, "because there are certain things you don't want to do, and everything has a limit." He looked at me and smiled. "You might not understand, because you are young and don't place a lot of importance on material things. But believe me, when you're a few years older, you'll want to live in a place like this, where everyone looks at you with respect."

I was the one to smile this time. "Everybody who respects me now will always respect me, even if I live in a palm tree house with a dirt floor, because I respect everyone around me. Of course, it would never bother me to live in a place even better than this. There's nothing wrong with that."

He looked at me skeptically. "Well," he said in irritation, "I just give an example."

I didn't reply, but nodded.

He said in an exasperated tone, "Well, what I was trying to say is that we have to do certain things that we're not proud of in order to maintain all that we've accomplished in life to give a solid future to yourself and your family."

I leaned back and stroked my chin with my right arm. "Even putting at risk the life of your son, as well as your own? And have on your conscience heaven knows how many other lives? Is all of this worth that?"

He stood up and yelled, "They guaranteed me that nobody would get hurt!"

I calmly asked, "And you believe that stupidity

without question? A ship full of explosives?"

"Of course! Why wouldn't I believe them!? Why would they do something like that? Only a deranged person would do something like that!" he screamed.

I smiled and looked at him. He realized what he had been saying and paled. He had fallen into the trap that I had put in front of him. He was completely mute, petrified, and full of guilt as he stood before me. He was speechless.

We heard a door open, and Daniel came into the room. Apparently, he had been awoken by his father's yelling. "What is going on? Why are you screaming that way, Papa?"

"Oh, nothing," said Lazaro, ashamed. "I'm sorry we woke you up, son. We were just talking loudly. Go back to bed."

Daniel looked at him in disbelief and then looked at me. I stood up with a very ugly expression on my face. Ignoring what his father was saying, Daniel asked me, "That is true, Commandantico?"

I looked straight into his eyes. I couldn't lie to him. I shook my head, picked up my beret and started to put it on. "The screaming you heard from your father—they are the screams of justification for some terrible guilt he has in his mind. Something he says he has to do, or he will lose all of this." I gestured around in the same way Lazaro had. "I only tried to help, but your father blew his fuse before he turned on the radio, so I cannot hear the program. Evidently, all of this is more important than your life or his own."

I pointed at Lazaro, who stood by mutely. He couldn't even dare to contradict my frank relation of the conversation. "You remember what I told you about the commander who is in jail for murder? Be careful in whom you put your trust and loyalty. Remember also that you can lose not only all this but a lot more precious things like your honor, dignity, et cetera. I hope you have time to reflect."

Daniel kept looking back and forth between the two of us. He was expecting a reaction from his father, who remained petrified and mute.

"I'm sorry, Daniel, but I'm going to sleep with my family," I said. "Thank you very much for your invitation, but due to these circumstances, I think the most appropriate thing to do is to leave you guys alone. Maybe this little conflict can help to Lazaro reflect and open his heart to you, Daniel. Maybe he'll ask your forgiveness and tell you the real reason he disrespected you when you mistakenly opened that letter."

Daniel looked at me in surprise and admiration. He tried to stop me. "It's very late, Commandantico. Please, don't go. You can leave in the morning."

I shook my head and smiled. I raised my right arm. "Thank you very much, my good friend and my brother. Think very carefully about what we talked about today, and open your mind, please, to reason. I think the best thing for everyone is that I leave and you guys have a little talk. Good night, and please excuse me."

I turned and headed towards the door. While I walked toward the door, I heard Daniel yell, "Papa, please don't let him go like this. Whatever he said to you, he was just trying to protect you. Even if what he said was wrong and he offended you, please stop him. It's past midnight—please don't let him go into the street like this, with this anger in his heart."

I continued to walk to the door. As I exited, I heard Lazaro say, "Commandantico, please!"

The Havana Conspiracies

Chapter 5: The Intelligence Exit Contact

I closed the door behind me and walked quickly through the garden. Everything had gone so well, and this was the perfect excuse for me to leave and let them communicate with each other. Maybe I had accomplished something. If Lazaro had second thoughts, we could thwart that plan to commit mass murder.

I was extremely anxious to get in touch with my uncle and the General with the details of what had happened in there. I rushed to my jeep and drove away as fast as I could with sadness in my heart. But I also felt a great satisfaction at having done everything possible—and a few things impossible—to save the lives of my friend and his father. I didn't know exactly how deeply Lazaro was involved, but I believed he could be a patsy for the larger, sinister plot.

I looked at my watch. It was half past midnight. Even though it was very late to call anyone, I decided to call Chandee at the emergency phone number she had given me in Caibarién.

I drove to the heart of the city and stopped the jeep in the parking lot of a restaurant named The Three Brothers, located at the fork of Calzada de la Infanta Street, one block from the Astral Theater. I parked and went to a public pay phone booth at the point in the fork. I dialed Chandee's number, and a half-asleep male voice answered, "Hello, who is this?"

"The voice of Caibarién," I answered. "Is Chandee at home, please?"

His tone immediately changed. "She is sleeping," he said agreeably, "but this is her father, Xiang, and a personal friend of your uncle's. Can I help you with anything?"

"Yes. I'm here in the capital by an unexpected emergency, and I have information of the highest priority that my sponsors should know immediately."

"Do you have paper and pencil?" he replied.

"Hold on one second." I pulled a small notebook out of my shirt pocket and my pen. "Very well, I'm ready."

"I need you to come to this address." I wrote down the address he gave me. "Don't knock on the front door of the business. Circle around the block and come in through the back door in the alley. There you will find a large green metal gate. I will be waiting for you. How far away are you?"

"I'm very close, and will be there in ten or fifteen minutes. I'm driving an Army jeep."

"OK. See you in a little while."

The Havana Conspiracies

Havana's Old Chinatown district

I hung up and headed to Chinatown. Once there, I turned onto Zanja Street and found the address. I went around the block, but before I got to the alley, I saw a local police car with a couple of patrolmen inside. They drove slowly in my direction. As they passed me, they saluted me with friendly smiles on their faces and continued their patrol.

I entered the alley and stopped at a green gate. I did not shut off my lights or my engine, because I saw three separate gates of differing shades of green. Xiang had neglected to tell me which tint of green his gate was, and I didn't see him waiting for me. I shook my head in mild exasperation.

Then I saw, in the distance, an Asian man with a Fu Manchu mustache waving at me. I drove slowly down and entered through the gate he had opened—an olive green gate, much the same color as my jeep.

Inside was a small plaza with a meat packing plant. He pointed to where I should park. After I got out, he formally introduced himself to me.

"It is a very great pleasure to meet you," he said in a voice only slightly accented in Chinese. He bowed to me in greeting. "I've seen you from a distance several times."

"The pleasure is all mine," I said with a smile, duplicating his bow.

In a gesture of affection, he put his arm around my shoulder and said, "Come on, follow me."

He opened a small gate at the right side of the building. It opened into a vast warehouse with the carcasses of cows, pigs, and sheep hanging from hooks in the ceiling.

We entered a long, semi-dark corridor. He closed the gate behind us, and we walked down the corridor that was lit only by naked light bulbs hanging from the ceiling. Most were burned out. Only one every ten or fifteen feet still had working bulbs. Boxes, buckets, dusters, and other janitorial equipment rested against the walls.

We entered a large room that appeared to be connected to another business—a textile firm. By the dim light, I could see industrial sewing machines on the floor with bolts of cloth and boxes of fabric lining the walls.

We passed through and entered another corridor. This time walked into a darkened, filthy room. The only lights hanging from the ceiling here were suspended by extension cords. Junk lined the walls of the narrow corridor.

Finally, Xiang stopped by the wall. There was a single hole and a faint line in the wall. It looked like a utility panel of some kind. He pulled out a key, inserted it into the hole, and pushed. A double door opened up in front of him. Very slowly, the wall pivoted open so we could walk in. He gestured with his right hand to follow him and held his index finger to his lips to communicate silence. He pointed at his watch and whispered, "It's very late. Let's not wake the family."

I looked at my watch and saw that it was one-twenty a.m. He closed the door from the inside, and I saw that the interior side of the door was a china cabinet filled with dishes. I smiled and thought how smart this Chinese man was and wondered how many people had been saved through this secret door from the time it was built. I knew from Chandee that Mr. Xiang had been doing this since at least World War II, when he had started working with the global intelligence community. This man was the grandfather of spies, I thought, since he had been doing it long before I had even been born.

I followed him closely through the antique store. Through a small crack in the curtain covering the front window I could see the main street I had just crossed. I followed him into a small office, and he switched on a desk lamp. He gestured to a chair. "Please, sit down."

"Thank you." I sat in the chair and began to give him the details of everything that had happened since Chandee left Caibarién and what I had discovered concerning Mister X in Daniel's house.

When I finished, he said, "The first thing in the morning, I will communicate this with your uncle and the General. However, since it's so late, you should stay here with us. That way, you won't call any attention to yourself by driving around the streets at such a late hour."

He brought me some blankets and a pillow and pulled out a sofa bed. "Please, until I communicate with my contacts, do not return to your friend's house. You caught Mister X by surprise. Your work with him was psychologically superb. But if you return there, you run an unnecessary risk, because this time he might be prepared for you. If he's a spy, he has as yet no proof of what you said to give to his superiors. It's simply his word against yours. The next time, though, he could be ready to record your conversation. He could create problems for you or at least plant doubts about your loyalty. Then Fidel or Che could order you held for questioning. They'll definitely want to know how you acquired the basic information, which could jeopardize not only yourself but the rest of us and what we're doing.

"Tomorrow, after your meeting with Fidel, go to the Astral Theater on Infanta Street. Do you know where it is? Chandee will be waiting for you there with two tickets. Take her hand like she's your girlfriend, go into the theater, and there she will give you instructions on how to proceed. But don't leave the theater until the movie is finished. Don't go back to Daniel's house until she gives you those instructions."

"Very well," I said sadly and in resignation, "I will do as you instruct." In my heart, I felt certain that I could take Daniel with me and convince him not to return to the pier.

The good Chinese man looked at my compassionately. He put his hand on my shoulder as I sat on the bed he had prepared for me. "Your optimistic eyes may want to see Mister X as a good guy and perhaps another victim, because he's the father of your best friend. But think of this, my son—what if Mister X is just another unscrupulous assassin with ambitions of power like the rest of these delinquents?"

He nodded his head sagely. "What if he prepares a trap for you and when you come out of that house the best scenario is to be handcuffed by the G-2 or in the worst scenario, killed by the MQ-1?"

He shook his head and said in a very firm voice, "The risk is too high. It's not worth it. You've already done more than what you were supposed to do. You are too valuable to us, OK? Don't make that mistake!"

I looked at him and nodded my understanding. "Thank you."

He turned the lights off and said, "Good night and rest well. You'll need your mind fresh for tomorrow." He left the office and closed the door behind him.

I lay there in the darkness, thinking. I understood perfectly what Mr. Xiang had told me. It was a very sour reality, but it was still the truth before my eyes.

I fell into a deep sleep, exhausted from my trip. In spite of the worries and problems in my head, I slept the night through and didn't wake up until a sweet voice said in my ear, "Wake up, Sleeping Beauty, or you're going to sleep all day long."

I started awake. "What? What time is it?"

Chandee picked up my wristwatch off of the desk where I had laid it the previous night and showed it to me with a smile. "Oh, my God! Twelve-thirty!" I sat bolt upright in bed. "My God, I haven't slept that long for a long time." Though I didn't like to get up early, I disliked sleeping too late.

She smiled wickedly. "Well, that means you'll feel guilty all day long, and I'll be able to take advantage of you. Even if I'm obnoxious with you, you won't defend yourself."

I bowed slightly as if at court. "Whatever you say, my queen."

She tilted her head and smiled. "Don't worry, I'm just joking with you. I know you went to bed very late. My father told me to let you sleep. I'm sorry if I woke you up before you were ready, but he also told me to take you to meet somebody very important for your future. Because we're going a little distance from the city, I don't want you to be late for your important meeting tonight."

"Where are we going?"

"We're going to Playa de Guanabo." She pointed to some towels at the food of my bed. "You can take a shower, and when you've finished, my mother has prepared a brunch for you. We've already breakfasted and lunched." Before she left the room, she bowed once more. "Your Majesty, we will await you in the dining room."

I nodded and smiled, thinking, *Esta chinita es algo serio[7]*.

After I took a shower and greeted Mrs. Xiang and Chandee's little sister, Yein, I enjoyed the excellent soup of shrimp and fish and other exquisite things Mrs. Xiang had made for me. I felt stuffed and thanked her for all of

---

[7] This little Chinese girl is too much for me

her hospitality.

The lady had extremely exquisite manners and said in an even more marked Chinese accent than her husband, "Thank you, and have a good trip. Please be very careful on the road."

We left towards Playa de Guanabo. On the road, Chandee explained to me that we were going to the home of a doctor who was supposed to be the direct contact with the world outside of Cuba. He was a member of global intelligence in charge of all insertions and extractions through the American naval base at Guantanamo.

"What is the reason for all of this?" I asked her with a certain amount of worry. This meeting seemed a little out of the blue, and I couldn't help wondering why they wanted me to meet this man. I had no plans to abandon Cuba, nor any desire to do so. "Since yesterday, when we spoke in Caibarién, until today, has there been some dramatic change that I don't know about?"

She shook her head. "No. From what my father told me, they only want to make sure that, in case something rapidly deteriorates for the worst, you don't wind up arrested and in the hands of our enemies. They want to give you the option to use this door in case your common sense tells you that things have gotten that bad. Only use this in case your life is in danger."

I shook my head and smiled ironically. "My life has been in danger from the very moment I decided to do all thing things I'm doing now."

She smiled. "I know, I know—but you know what they mean. In an extremely urgent, immediate situation, you will now have an alternative."

I smiled and nodded. I looked at her for a moment, extreme irony still in my expression. She patted my cheek and turned my face back towards the road. "Keep your eyes on your driving. I know I'm exotic and very beautiful, but I want to make it to Guanabo in one piece."

"Chinita, you are impossible! You are so conceited it's disgusting."

Thanks to our joking and conversation, the trip went by very fast, and we were entering the town of Guanabo. She guided me to a small hill, on top of which stood a beautiful chalet in which this important individual was supposed to live.

As we went up the driveway, I saw an older, beautifully preserved Jaguar XJ-6 parked outside. We also noticed a curtain in one of the windows moving, as if someone inside was watching us. We parked and walked up to the door, and Chandee rang the bell. The door opened immediately, as if someone were just inside waiting for us. A tall, thin woman in her thirties greeted Chandee with joy and a smile, giving her a big hug.

"I am Margot," she said, turning to me. In spite of my uniform, she was greeting me as if I were one of the family. "I know who you are, and we're all very proud of you and your work."

"Thank you for your pleasant words, Margot," I replied with a satisfied smile.

"Come in," she said. We entered the chalet behind her and followed her through the house to the backyard, which had a breathtaking view of the ocean, a garden, and a white, curtained gazebo. A man with a receding hairline sat there, dressed all in white, with canvas shoes and no socks. He looked very refined and wore dark sunglasses. Around the gazebo was a beautiful waterfall and a meditation pool.

As soon as he saw us, he stood up, removed his sunglasses, and received us with a big smile. "Welcome to my humble shack. *Mi casa es su casa*[8]."

"Thank you very much." I looked around the room. "You have a beautiful home, and I would absolutely be delighted to live in your humble shack for the rest of my life. Emotionally, I don't think it would scare me in the slightest."

He smiled broadly and took my hand in an iron grip. "Dr. Vallarte is my name. Everyone calls me el Professor. I see with great pleasure that, on top of being a patriot of great eloquence, you also possess a sense of humor."

I smiled. "Oh, well—I don't know whether all that's true, but I will agree with one thing. A man or woman without a sense of humor is like a lemonade without sugar."

He laughed at that. "If you don't have sugar, at least put a little honey in it." Everyone smiled, including Chandee.

Margot said, "Life is sour enough most of the time; why leave out that sugar or honey?" She smiled. "By the way, we have lemonade with sugar that we can offer you, unless you prefer something else to drink."

---

[8] My house is your house

"Lemonade with sugar is fine with me. Thank you very much."

Chandee said, "The same for me, but I'll help you in the kitchen." She put her arm in Margot's, and the two women left the Professor and me in the garden so that we could speak alone.

The Professor said, "I've been wanting to meet you in person for a long time, but your uncle didn't even tell me until today that you were his nephew. He and the General are so protective of your security that they made me promise on my family honor that this was going to stay with me. They want nobody, and I mean absolutely nobody, to know your identity. I believe that this is very important to your survival, but I also believe that you and I meeting is equally vital. I'm the door in and out of this island. I'm not the only one, by any means—but I'm the most secure." He pointed at me firmly with his index finger. "Guantanamo." I smiled and looked at him with a little irony in my expression. He leaned back with a surprised expression. "What—you don't believe so?"

I also leaned back in my rattan chair, beautifully decorated with floral patterned pillows. I raised my arm. "Oh, oh—no, no, no. Don't misunderstand either my expression or my smile. First, from my modest point of view, when it comes to the point we have to abandon this island, I don't think any door will be sufficiently secure. Second, I hope that I never have to use any of these doors. Don't take me wrong—I sincerely and profusely appreciate your keeping that door open not only for me, but for those around me that are risking their lives by my side."

He looked at me piercingly. "I'll give you all the details

and codes that you can use in an extreme emergency. If everything's OK, we'll send you the green light, and you don't need to contact us. If, however, you get a yellow light, get in touch with us because we need to let you know what's changed.

"Not even my superiors know who you are," he added with paternal pride, "because that is the condition put on the table by your uncle and the General, and we will maintain that for your own security."

I breathed deeply. "Thank you very much. You don't know how good those words make me feel."

"You're welcome. It is our duty to protect you as if you were a rare Cuban diamond, probably created by the lightning in the sky. We have to guard that with a big safety security box."

Margo and Chandee returned from the house with a large pitcher of lemonade, some sandwiches, and some hors d'oeuvres. "This will help you recharge your energy," said Margot, "and you can keep talking in a relaxed atmosphere."

We all smiled, and I said, "Thank you very much, ladies, both of you."

"When Chandee visits us, it makes Margot very happy," the Professor said. "She's not just a guest; she's like a part of our family. Not only that, but she's very efficient. She knows how to do everything, and she does it very well." Chandee blushed and smiled, and then bowed slightly.

Even though she typically spoke with no accent, she replied in a comic Chinese accent, "Thank you velly much, thank you velly much." She bobbed and bowed in Chinese fashion.

I seized the opportunity to tease her, saying, "Oooh, this is the first time since I've met her that she's blushed." At my words, she blushed even more furiously, and I knew I had gotten her as well.

"OK, OK," she said in mock surrender. Both women walked back into the house, laughing as they went, Margot's arm around Chandee's shoulder protectively.

After they left, the Professor continued to speak as we ate and drank the wonderful canapé and the delicious lemonade. He went over the ways to escape the island, the primary route as well as the secondary routes in case the principal one had been compromised. We spent several hours going over the topography, mine fields, and the camps in detail. He insisted that I memorize all of these features, as I could not leave his house with notes or any papers in my possession about this. If I were stopped and searched with these notes on my person, they would have no mercy and would execute me on the spot as a spy.

Between the Professor explaining things into such detail and questioning me and quizzing me to make sure I got it all right, we didn't even realize how much time has passed. Chandee came out, and said, "I'm sorry to interrupt, but we should get back to Havana. It's almost six o'clock."

"What?" I looked at my watch. "Oh, my God! Yes, we have to get out of here immediately. I have to be at Che's office at seven."

"Yes, go at once," the Professor said. He stood and gave me a hug. "It's very important that you be punctual.

The Havana Conspiracies

Punctuality says a lot about the personality and responsibility of an individual. Whoever is not punctual cannot be trusted."

"In that case, I'm very, very trustworthy, because I'm known by everyone in my circle to be sometimes half an hour early to my meetings."

"It's better to overflow the glass than to not have enough to drink," the Professor agreed.

After we said our farewells, we headed back to the capital. When we got back to Havana and reached Chinatown, I drove to Chandee's place and stopped in front of the antique store.

She leaned over and kissed me on the cheek. "I will be waiting for you in the movie theater tonight after your meeting," she murmured in my ear. "Don't worry if your meeting takes longer than you expect. I know how these leaders of the Revolution are—they love to talk forever until their tongues drop out of their mouths. I will be waiting for you. Even if it's after midnight and the theater is closed, I will be there. Go, relax, and have a good meeting."

"Thank you," I replied.

I left and drove to Che's office. Shortly afterward, I arrived at the building. Silvano wasn't there yet; at least, I didn't see his olive green Volga anywhere in the underground garage where we had agreed to meet. I looked at my watch, and saw it was 6:45. There was a service station just for the executives, and decided to go there and asked the man in charge to please fill up the jeep's tank. A tall, skinny, pleasant mulatto smiled and said, "It will be a pleasure, Commander." He gestured to two assistants, and they performed a full service.

When they were finished, I looked at my watch. It was 7:10, and Silvano was still nowhere to be seen. I went into the underground parking structure, and parked my jeep next to the Volgas, Buicks, Fords, and other cars parked there. I turned the engine off and waited for another fifteen minutes. Finally, at 7:25, Silvano pulled his Volga into the structure. As soon as he saw me, he blew the horn and waved to me from the window. He parked and looked at his watch.

Soviet Volga issued to government officials

"Don't worry about the time. It's only ten minutes or so from here. Besides, you know Fidel is never on time. We'll probably have to wait an hour for him anyway."

"I don't care when he'll get there," I said seriously. "We should be there at least thirty minutes early. Our meeting is at eight. We should be there now."

He looked at me in surprise. He went to the trunk and pulled out a brand new shirt still sealed in plastic. "Can I at least change my shirt?"

"You can change your shirt, take a shower, whatever, as long as we get there half an hour beforehand," I said, still serious.

He shook his head, evidently not liking what I was saying.

"You know what?" I added. "You can do what you like, and I'll go on ahead."

He didn't like that, either.

"Fine," he said in resignation. "I'll change my shirt right here in the goddamned garage." He ripped open the plastic in annoyance, whipped off the shirt he was wearing, wrapped it around his fingers, and flung it violently into the trunk of the car. I wondered what fly had bitten this guy to change him from such a pleasant man into a jerk within a mere twenty-four hours.

"Goddamn it," he muttered to himself, "I only wanted to go to the bathroom, wash under my arms, and put on a clean shirt."

I controlled my own rising anger. Even though he hadn't been addressing me, I replied, "Why didn't you come in earlier, then? You could have taken a shower or done whatever the hell you wanted. What if we get a flat tire on the way? Then you wouldn't have to apologize in shame because you came in late, because you took your time getting here like a stupid moron!" I got into the car and slammed the door to display my grievance.

Realizing I was angry, he got in the other side in

silence. He drove dangerously fast—so fast that I held on to the sides. He made the trip in five minutes, and when we got there, I felt a small surge of satisfaction when we were told that Fidel had returned early and was waiting for us. To our great surprise, we were also told that Che was there with him. I looked at my watch, and noted that it was 7:30. I looked at Silvano gravely, and made no comment. Silvano avoided my eyes and bowed his head in embarrassment.

The escorts took us through the office and into the conference room, where Fidel and Che were sitting with the rest of their escort. "Well, well, well," Fidel said as we walked in, "it's good that you guys came early, because I have to leave for Mariel in less than an hour."

This was magnificent, since it meant I would be able to get out of there early to meet with Chandee. After we greeted each other, Fidel turned to address me. "Who had the idea to come in early? I left the message that I wanted to see you guys at eight. I know it's not him," he said, pointing to Silvano with a grin, "because he'll be late to his own funeral!"

I didn't know why he seemed intent on humiliating Silvano, but he continued, "He's late to every meeting. I don't know why—maybe he likes to have people wait for him."

My spy instincts told me that Fidel was doing this to indicate that he didn't like Silvano much, so that Che would like him more. He was using reverse psychology so that Che wouldn't suspect Silvano of being a spy for Fidel.

I decided to ruin his head game and raised my arm to say, "Excuse me, my Commander, but Silvano is the one who suggested we come in early. He said you were accustomed always to be early or on time."

Fidel burst out laughing. "He said that?" he exclaimed in disbelief, looking straight into my eyes. "Really? That's what he said?"

I held his eyes and nodded my head. "Yes, I wanted to stop in the Havana Libre to change my shirt and clean my underarms." I smiled with irony. "This shirt smells like hell—I've had it on for three days! But Silvano insisted that I should do that later, since we didn't have too much time. He wanted me to be here at least half an hour before you were."

Silvano was looking at me in absolute disbelief.

Fidel laughed again. "You have to tell him, '*Carajo*[9]! Who is the Commander here?' You should tell him, 'You better watch out! You're not the Commander here, I am!'"

Che and the others laughed. Silvano forced a sickly smile.

Fidel continued, "And after you've been saving the life of Che, from what he just told me, Silvano had better keep walking the tightrope, because you, Commandantico, are going to take his position away. No more assistant to Che, if he doesn't get his act together." Fidel pointed to the chairs. "Come on, you guys, sit down, sit down!"

We sat and I said, "No, my Commander. It's OK that Silvano should keep his assistant position. I prefer to do something else, because to me, I think it would be better to be the head of the mind than the tail of the

---

[9] What the hell

lion."

Everyone, including Silvano this time, laughed. Che almost choked, as he was lighting a cigar. After he regained his composure, Che wiped his eyes with the back of his hands and raised his hand high. "Thank you—thank you very much. I've been compared with many things before, but never to a lion!"

I shook my head slightly and wondered how this man could be so conceited and not bother to ask me what I meant by that. The truth was that I would rather be the minutest part of those who did the thinking than to be in a position where I had to smell the worst he had to offer. It was absurd to me that he should glorify himself, and so I ignored him for the moment, noting that the only way he resembled a lion was that he disliked taking showers and so smelled like one after a few days. The escort called him "the Cat" because of his dislike for water; at least, I thought, the cat and the lion were in the same family.

Fidel asked me, "Do you want to go to Mariel? We've prepared a new base for modern torpedo helicopters with long- and short-range missiles. They should arrive soon from the Soviet Union."

I graciously declined, saying, "Thank you, my Commander, but I've already arranged to have dinner with my family here in Havana tonight."

Finally, Fidel came to the point, and asked us for the details of what happened with Nogueira. "Even though Che has briefed me extensively, I want to hear it from your own mouths."

After we gave our statements, Fidel summoned two military auditors, who examined us and took down our declarations. They took a picture of Silvano's foot, and Fidel raised his right hand up high to pronounce his sentence. "OK, I think Nogueira should be interned in the psychiatric hospital. He is a great Revolutionary and a friend of my brother, Raul, but there is no doubt that he has termites in his head. Let's put him for a while in Mazorra, and see if he gets any better."

There was no doubt in my mind that Fidel had some sympathy for that crazy maniac, but he had no alternative after what Nogueira had done. He said goodbye to us and left with his escort.

After Fidel left, I said to Che, "I'm really caught by surprise to see you here."

"The surprise was all mine," he replied, "when they came in helicopters to bring me here from Caibarién. Fidel wanted me here today. We have other big problems and one matter of high security we have to take care of immediately.

"Can I help in any way?" I asked.

"No, no," he said, "I believe that Silvano and I can take care of this. Thank you for your offer."

"No need to mention it."

"What do you plan to do tomorrow?"

"I'm thinking of stopping at the military hospital to check on some extreme headaches, some chills, and insomnia I've been having lately," I said, to head off any other ideas Che might get.

"OK," he said, with no alternatives. "Go and get yourself checked out. Very good idea, after all you've been through. Make sure they take all these tests, and don't eat breakfast in the morning. They can't do any of those tests if you have anything in your stomach."

"Thank you, I'll do that."

Che asked Silvano, "What car are you driving?"

"I'm driving the olive-green Volga," Silvano replied.

"Give the keys to the Commandantico, and you come with me. We have a great problem with your friend in the Union to resolve."

"I gave him the gifts and the message," Silvano said in surprise. "What is the problem?"

Che looked at me and the others and cut him off. "I will explain to you later."

Silvano handed me the keys to the Volga. He looked me in the eyes and murmured, "Thank you."

"You're welcome," I said. With the keys in my hand, I said to Che, "Probably the day after tomorrow, I'll return to Pinar del Rio. Where did you want me to leave the Volga?"

"Take it with you. Don't worry about it. Take it for the time you want it. You deserve that and a lot more."

"Very well—thank you very much."

He had just officially given me a car that only the top ministers were driving.

We said our goodbyes, and I left them in the conference room. I thought that, because of all of his security, the place looked less like an office and more like a military fortress. A short while later, I was driving the Volga and noting the difference between the jeep and that small Russian car. It was like getting off of a tractor and getting into a luxury recreational vehicle. That Soviet car, though, couldn't even be the dirty sandal to my father's 1959 Ford Ranch Wagon, but it was still better than the jeep.

I could tell that Mister X was having second thoughts. He might have digested what we had been talking about the night before. Even though I could only speculate, the pieces of conversation I had heard between Silvano and Che indicated that the operation was no longer running smoothly. As an optimist, I always preferred to think the best was happening. We had only a few hours, perhaps, before that sinister sabotage would cost the lives of so many innocent people. I drove along Vedado until I reached Infanta and then headed to the Astral Theater.

March 3rd
8:45 pm
Astral Theater

The movie theater had no parking lot, so I found a spot across the street in front of the theater. I could see Chandee in one of the side entries, waiting for me, leaning patiently against the wall. She saw me trying to cross the street, dodging the few cars that were still on the road. She waved at me. I returned her wave as I crossed the street. I walked up to her, and she hugged me with a smile.

"Hi," she said. "It's great you finished your meeting early—I wasn't expecting you so soon. I only got here five minutes ago."

I smiled and kissed her on the cheek. "Good, I didn't make you wait."

She returned my kiss with one on my cheek and took my hand as if we were dating. We walked into the lobby and gave our tickets to the usherette. The usherette used her flashlight to help us find seats.

The theater was half full, so we picked two seats in a virtually empty row. There was only an elderly couple sitting in the aisle seats, and so we crossed all the way to the other side of the row. Chandee leaned against my chest and put her arm around me as if we were lovers. She leaned her mouth near my ear as if she were kissing me, and said, "The message is from your uncle and the General, and is as follows: under no circumstance should you go near your friend Daniel or his father, Mister X. Our intelligence indicates that after you left last night, Mister X tried to disassociate himself from the whole thing. He might have remorse, he might have conscience, but all we know is that today, at five-thirty in the morning, contrary to his usual custom, he left the house with Daniel and they went to the docks. From his office, he called one of his contacts, Fausto Pijirigua, because he could not get in touch with Silvano. He told Fausto to tell Silvano and Che that the operation has to be stopped because there's a leak. He said he knows for sure that another person knows the details of what they're planning."

I shot back and looked at her in the eyes, shaking my head with an expression of blended irritation and shock.

I stayed like that for a few seconds, and then I leaned in close to her ear. "Did Lazaro mention any name?"

She put her hand on my face, trying with some compassion to alleviate my tension. She shook her head negatively and mouthed the word "no" to me.

I leaned back in my seat and breathed a quiet sigh of relief. I rested my neck on the back of the chair and breathed deeply. She embraced me once more with her arm and tried to bring me close to her. I understood and leaned in to her. She put her lips on my ear once more and said, "We also know that after the conversation with Fausto, Lazaro visited the French and Belgian embassies. He tried to get in touch with both ambassadors. We do not know what his intention was in those visits. This is not going to be the end of this. Che and his accomplices will make sure they get Lazaro to get a detailed explanation of what he told Fausto, but they will also demand the name of this leak who knows about the operation."

I turned away from her mouth and moved to her ear. "That is why Che was in the meeting today with Fidel, even though he wasn't supposed to be back for two weeks. It makes perfect sense now. Tell my uncle and the General they are expecting very sophisticated helicopters with short- and long-range missiles as well as torpedoes, that the construction of this base is almost done, and that the place is the port of Mariel."

She nodded. We parted for a few seconds, and I sat there thinking as I watched the movie screen. The movie was Some Like It Hot. A gangster with white spats was coming into the room.

I didn't hear any of the audio, so sunk into my thoughts was I. I was wondering what Lazaro would tell Silvano and Che when they confronted him. A great guilt grew in my mind, and I regretted that I had pushed it so far across the line to find out more about that operation. My goodwill in trying to save my friend might have resulted in pushing my luck too far.

Chandee touched my shoulder, breaking my train of

thought. I leaned in to her, and she whispered, "What do you want to drink?"

"Nothing. I'm fine." I started to get up. "Let me go—what do you want?"

She held me down and pushed me back by my shoulder. "Relax, and stay quiet. I will bring us something to drink, OK?" she said with a smile. "Please—relax! You are very stressed. I can tell from your respiration."

I leaned back into her ear and whispered, "Coca-Cola."

She smiled in satisfaction to see that I wasn't fighting her any longer and was being cooperative. She stroked my face and said, "Calm down."

I smiled as she left towards the concession stand in the lobby. I sat there thinking that perhaps if Lazaro decided not to go through with his part of the plan, Che and his accomplices might be forced to abort the sabotage. But if Lazaro implicated me by telling them what I had said, even though I had left it open to his interpretation, things could turn ugly for me. I had to be very prepared, because Lazaro was a question mark in my mind at that moment.

Chandee returned with her hands full of hot roasted peanuts in a paper cone, popcorn, and two large cups of Coke. As we ate, she leaned into my ear once more and asked, "Do you have any idea what time this sabotage will take place if Lazaro doesn't stop it?"

I leaned away from her and silently shook my head. A few minutes passed as we ate and drank our snacks.

I leaned into her and whispered, "Can you please send this message to my uncle and the General? Che and Silvano might be interrogating Lazaro at this moment, wondering what turned him one hundred eighty degrees so abruptly, why the hell he's gotten cold feet, and who is behind this. Tell them that, in my opinion, they should allow me to get close to Lazaro again, perhaps tomorrow afternoon. I don't think this sabotage will take place until the evening. All crimes seem to take place at night. I assure them that if I can get close to Lazaro, I can get from his own mouth to what extent he involved me in his excuses and get him to put his car in reverse to get out of the situation. I believe he'll listen to what I say after our little difference last night."

I leaned back a little bit. She kept looking at me, eating her popcorn with a slight expression of agreement on her face. She touched her temple with her right index finger and nodded.

She handed me a bag of peanuts. I opened the bag and emptied it in my mouth. As I chewed, I said, "Thank you."

The movie was concluding. Jack Lemmon said to Joe E. Brown, "I'm a man!" He took off his wig to prove it, and Joe Brown replied with a shrug, "Well, nobody's perfect!"

We left the theater, hand in hand, and before we crossed the street to the Volga, all the young couples leaving with us looked at me with my uniform, pistol, long hair, and a car driven only by those at the top of the hierarchy, and Chandee smiled at the jealous looks from some of the other women. Moved perhaps by that pride, she hugged my arm to her and kissed me on my cheek. I looked at her and asked with a smile, "What was that for?"

"For everything you do, and for being a hopeless

optimist," she replied, then elbowed me. "Oh! You made me blush again!"

We got into the car and drove to her house. When we got there, I slowed down as we passed in front of the store. Xiang's green and white Ford Fairlane approached in the opposite direction, also slowing down. He didn't recognize me in the Volga. He looked at us with a blend of curiosity and fear, as what I was driving could be anyone from the G-2 or a big honcho in the government.

As he drew close, our eyes met through the windshields and he smiled in relief. He didn't acknowledge me openly but only gave a very slight nod of his head. He continued on and turned around the block.

As I watched the taillights disappear around the corner, I figured that he was bringing in something through the secret entrance that he didn't want anyone to see. I parked in front of the store and said to Chandee, "Don't forget, tomorrow at two-thirty in the same place. I will be waiting for the answer to my question from you guys. Daniel gets off work around three. I want to see if I can talk to him at work and pick him up from there. But I might also get lucky and be able to kill two birds with the same shot."

She smiled and kissed me tenderly on the cheek. She shook her head. "No doubt, you are an incurable optimist."

I smiled tenderly and nodded. "Claro, chica. Better to be an incurable optimist than a faithless pessimist."

She shook her head once more, got out of the car, and walked into the shop. I watched her walk away, admiring her for a few seconds. She walked all the way to the door, turned around, and waved to me. She realized I was watching her, whether in admiration or protectiveness to make sure she safely made it to her door.

I drove away slowly to avoid attracting attention. I also wanted to check out the area and see if I could notice any suspicious car in the street or any of the adjoining streets nearby. I realized that the same way our people had been checking them out could be used on me by my enemies.

Everything, however, looked clean. I drove towards my family's house on Carlos III.

A Very Dangerous Man

We classify the most dangerous men as those who think they know everything and can get away with anything because they have a superior brain. That superiority makes him believe that you and everyone else are fools. He uses elaborate lies to put a veil over your eyes, making you blindly believe his lie. He convinces you that in plain daylight he can pull the cover off of the table and not break a single plate.

This man, in his profound stupidity, crosses a double line. He assumes in his mind that you and the others believe his elaborate lies. Without the barest provocation he pushes one person against the other more and more in his deadly games, not knowing that you and the others don't believe a word he says. You pretend to play his game like a hunter waiting for his final move to destroy him. Unfortunately, you and the others have no other choice, because that is the only way to deal with this very dangerous man. It is the only way to stop his dangerous games.

Dr. Julio Antonio del Marmol

Chapter 6: *La Coubre*, the Deadly Bloodbath

After dinner with my aunt and uncle, my aunt took me to her son's room. He had died when he was only three, but they had kept the room up with all the toys and decorations as if he had been sleeping there just the night before. Batman and Superman figures lay on the bed. My uncle had on several occasions tried to convince my aunt to get rid of it all, but she wanted to hold onto the memories. She visited that room each day, consoling herself.

Now my aunt put her arm around my shoulders and said, "Sometimes, trying to protect the person you love most will destroy them and we don't even realize it."

"Why did you tell me that?" I asked.

"Because after so many years of trying to start a family, God finally rewarded us with a wonderful baby boy in our middle age. He was the most gorgeous creature, so beautiful and perfect—we couldn't even believe God's grace. We were so ignorant and overprotective. We wanted to isolate him from all forms of bacteria, so we sterilized ourselves before we even touched him. But he needed certain bacteria in his body to activate his immune system. In consequence, he had none, and he became so weak and vulnerable that his body couldn't fight off very mild infections, like a common cold. Eventually his whole system collapsed, and he died."

I shook my head sadly. I picked up a picture of my little cousin from the dresser and looked at it. He was a beautiful, red-headed kid that looked very much like I did when I was a little boy, with light eyes. I thought of the irony. My poor relatives who had wished so hard for that boy were moved by their vast love to protect him so much that it resulted in his death. The worst part was that they both had to live with that death on their consciences for the rest of their lives. My eyes grew moist at that thought, and I gave Aunt Violeta a strong, compassionate hug, much as she had given me the previous day. She had probably felt the same kind of love for me before and did that to avoid bursting into tears.

Finally, she pulled herself together, dried her eyes, and said, "Please, don't tell your uncle about this. Pancho never set foot in this room after our boy died. He was so psychologically affected by the trauma that every time he sees a boy about his age, he breaks down in tears. He took our little boy with him everywhere he went, even to work, he was so proud of him. It was like he lost himself when our boy died. For a while, it even seemed like he had lost his will to live."

"Don't worry about it. All our family knows about this, and my mother and father told us never to mention this subject to you unless you brought it up first."

My aunt ran her fingers through my hair tenderly. She looked into my eyes. "You know what? Your Mima and Papi are the most beautiful people I've ever met—generous, lovely, and the biggest hearts I've ever seen."

I nodded my head and smiled, delighted at hearing such praise of my mother and father. "I thank God every day to be so lucky that He gave me such great parents."

We sat for a while and listened to some Beethoven. After a while, we retired for the evening.

The next morning, I drove to the military hospital after saying goodbye to my relatives. I knew that whatever was causing those headaches was nothing important—more than likely, it was stress as a result of the double life I was leading each day. I went because I had told Che that I was going, and I needed to make sure that it checked out in case he sent someone behind me to check on my movements. I realized that the more I got involved in the spy business, the more carefully I had to tread each minute of every day, taking care that I never contradicted myself.

I spent several hours in the hospital while they took blood samples and ran a battery of tests. It was almost noon by the time I went to the hospital dining room for lunch. I hadn't had breakfast, in anticipation of the blood draw.

Finally, around 1:30 in the afternoon, I left the hospital. To ease my mother's mind, I decided to call my home in Pinar del Rio. She had told me repeatedly to call her to let her know I was all right anytime I was going to spend a lengthy amount of time out of the house.

I drove to the Havana Libre. I gave the car to the valet to park and entered the lobby. I went to a public phone and dialed 3504, my home number. After a few rings, my mother answered.

"Hello, who is this?"

"It's your son, Julio Antonio."

"Thank God, my boy! Why haven't you called me before? You've kept me on the border of desperation and worry."

"I'm fine, Mima. I'm fine."

"Claro! But I have to worry about it when you don't call for several days. You're neglecting your studies and your music lessons, for these ignorant, flea-infested people in power. They want you to be ignorant and flea-infested like they are! For God's sake, my son—I beg you, don't become a fanatic as your father has become to this stupid Revolution. Your father is a great man, honestly, and he has a wonderful heart, but his naivety is going to lose him everything he's worked for all his life."

I smiled out of my admiration for my mother, who had been able to see the rain before the dark clouds had gathered and called things plainly as she saw them and who was so concerned for my education. She was right—I had been juggling not only the responsibilities placed on my shoulders by the Revolution, but also those placed there by my double life as a spy.

"Don't worry," I said, trying to calm her down with love. "I will be back in a couple of days and will continue my studies. I'm starting to get a little tired of all the rhetoric and lies. These people—if one is not conniving, another has a deranged mind. They don't have any scruples at all."

"I know you will be one of the first to wake up from this morbid nightmare, but please don't repeat what you just said to anyone. Do you hear me?"

"Yes, Mima, I hear you."

"OK, take care of yourself, and please don't open your feelings to anyone."

"Mima, I only told this to you. I'll never share it with anyone."

"Good, my son. Hurry home."

We talked for a while and I explained to her I was staying at Violeta and Pancho's house.

"Give them my regards and a big hug from me," she said, "and you be safe. I love you very much."

"I love you, too, Mima."

I hung up the phone and left with a big smile on my face. I knew what I had just done wasn't prudent, but it felt so good. I had finally gotten a lot of things off my chest. I couldn't simply unburden myself to anyone else, not even Yaneba. In spite of how well I felt now, I knew that I could never do that again.

I looked at my watch, and saw that it was 2:45. I rushed out of the hotel and drove the Volga towards the Astral Theater.

When I got there, Chandee was pacing impatiently from one corner to the other, continually looking up and down both sides of the street, keeping a lookout for me. I parked in the same spot as before across from the theater. She waved at me, and I locked the car and crossed the street. As I navigated the street, I realized that there was more traffic than usual, and I thought that perhaps it was the afternoon rush, and people were leaving work to head home for the day.

Once I got to her, she hugged me as if she had not seen me in months. She kissed me tenderly on my neck and murmured in my ear, "I thought something horrible might have happened to you."

Her voice trembled, and as we embraced, I noticed that her whole body was shaking. I leaned back from her a little after a few seconds, completely surprised. "What happened? What's wrong with you?"

Her beautiful, bronze Asian skin was very pale—white as a sheet in fact—and her eyes were wide open. She took a deep breath. "Not even ten minutes ago, two cars from the G-2 came here and arrested a couple in the theater. They practically dragged them out of the building. On top of that, you're never late!" She looked at her wristwatch and showed me that it was 2:50 on the dot.

She breathed deeply once more. "The worst things have crossed my mind. I thought they had arrested you, tortured you, and for a moment after they piled out of that car, it looked like they were coming towards me." She crossed herself. "I thought I was dead! I almost started to run, but thank God I didn't. I would have incriminated myself if I started to run because I saw them. I would have completely given away my guilt. But I was so paralyzed, I just stood there. The men went right past me, but my heart had stopped completely."

I stroked her cheek with my fingers. "I'm sorry, honey—I'm really, really sorry that I'm half an hour late. I hadn't spoken with my mother since I left Pinar del Rio, and I didn't notice the time. It melted right through my fingers like butter. I feel so bad about what you just had to go through."

"Don't worry about it. Your mother deserved that, and a lot more." She crossed herself again. "Thanks be to God that nothing bad happened. Is everyone OK at home?"

"Yes, everybody is fine, but my mother is waiting impatiently for my return."

"Claro," she said with a smile. She took my hand. "Well, let's go inside the movie theater. We've drawn enough attention by standing here."

"Very well," I agreed. She already had the tickets in her hand. We went inside and gave our tickets to the usher. A young usherette took us inside, and we went to the same seats we had claimed before.

We sat down, and she leaned against me, putting her lips near my ear as before. "The message is practically the same. Do not get close to Daniel, even less near Lazaro. He's being followed. Also, he has been avoiding Che and Silvano's gifts. Your uncle and the General are both of the opinion that you did an extremely good job. They told me to give you a little pat on the shoulder for your extraordinary powers of persuasion." She gave me a little pat with her fingertips. "Evidently, the seed you planted in his brain and heart has grown rapidly and has rooted deeply in him. According to our contacts' information, he's been turned around almost ninety percent. He could be the key to stopping Che's plans or at least handicapping the sabotage."

I shifted position in my seat and put my lips near her ears. "Lazaro hasn't spoken with Che and Silvano yet?"

She shifted back. "No. They haven't been able to locate him. He's given orders to his people in the port to not tell anyone where he is. He's been moving from one ship to another, hiding from Che and Silvano. He's even sleeping on different ships each night, protected by his union guys, who are really loyal to him."

She leaned back a little and smiled, which I could see thanks to her white teeth in those shadows. I smiled back, and she pumped her right fist in a symbol of victory.

She leaned back in and said, "That is the reason your uncle and the General want you to stay away from them and let things take their natural course. Your presence close to either of them can draw suspicion and complicate everything unnecessarily. It remains to be seen if Lazaro will use your words to incriminate you and throw suspicion off himself, but we think he would have done that by now if he was going to take that path. Do you think so?"

I leaned back a little and nodded. Chandee had taken a huge weight off my shoulders and untangled the large knot that had been in my stomach for the last twenty-four hours. I had been constantly concerned about how Lazaro would use my information and my words when he spoke with Che and Silvano. The best scenario would have left tremendous doubt about my loyalty to the Revolution and to the individuals in charge of the country like Che.

I looked at the screen; the movie playing was

Spartacus and the final scene in which Kirk Douglas killed Tony Curtis to save him from the fate of crucifixion was playing.

Suddenly the entire movie theater shook violently. The movie continued for a few more minutes and then ended as the credits began to roll. Another tremor, more violent than the last, shook the building once more, and this time, we heard the roar of a vast explosion. The lights came on as the projector switched off. Everyone stood up in confusion. Some people who had already started to leave the theater hurriedly completed their departure. People began to murmur nervously to each other, and I noted by my watch that it was 3:15. I looked at Chandee with a very sad face, and she returned my look with understanding.

The damaged *La Coubre*

"Do you think that was it?"

I nodded slowly. "I think so. Evidently something precipitated things, and I was completely wrong in my calculations. These people are not common criminals—they don't need the night to operate, because they feel protected by the law."

We pushed between the people shoving to get out of there and emerged to a commotion of people rushing in the street, police, fire, and ambulance sirens, and ash falling to the ground. We ran across to the street to my car, and the squealing of brakes alerted us to a car that almost hit us. I slammed my hands down on the hood to protect Chandee.

"I'm sorry," the driver apologized. "I didn't see you."

"It's OK," I said, "just be more careful. What happened?"

He replied, "I don't know. There was a big explosion, and everyone's running away from the port."

We turned around to face the ocean, and there was a huge column of black smoke and ash rising up from the port area that eclipsed the afternoon sun of that terrible day. We jumped into the Volga and drove towards the port to discover what was going on.

The closer we got, the more we looked at each other. We realized that what we had been trying to prevent had happened anyway. I felt a really strong knot of defeat in my chest. No matter how much we had tried to stop that criminal act, this psychopathic Che and his miserable associate had ultimately been successful. At least, that is what I thought at that moment.

In silence, we reached the old Pan American Pier. Between the people and debris cloud, it was so bad that you couldn't even see the entire port. I pulled over to what looked like a secure location and got out of the car. The sight that greeted us was one of horror: decapitated heads, legs, and arms, disemboweled torsos, bodies torn in half. It looked like a plane in a war movie had just dropped a large bomb in a large crowd of people.

Damage to harbor facilities

Chandee had been walking behind me and stopped for a minute. I turned to her. She gagged, turned away, and vomited. I went over to her and held her head with one hand on her forehead and the other massaging her neck to relieve the tension.

"Do you want to go back to the car?" I asked her compassionately. "You don't need to see all this, but I have to find Lazaro and Daniel."

I took a couple of handkerchiefs out of each pocket in my uniform pants, and handed one to her. The other folded into a triangle and tied around my nose and mouth to block out the smell of charred flesh, bowel, and chemicals, which was worse even than that sarcocho tank I'd hidden in after stealing Che's portfolio several months before. "Are you OK?"

"I'm fine, I'm fine," she answered. "I'll follow you.

Keep going." After she cleaned her mouth, she folded the handkerchief in the same manner I had.

The volunteers transporting the wounded and the body parts crossed by near us. One was bearing only a head and an arm on his stretcher and another just a torso. The smell of Sulphur, propellant, and hydrochloric acid made the air difficult to breath. The partially dissolved organs and flesh which coated the ground made movement difficult.

We heard loud, desperate screams of agony underneath a vast pile of steel and iron in the debris. Chandee held me, and between the two of us, we began to remove the various bits of metal from the pile. A heavyset man with a dark, immense beard had been cut in half. He was missing everything from the waist down, his intestines lying loose on the ground beneath him.

He was still alive.

Some of the volunteers with stretchers came over to help us and remove him from the debris. However, a gigantic support beam was too heavy to move.

One of the volunteers yelled, "Bring a portable hand winch over here!" Another one left to find one.

The heavyset man said to me, "Will you please give me your pistol? I don't want to live like this anymore. For the love of God, please!" He held his hand out to me.

"Are you crazy?" I asked, shaking my head. "You should thank God you're alive. We'll get this beam off of you, and then we'll take you to the hospital, sew you up, and you'll be OK."

I breathed deeply; I knew it was a lie even as I uttered it. I felt a strain in my chest. "You'll see—in a few months from now, you'll look back and think of this as a bad dream that you've woken up from. They won't take too long with that winch, and we'll get you out of there in no time."

He replied more calmly, "Sure, you'll only take five minutes." He looked down at his own intestines. "It will only take five minutes, eh?" he repeated sadly.

I recognized the man's voice. The mafioso had said those exact same words to me when I had called Lazaro's office. I asked him, "Where are Lazaro and his son?"

He screamed in pain once more. "Let me die, please!"

One of the volunteers returned with morphine, and at great personal risk climbed around the beam and injected him with it. A few minutes later, he asked me, "*El Jefe*?"

"Yes," I said, "Lazaro! El Jefe. When was the last time you saw him?"

"Over there," he said, pointing off to a pile of debris. "We were both in his office when that crazy son of a bitch Silvano shot him. Just a few minutes before the first explosion."

Chandee asked in surprise, "Silvano shot your boss?"

"Yes, yes! Something Silvano wanted him to do, and my boss told him to count him out. Said they were all a bunch of liars."

Chandee asked, "That's all? What happened after that?"

"Silvano told him he was a coward." He started to cough up blood. He caught his breath. "He took his pistol and shot him twice."

I asked, "Where is Silvano?"

He raised his right arm and pointed to the same place. "With the first explosion, I saw Silvano fly through the air."

Chandee and I looked at each other in surprise, still wondering what had happened there. The volunteer arrived with the hand winch, the chain clanking against the frame wildly. They told the man with the morphine to grab the chain. Slowly they let out the slack so that the man down there could wrap it around the beam.

After he had secured and locked the chain, they slowly started to crank the winch, and the beam slowly lifted off of the unfortunate man's stomach. He breathed in relief as the beam began to move over and away from him. Other volunteers moved down and began to clean up the debris. Two of them started to scoop up his intestines with a plastic shovel and put them into a medical bag.

Just as it appeared to be a success, the knot in the chain completely snapped and opened. The volunteers jumped out of the way, and the beam crashed down right on top of his chest and skull, killing him instantly.

We all stood there in silence. Perhaps the man had what he had wanted all along—release from that agony. He didn't even cry out when the beam hit him. He couldn't have seen it coming or reacted if he had. All that could be seen of him were his arms on either side of the beam. The man who had been guiding the winch let go and recoiled in horror, placing his hands over his face.

"Oh, my God! Poor man! What a horrible death!" He had tears in his eyes, and some of the dead man's blood had splattered all over him. He himself had nearly been injured by the falling beam.

Chandee looked at me in horror. We were all frozen and then heard a voice by the pile of debris where Lazaro and Silvano supposedly had been. The voice was crying for help, and all of our heads turned in its direction, snapping us out of the limbo of that terrible moment we had just witnessed.

As a natural reaction, we all scrambled out of there, and moved towards the voice. We began to remove debris from the pile, searching for the person in distress. The voice sounded desperate but still had the strength of life in it. Piece by piece, we began to dig the debris away. A few minutes later, we had added another group to help us, and together we uncovered two men.

One man I could recognize at once. He was facing up, and I could see it was Silvano. He was dead, a piece of steel piercing his neck all the way through. The other man had been lying on his stomach. As they turned him, we could see his profile. It took several men to remove the large piece of iron off of his back and slowly turn him around. The flesh of his cheek was entirely missing as well as one ear.

Chandee shuddered in revulsion. The bone of his lower jaw and the molars were completely visible. One volunteer poured a little water on his face and began to clean the ash off of him.

"Be careful," I said, as he began to cough from the water entering through the hole in his face, "don't put too much water on his mouth. You could asphyxiate him."

At the sound of my voice, the man opened his eyes and looked up at me. A shock of recognition went through me. "My God," I said to Chandee. "It's Lazaro!"

He coughed a couple of times. "Commandantico, Commandantico," he said. He coughed some more.

"Yes, Lazaro, it's me. Where is Daniel?"

"That bastard Silvano killed him. His body should be around there." His body was completely fried by the heat, and he couldn't move his arm without pain. He gestured feebly with his finger. "That bastard tried to kill me, too, when I refused to place any more explosives." He paused. "You were right. They're all the same."

A volunteer came up and gave him some morphine and began to dig him out of there. "The sons of bitches are cut from the same cloth." A couple of volunteers started to move him and he screamed in agony. It looked like it had been cooked by the heat of the explosion.

One of the volunteers called, "More morphine and a pallet!"

Another said, "No more morphine—you'll kill him."

I could see two bullet holes, one in his left shoulder, and one close to his abdomen. "What happened here?"

He tried to smile, but it was more a grimace and a grunt came out. "I ruined their party," he said bitterly. "In his last act of desperation, Silvano grabbed Daniel and shot him in the head."

I winced and turned my head at the thought. He saw my expression. "I grabbed the crank from my jack and stuck it in his neck. But not before he shot me two times. I can die in peace now, because the ship is still there."

He pointed out to sea, and I could see that the ship was still floating out there, smoking. "She's still afloat.

The damage is nothing that can't be repaired." There was indeed very little damage. It looked like Silvano, in desperation to please his masters, had attempted to create an explosion himself. However, it was nowhere near the level of devastation they had planned, and *La Coubre* still rode majestically in the waves.

I smiled—as the Bible says, those who live by the sword die by it, and this certainly had happened to Silvano. The volunteers put the pallet under Lazaro to raise him up, and he screamed even more loudly. The morphine wasn't sufficient. Two volunteers took each arm to attempt to carry him differently. His body lifted partially off the floor, and then both arms snapped off at the shoulder. Lazaro's scream of pain reverberated throughout the entire area and could probably be heard blocks away. The scene that played before our eyes was one I don't think anyone had ever seen before. It was so hideous; when the arms detached from the body, the ligaments were plainly seen dangling from the stumps like long strands of spaghetti, only these dripped blood. More blood spurted from multiple wounds.

Chandee held her right hand to her mouth and raised her handkerchief. She couldn't hold it in any longer. She began to retch and lose whatever was left in her stomach. I was extremely nauseated myself. A couple of the volunteers likewise started to vomit.

I understood in that moment that this was too much for her, and I realized that there was nothing I could do there anymore. According to Lazaro, Daniel was dead, and I could tell that the father would soon follow his son through that door. His body was completely cooked by the heat, and there was nothing that could be done for him. Each drop of blood brought him closer to death, and it was a race between which would kill him first—the blood loss or the shock to his system from all the burns.

The memory flashed into my mind of the dinner at Daniel's house in Pinar del Rio, and it was chilling how accurate his grandmother had been in her prediction of both their deaths. Lazaro had completely dismissed the incident, and I wondered if, in the midst of his horrendous agony, if it also was flashing through his memory as he drew his last breaths.

I took Chandee by the hand and said, "Let's get out of here. This is enough. May God have mercy on his soul and forgive him for bringing his son with him to this horrible death."

Chandee crossed herself at my words and nodded in agreement. "Amen." We walked away from the grisly scene.

On our way back to the Volga, we continually had to avoid groups of volunteers scrambling from one victim to another. I could see through this chaos Che and his assistant Fausto Pijirigua, along with his escort. The short, paunchy Fausto walked carefully in his shiny boots with silver metal toe caps, trying not to slip in the bloody carnage.

They had just arrived and were in time for the photo op and propaganda moment. Photographers and journalists busily recorded Che tending to the wounded as a first responder, trying to demonstrate to the people the sacrifice he had made and the risk he had taken to go to that macabre scene. The press at that time were in the process of being nationalized by the government. They had already been intimidated and were anxious to release a story exactly like this that would show the new government in a positive light. Those who weren't afraid were already in bed with the new dictator.

One of those pictures became the iconic photo of Che through a very well-organized piece of propaganda by the communists. The photographer who took the picture maintained his silence, as he disliked the communist system, and even less the Castro brothers. However, he had to maintain the façade of professionalism or suffer repercussions and retribution. No one could agree with the strangulation of free expression, especially of artists, by the new regime in Cuba.

That picture was ironically titled *Guerrillero Heroico*, or the Heroic Guerrilla Fighter. My opinion has always been that giving it the title of "the Machiavellian Guerrilla" would have been more appropriate. I knew full well that the real intention of Che's plan was not to just kill a few people; he wanted to sink the entire ship, which would have killed many more people. Had all the munitions in the ship been detonated as planned, the blast would have destroyed the entire harbor facility. The death toll could conceivably have reached several hundred at that point, with overall casualties of very nearly a thousand. The physical damage to the area would have been irreparable.

Covered by ashes and smoke, I was not spotted by

Che as I opened the door of the Volga and let Chandee in through the passenger door. I then ran to the driver's side, and got in. We drove away quickly from that place in our attempt to avoid a chance meeting with Che. Luckily for me, Che was distracted by the attention of all the photographers and never realized that I was there. We drove away towards Chinatown.

As we drove, I asked Chandee, "Are you feeling better?"

She didn't answer but just nodded her head. Her face was still pale.

I reached out with my right hand to hold hers. It was sweaty and trembling. "When we get to your house, you should take a hot bath and try to relax your nerves."

She nodded again in silence. She held her right hand to her stomach and rubbed it as if she were in pain or discomfort.

"Did you want me to pull over?" She nodded silently. I pulled over close to the sidewalk on the Malecón, which was our boardwalk by the sea.

She didn't wait until the car was completely stopped. She jumped out, ran to the old wall, and leaned over it to vomit. By this point, her stomach was completely empty, which made it an agony for her.

After I parked the car, I got out and walked over to her. She was shaking her head and allowing the cool ocean breeze to caress her face and set her long hair blowing in the north wind. It looked like she was feeling a little better; the sun was out, but the gathering clouds hinted at rain in the near future. At that moment, I felt it was God's gesture of sadness for the pain and suffering these people were going through and the unnecessary waste of so many innocent lives. I put my hand on her shoulder and asked, "Are you feeling better?"

She turned and tried to give me a smile. Instead of a smile, it really conveyed to me a combination of anger, defeat, and sadness. "I don't think I'll be able to sleep for a long time," she said finally, "thinking only of that man cut in half, and the other, with his arms ripping right off of his body." She turned around, put her head on my shoulder, and began to cry. "How can God allow these things to happen? Why does any human being have to die this way?"

"Cry," I answered, "if it will make you feel better. Let the tears wash the pain out of you."

She cried for a few minutes, releasing all of the pain and depression she was feeling and letting it run out of her eyes.

She pulled herself together, and we got back in the car to continue on to her house. As we arrived there, I stopped in front of the store with the intention of dropping her off, but she insisted I come in. She had just received a record by Paul Anka from Canada. Unlike most LPs, which had twelve tracks, this one had fifteen, and she wanted to play some for me. "You'll love it," she said, "I know you like slow rock."

I could not resist this temptation, but I told her that I was going to park the Volga a block away, so that it wouldn't be in front of her family's business. I didn't want to call the neighbors' attention to it.

After we parked, we walked back to her house. Her mother and sister were extremely happy to see us, as the disaster was all over both television and radio news, and they had been worried about our well-being. Xiang was not at home, but Mrs. Xiang offered us a delicious cinnamon tea. Chandee told them the horrific details of what we had gone through this day, and they expressed their compassion and sympathy.

Chandee went to one of the bathrooms to clean herself up, while I went to another one to take a shower myself. I wanted to get rid of the stink of that horrible place and wash away any ash still caught in my hair.

After we were done, Chandee took me to a small room that connected with her room. There were a lot of books on different topics and a very nice console record player. We sat down and listened to Anka's new record. I heard for the first time with her the song "Put Your Head on My Shoulder." Even though I did not at that time understand a word of English, the music nostalgically took me back to another time, before the Revolution, when life was happier. We listened to it several times for hours, until Mrs. Xiang knocked on the door to inform us that dinner was served.

I looked at my watch. "Oh, my God, it's eight-thirty! Time flies when you're having fun."

Mrs. Xiang said, "Time flies even when you're not having fun." She tapped her temple with her index finger and said, "Everything is here. Good time or bad time, doesn't make any difference. Time is the same."

"Yes," I agreed, "you're probably right. The time is the same. Whatever is not the same is within us, according to the moment we're going through psychologically."

Mrs. Xiang pointed at me and said, "That's right, that's right. You've got it. Xiang is back now and waiting at table for you two. He is very happy that you're here with us today, and that we will all have dinner together."

"The pleasure is all mine, and I'm really happy to be with you guys, too," I replied.

Chandee turned off the record player, and we followed her mother into the dining room.

After we said hello to Xiang, we sat down to a delicious dinner of fried rice and seafood. The soup was shark fin, and we also had chicken with almonds. I ate until I could not even take another grain of rice, and I excused myself.

"Come with me," Xiang said, "I need to talk to you." He led me into his office. Once inside, we sat in comfortable chairs.

"We are very proud of you," he said, "and you should be proud of yourself. Even though we could not completely stop this terrible sabotage, you made something happen that appeared impossible. You derailed the main source and reduced the whole thing to be of minimal effect. While it's not a victory, it's still a very great accomplishment."

I shook my head. "I don't know if we can call it an accomplishment with so many dead and wounded. On top of that, my best friend and his father lost their lives. But I know it could be a lot worse. In the house of the blind, the man with one good eye is the king; but having only one eye still doesn't make me happy when I look around at all the blind people around me."

"You are very savvy like a Chinese," he said sympathetically. "That's true, and you're right." He shook his head. "I'm sorry. But you must take into consideration that you are in the clear and have no problems. We all know you did whatever was in your power to save your friend's life, even at risk to yourself."

I shook my head. "If only he had listened to me, he would be alive now."

He replied, "Yes, but that is the problem with mankind. Nobody learns from other people's experiences. I want to warn you, though, that Lazaro left some notes with the ambassadors of France and Belgium. He mentioned that if anything should happen to him and he should die, that they should ask you, since you would know the reason for it and who was behind it."

I leaned back in my chair and rubbed my cheek. "I cannot talk about this without incriminating myself! What can I do, even if they ask me?"

"Exactly!" He emphasized his point by pointing at me. "Nothing! That is why I wanted to bring you in here to talk to you. You have to be prepared, because what Lazaro did not know is that the ambassador of France and Che are best friends; not only are they best friends, they both work for the international Marxist communists. The French ambassador is on the payroll of this government as a spy in Europe. That's not enough; these people have private meetings with the internationalists and the Soviet KGB. Among them are writers, politicians, and intellectual *de sobaco*[10]." He paused and smiled. "You know why they call it the *Sobaco*? It's a code, a signal—whenever they meet, they should bring a book. It doesn't make a difference whether they've read it or not, but it must be tucked in their armpit. Moreover, it must be

---

[10] The armpit

held under the left armpit."

"Oh, my God!" I exclaimed. "What can I do with this?"

"Nothing. Like I told you before, under no circumstance can you ever admit to the ambassador, if he comes to talk to you, or to Che, or to anyone else, that you had that conversation about *La Coubre* with Lazaro. You will deny that, even if they torture you. You don't even know why Lazaro created that fiction and mentioned your name in that note. You let them think whatever they want, and you pretend to be completely ignorant of everything. In the end, the only ones who can contradict you," he leaned in to me at that point for emphasis, "are Daniel and Lazaro. And, according to our information as well as yours, they're dead. For good or ill, that is the reality, and when you deny this, Che and the others will have to come to the conclusion that Lazaro got cold feet and created that story to get out of it. We don't know for certain yet whether the ambassador to Belgium is involved in this plot. We don't know the reason, either, why Lazaro chose to visit him. You therefore have to consider him as a question mark. If he approaches you for any reason, you maintain the same line you're going to maintain with the French ambassador until we can verify with the insurance company for the ship. They will be doing their own exhaustive investigation into what happened and what was behind the whole thing. The only thing you know about *La Coubre* is that your friend and his father both worked on the ship when that explosion occurred. Nothing else. Do you understand?"

"Absolutely," I replied. "I hope we can find a way to directly or indirectly expose the Cuban government and Che and bring the truth of what happened to the entire world."

He smiled sadly. "In a perfect world, it should be that way. Unfortunately, we don't live in a perfect world. Not even an imperfect one; we're living in a rotten world, full of maniacs and sick men with power and egos like Che, Fidel, and Raul. We have to play the game of cat and mouse, and unfortunately, right now, we are the mouse." He stroked his beard. "I hope this is not the case for very long."

I made a sour face. "I don't like being compared to mice at all. Let's hope this doesn't last for too long, indeed. But if we're going to be the mouse, then let's at least be the head. Let's be the leaders in this game for as long as it lasts."

He smiled and nodded. "Do you know the exact location of that helicopter base?"

"Not exactly, but I have an idea. I overheard Fidel tell Che where it's situated. Apparently, Che has not yet been there. According to Fidel, they're establishing the base in the old cavalry fort used by the Dictator's army. It's about ten kilometers before you get to the port of Mariel, after you pass an observation tower built by the Spanish colonial power in the eighteenth century."

Mr. Xiang raised his right hand. "Ah! I know where that place is! I've been there. It's about twenty-three kilometers from the Mariel Highway on the left side. They might decide to install this in there, because the cavalry has become obsolete. Even though the Dictator's government tried to maintain those units to patrol the rural mountain areas, they probably came up with the idea to use the installation already there." He looked at me in silence and stroked his beard once more.

"What are you thinking?"

He continued to stroke his beard thoughtfully. "Hmmm." I continued to look at him, but asked him nothing more. I patiently maintained my silence and waited for his answer. After a few seconds of thinking, he asked, "When are you thinking of returning to Pinar del Rio?"

"Tomorrow morning," I replied, "unless something unexpected comes up."

He leaned back in his chair. "You said that Fidel invited you to go with him to the base."

I nodded. "Yes, that's right."

"I know you did what you're supposed to do and more according to the circumstances. You declined the trip because you were scheduled to meet with Chandee yesterday." He shook his head and clucked his tongue. "What a pity—that was a perfect opportunity to go there and take pictures of what they're doing in that installation." He raised his right hand up, pointing upwards. "Perhaps not everything is lost. On your way back to Pinar del Rio, perhaps you could come up with a way to make a detour to Mariel."

"What excuse?" I demanded. "Could you please tell me? This sabotage that they're probably screaming the Counterrevolution is responsible for, and that the reporters on the TV will be yakking about for a long time, gives them the unique excuse to bring in anyone they want to accuse, sentencing them to thirty years to life in jail or the firing squad. You tell me, what kind of excuse can I possibly invent to be around that strategic base, uninvited, that not even Che has visited yet?"

Xiang looked at me in surprise, not expecting this reaction from me. Embarrassed, he tried to calm me down. "I'm just trying to give you an idea. You, and only you, know what you can or cannot do, taking into consideration your security as the most important priority."

I squeezed my lips and stroked my chin gravely, trying to analyze that last sentence. "All of this is without taking into consideration that in the last twenty-four hours I've been very close to one of the key individuals connected with this sabotage. Practically with no explanation or logical reason, he retracted something he had previously been willing to do with these people, taking it into his head to ruin their plans. I have to walk on glass with my shoes off from now on for a little while. Even though all of these people are sons of bitches, they are not stupid. We cannot underestimate them. That would be very dangerous, not only for me, but also for all you guys around me."

After a few seconds, I furrowed my brow and said, "If Chandee released my worries before, your information about the French ambassador just multiplied them. The question mark over the Belgian ambassador, since it's not clear which sea he's swimming in, definitely means I'm not in the clear zone like you said before. On the contrary, I'm in extremely high doubt. If I were them, I'd be wondering right now why the hell Lazaro had given them my name in the event something tragic happened to him."

Xiang scrutinized me in silence. "You don't have to say anything more. I understand you perfectly. Go back to Pinar del Rio, lay low for a while, and don't move. Let some time pass and see which way things turn."

I didn't reply, and we sat there in silence for several seconds. Finally, he broke the silence. "If you want, you can spend the night here. You're probably tired, angry, and frustrated from everything you saw today. But, if you decide to stay here tonight, please take your car and bring it around here to the back so that we don't call any attention in the neighborhood. The car will also be more secure there."

"Thank you. I will take you up on your invitation. I'll leave very early in the morning. If I don't see you, we'll maintain contact through Chandee. Please say goodbye to her for me, and to the others. I'm really tired, and I think I'm going to go to bed in a little while. I'll go and park the car in the back like you asked."

I stood up and walked to the door. When I got to the door, I looked back. "About those pictures you want from the base, let me see what I can do. If I can accomplish anything, I'll be in contact so you can send Chandee to pick them up."

He was about to say something, but I walked out of the door to head him off. I left the little office and walked towards the front entrance and into the store. I walked out to bring the Volga to the usual storage location for the coming night.

After I parked the car in the back and re-entered the store, I looked through the window in concern at my surroundings. I knew that it would be a matter of time before Che or someone around him placed somebody to watch me. Evidently, everything was quiet and clear—at least for now.

I went inside the office where I had planned to spend the night and went to bed with the hope that those horrific moments we went through that day would not persecute me in my dreams. I tried to blank my mind, tried to substitute those terrible scenes with those beautiful memories of Yaneba on the beach at Las Canas while we swam under water and discovered a dozen lobsters, and the beautiful night on the front porch of the beach house. I hoped I could leave the image of *La Coubre* behind me in the past.

Soviet helicopter given to the Cuban military

Chapter 7: The Sadness of the Goodbye

My approach worked; I had great dreams. There were only a few flashbacks to Nogueira and his revolver against my head, but otherwise I slept exceptionally well.

I awoke at 5:30, and everyone was still asleep. I washed my face and brushed my teeth, and then put together everything in my travel bag. I wrote a note of gratitude to Chandee and instructed her to give to her mother, sister, and the others in the house my most sincere thanks for their hospitality. I crept silently out of the house.

I got in the Volga and left Chinatown behind. I stopped at a bakery and bought a large box of Cuban pastries. I also ordered a midnight sandwich of sweet bread and a large glass of orange juice, taking some for the road. Even though I had ordered more pastries than I was supposed to, I decided to take the extras to Mima. Pastries were her favorite, and I had inherited that fondness from her.

I drove for a while, and when I got to the T intersection to turn off onto the highway to Mariel, I could not avoid having a pang of remorse at telling Xiang that I could not do what he had asked. I knew I really could, but the stress and my emotional frame of mind the night before had made me upset at that moment, more so than was ordinary for me. They had already asked so much of me. I had not even yet concluded what I had been sent to do when they were asking me to take on more responsibility. The coming investigation with the ambassadors really concerned me, and I might have been a little harsh towards Xiang.

I made a decision. I turned to the right and drove down the highway with a sign marked "Puerto del Mariel."

I smiled, wondering what Xiang had thought after our conversation the previous night. He probably thought I was a little neurotic.

I established in my mind what I would say when I arrived at the base. I believed I should maintain the excuse of accepting Fidel's invitation. Follow the truth, and the truth would set me free. I determined that this would be the safest course for me to adopt. Following the same instructions Fidel had given to Che, I reached the base without incident.

When I arrived at the main gate of the base, I identified myself to the soldiers on the other side. They approached me and saluted upon seeing the vehicle I was driving. They called Captain Martinez, the man in charge of the base, and he immediately authorized my entrance over the radio.

They opened the gate, and I drove inside. Extensive

remodeling was still in progress. Walls were partially torn down, and large landing pads for the helicopters were partially erected, with microwave communication towers and a single air traffic control tower already in place. I arrived at the half-constructed building that was clearly intended to be the Central Command. A tall, distinguished man, white skinned, slim, with black hair, came down to greet me followed by a sergeant, a couple of corporals, and a few other soldiers. His epaulettes bore the three Vs of a captain's rank. He walked up to me and saluted as I got out of the Volga, as the others likewise saluted. I returned the salutes.

"I've seen you many times on television and other places," he said, "but I've never had the pleasure of meeting you in person. It's a great honor. What brings you to this *parajes*[11]?"

I smiled and replied, "Well, this *parajes* you are in charge of is the last kick in the butt to the rear end of the Yankee Imperialists. It is also the latest pride of our Commander-in-Chief. He actually invited me yesterday to come here with him to visit you. Unfortunately, other responsibilities prevented me that pleasure. On my way to Pinar del Rio, I decided to stop by and see this great new wonder. I hope our Commander-in-Chief had a great time with you yesterday and left with a great impression," I waved my arm around, "of the magnitude of all this." I pointed to all the dormitories, landing pads, and the

---

[11] Humble place

works in progress. "This looks magnificent."

He looked at me, his face positively beaming like a kid in an ice cream shop. "Yes, yes, indeed! Our Commander-in-Chief is impressed and very happy with the progress we've made preparing this base in such a short time. As a matter of fact, we're almost a week ahead of schedule! He told me that he was only expecting bulldozers and construction equipment, but he was completely surprised at what all we've done in such a short time."

I smiled. "He's not the only one. They told me it wouldn't be done until next month—that it was only in progress. But you've already got the things standing up! You've not only surprised the Commander-in-Chief, but me as well."

Captain Martinez smiled. "Come on, let me show you around. I want to give you a tour."

"Very good," I replied with a grin.

"I want to show you the Jacuzzi, the sauna, and the Olympic swimming pool we have under construction for the recreation of our pilots." He put his arm around my shoulder in a gesture of affection. We walked through the construction of the hexagonal building. I got my book out of my shirt and took my pen out. I started to write notes as he explained everything. Whenever his attention was diverted, I also surreptitiously took pictures of everything.

"Very smart," he said to me.

"What?" I replied.

He put his finger wisely to his temple. "Whatever we put here, we might forget. Whatever we write down goes to history!"

I smiled and nodded. I laughed inside at how true that was, although it wasn't what was in my book that was important—it was what was going into my pen.

His tour took us almost two hours, and he insisted that I stay with him for lunch. I firmly and politely declined his invitation. "I need to stop by my brother-in-law's house. I haven't seen him or my sister for a while, and I promised my mother to be home tonight for dinner."

He nodded understandingly. "OK, I will give you a rain check. When the base is finished, you come any time you can, and we will have lunch together."

After I said goodbye to the men in the base, I slowly drove out towards the gate with a big grin on my face. I had another invitation to come back once the base was completely functional and get an update.

I continued my trip towards Pinar del Rio. I went onto the highway and headed towards La Leña, where my sister Disa and my brother-in-law Canen lived. About an hour and a half later, I arrived there, where they received me with much love. My childhood nanny Majito was living with them on my mother's instruction, and she showered me with affection. We sat down to lunch, and I was told that everything that I was eating had been grown there on the property—the house appeared to have belonged to one of the very wealthy who had left.

As we sat on the porch, I looked around and took note of their home. The circular house was in the middle of the mountains, and the porch completely encircled it. It was surrounded by cedar trees, and looking down from the porch, one was given the impression of being in the jungle on the Amazon. It was breathtaking and would appeal to anyone who loved nature in its most pristine virginity. It was captivating.

After everyone drank the Cuban coffee, which I diplomatically declined, four soldiers who took care of security for my brother-in-law appeared on patrol. According to my brother-in-law, Commander Escalona insisted that he have at least four men with him, as he was now the chief of the tribunals for the province. There could always be those unhappy with a sentence he had handed down, and so someone might attempt to retaliate against him. It was also one of the reasons he had taken that remote house.

The four soldiers were the best snipers in the whole regiment. After we spoke for a while on the porch and I told them of my trip with Che to Caibarién, the crazy Nogueira, and all that had happened at the pier the previous day, they told me about their honeymoon and other pleasant subjects. After a little while, my sister went inside the house with Majito, and Canen told me that he wanted to speak with me in private.

"Let's go—I want to give you a tour around," he said. We walked around the house, and the pure, mineral waterfalls provided a good white noise in the background to cover our conversation. He showed me huge cages with fighting cocks and the horses' stables. Two soldiers followed us at a distance, while the other two remained at the house with the women.

"We only have to go to the city when we wish to."

He showed me another cage with hens and fresh eggs all over the place, a beautiful pond with all kinds of freshwater fish, a stable with dairy cattle, another stable with pigs and goats, and cages with Cornish hens and pheasants. The area with the pheasants was surrounded with fish netting in the trees, so that the birds could fly around and avoid having their meat grow tough by enforced inactivity. There was no doubt in my mind that the person who had possessed this property before must have been filthy rich and very reclusive.

All of the property was about twenty acres in area, and it looked like a military fort, with twelve-foot-tall fences topped with barbed and razor wire.

It was also reminiscent of a zoo.

I wondered what kind of pain the person who had built all of this had felt at abandoning that magnificent property. His love of privacy was not as strong as his love for freedom; it was the only reason I could think of that would prompt him to leave behind all the fruit of his work.

I was completely abstracted in my thoughts, so Canen asked, "What do you think of our place?"

He caught me by surprise, and I smiled sarcastically as I answered in the same way I had replied to Argibay and his new car. "I hope you didn't have to pay too much for all of this."

He laughed and said, "What, you're going to make fun of me now?"

I hit him on the shoulder playfully. "No, no, chico— I just wanted to mess around with you a little." He looked at me unhappily and shook his head. "I see your conscience is still intact, because my joke bothered you."

"You have to be careful," he said. "With me, it's no problem—but somebody else could take your joke in a different context." He looked at me very gravely. "You want to see how my conscience is still intact? All those soldiers and the sergeant who tried to rape your friends are in jail."

I nodded and replied, "Thank you. I really appreciate that."

"You know what Argibay told me the other day when I ran into him at the regiment? He said, 'You should not be hanging around with the worms, because all the families of those young ladies are enemies of the Revolution and probably will be in Miami soon.' Of course, I sent him to hell and told him that it was not an excuse or a justification for the soldiers to be rapists, especially with minors, and that he's converting himself into their accomplices by defending them."

I replied, "It's great you told him that, because that's exactly what I told him in his office when we discussed the situation not too long ago."

We sat down on the trunks of some chopped-down trees, close to the horses' stables. The bodyguards following us went over to the horses, picked up some alfalfa, and began to feed them.

"Listen to me very carefully," said Canen, "because I'm not going to repeat it. Even though you are intelligent and wise beyond your years, I am older and more experienced than you." He glanced at the guards to make sure they weren't listening, and he lowered his voice. "I think your life is in danger. You have to walk very carefully, because you're swimming in shark-infested waters. The sharks, when they smell blood or feel in danger, will not only attack you and the others, but also devour themselves."

I looked at him seriously. This was coming out of the blue. In surprise, I said, "Brother, I don't know what you're talking about. I think someone is filling your head with erroneous ideas. Maybe if you can be more explicit in what you're referring to, I will understand you better and can assimilate what you're trying to tell me."

He looked at me with an ironic smile and stood up. He brushed his pants seat off and said, "Let's walk towards the back over there." He gestured to the soldiers to remain where they were and that we would circle back. While he signaled, I also stood up and brushed off the seat of my pants.

I followed him closely. We entered a banana tree grove, and he stopped. "Remember one thing: I will never betray you—first because of my moral convictions, second because you know I believe in God and Jesus Christ, and third because now we are family, and that is more important than anything in life. I don't know how I can get through to you, but I have been advised you are in extreme danger, because you've been leading a double life. You actually don't even realize how dangerous what you're doing is. I have information that they are soon going to put somebody behind you—I don't know if it's a woman or man—who you trust completely. This person will accuse you of treason and working in the service of foreign governments and will bring enough charges against you that the government will put you in front of the firing squad. Raul has given secret orders to Piñeiro that not even Fidel or Che should have knowledge of what they're doing, until they accumulate enough evidence. According to my source, Piñeiro has told Raul that he has complete assurance that you had something to do with the robbery of Che's portfolio."

I gave him a look that was deadly serious, but I maintained my calm. I could see genuine worry and sadness in his eyes.

"Damn!" Canen said. "I don't know how I can get through to you." He rubbed his forehead with his left hand.

I remained silently standing by his side. I moved over to a manzano banana plant and touched it to make sure it was soft enough to be ripe. I pulled a couple of bananas off the bunch, gave one to Canen and kept one for myself. I started to peel mine as he kept looking at me. Finally, I said, "Really, really, my brother—you have no idea how much appreciate your worry for me, and I value that information. But I have no clue of what you're talking about. Your reference that I'm living a double life." I shook my head and smiled in seeming bemusement. I spread my arms. "I don't have time to live one life, because the Revolution doesn't give me time for that. Between Che and Fidel, how the hell can I have another life?"

He threw up both arms in frustration. "Fine, fine! I see they've trained you very well. OK, what if I tell you to go and ask the General?"

"What?" I asked.

"You know—the General! The next time you see him,

ask him if you can trust me." He stroked his cheek, and I could tell he was looking for a reaction from me.

I moved around slightly and thought about what Chandee had told me in Caibarién of the MQ-1 penetration in the group. I swallowed and wondered if that spy was Canen. I couldn't figure out how he knew about the General, so I replied with a shake of my head and half-jokingly, "I don't know any general in Cuba. The generals don't exist anymore; Fidel and Raul took all those ranks out. Remember? Only Commanders. Are you just screwing around with me?" I slapped him playfully on the chest.

Canen's look was deadly grave and frowned. "*Carajo*! You are truly more than good—you are a master in this goddamn business!"

He shook his head once more. "I think I've been worrying about you unnecessarily, because I believe you are vaccinated already against everything I've been telling you. Believe it or not, this makes me feel a lot better. I can see you are a professional." He scratched the back of his head. "Cojones! I have another big surprise for you."

He grabbed two more bananas from the tree and offered one to me. "You don't have to admit anything to me—all I ask is that you check whatever it is you have to check. Reassure your position, and later on, we can talk in more detail. But I have to tell you that my group and my circle have information as fresh as the banana in my hand." He held up the banana and took a bite from it. "Let me advise you to be very careful with your other brother-in-law, Guerrero. He is considered extremely dangerous in our military circles. My colleagues call him the Pirate, since he's capable of selling his mother for a single Cuban peso."

I nodded and smiled joylessly. "Thank you for that information, but I know what Guerrero is already. I know of his weakness, unfortunately. You understand?"

"Yes—just remember, we all have good and bad members in our families. It's better to know who we can and cannot trust." This time, he looked more pleased, as we were in complete agreement. Even though he hadn't had any corroboration from my part about what he had been telling me, at least we were on the same page together regarding the danger Guerrero represented to everyone.

"It's really a pity to have someone like him in our family," he said. "A man can offer his life for his convictions. It's good for the majority. But he can never sell friends and family for personal ambitions or material rewards. Betraying your friends and family while pretending to be something you're not is the behavior of a conniving, deceitful person with no scruples at all. Speaking of scruples, be very careful with Che. He's another one like Guerrero but on a larger scale; he's the same monkey with different music."

I smiled and nodded again.

Canen raised his right arm and yelled, "Isleño!"

The taller, thinner guard with a long nose and a face full of freckles replied. "Yes, sir, Captain Canen?"

Both guards came over to us. Each was armed with a machete, a pistol, and a rifle slung over his shoulder. When they reached us, Canen asked, "Will you please let me have your machete?" The soldier drew his machete from its scabbard at his waist and handed it to Canen. Canen cut the bunch of bananas that we had been picking individual fruit from and gave it to the other soldier, a man of middle height, olive skin, and curly hair. He took the bunch and slung it over his shoulder. Canen cut the tree trunk into small pieces and scattered them around the other trees to fertilize them. He returned the machete back to Isleño and said, "Let's go back to the house."

On the way back, he put an arm around my shoulder. "Remember, anything you need, come to me first before you talk to anybody else. Any problem at all." I looked at him in confusion. He smiled and raised his other hand. "Of course, after you get the green light that you can trust me."

I smiled and shook my head. I looked at him noncommittally. "Thank you, brother." He smiled and squeezed my shoulder affectionately.

We walked into the house, and Disa and Majito insisted that I stay until the next day so I could have dinner with them that evening. I declined, telling them that I had promised Mima to return home that day, and I didn't want to unnecessarily worry her. After a few hours having a good time in their company, I said goodbye and continued on my journey towards Pinar del Rio. I was really anxious not only to see my family, but I had an extreme burning in my heart to see Yaneba, to hug and kiss her while she was still in Cuba. She and her family were planning to escape the island in a small boat once her father had collected the thirty-five gallons of gasoline required to make the trip to Miami.

As I entered the city, I realized that there had been some changes. There was a barricade at the bridge over the River Guama. I slowed down gradually with the intention of stopping. The soldiers recognized both the car and me and gestured for me to continue through. We saluted each other, and I drove on into the city. I turned left by the Jupiña factory and towards my house.

When I arrived, Mima received me with kisses and hugs full of joy, and I gave her the box of pastries. She appreciated that very much, giving me extra kisses. My brothers helped me unload the Volga, and my youngest sister, Marda, stored the produce that Canen and Disa had given me: eggs, vegetables, and fruit that had all been grown on the ranch.

After I spent a little time with my family, I left and drove towards Yaneba's house. I discovered that the house was closed up; no one was around, and it looked like nobody had been around for a while. A fear gripped my heart that she had already left, and that I had spent too much time away, causing me to literally miss the boat. Ordinarily, when they left for the beach, they would have somebody taking care of the house. Without thinking twice about it and with my head filled with anxiety, I drove towards Las Canas in the hope of finding them still there.

When I arrived at the beach house, I saw Martina, the family's black housekeeper, outside sweeping the porch. She raised her head and saw the Volga. As if she had seen a ghost, she put the broom against the wall and ran inside the house without looking back a second time. She closed the door behind her.

I had already raised my right arm to say an affectionate hello from the Volga, and froze in that position with an expression of surprise on my face. I drew near the house, parked, and shut off the engine. Before I got out, I realized that Martina had not recognized me because she had never seen me in this style of car. It was late afternoon and the sun was setting; she would not have been able to see inside the vehicle and know who was driving it. Considering the only people who drove Volgas, it was natural for her to jump to the conclusion that it was the G-2 coming, and the poor woman had run inside to warn everyone of the imminent danger outside.

I got out of the car, smiling to myself, thinking of the level of fright I had just given the poor lady. When I got to the porch, I noticed a curtain twitch, an indication that someone was peeking through from a side window. The front door opened, and Yaneba was there, grinning broadly. She turned back and yelled, "It's OK! It's Julio Antonio!" She ran to me and gave me a big hug and kiss. She whispered in my ear, "We are leaving very early tomorrow morning. Thank God you came back today! My main sadness all these days was that I would be leaving Cuba without saying goodbye to you."

I gently pushed her away a little and touched her face with the fingers of my left hand. I took her hand in mine and placed it on my chest. "Feel my heart and see how fast it's beating. This is what had been going through my mind all the way from Pinar del Rio to here, when I found your house closed up and nobody there. You don't know how happy you've made me to see you still here."

She smiled in pleasure.

Martina showed up at the door with a big smile on her face and a hand over her chest, demonstrating to me the fright I'd given her. "You scared me half to death! Where did you get that car, my son?"

"Just a little gift from Che for saving his life," I answered with a mischievous smile.

She shook her head and gave me a big hug and a kiss on my cheek. "Thank God it's you, and not what crossed my mind when I saw that car. Come on, let's go inside."

When I went inside, I was surprised at seeing one of my good friends, Arturo, sitting there with his father, Mayo, both of whom had been scared witless. Mayo looked at my uniform, his face pale and distrustful. I could see the fear and questioning in his eyes.

Apparently, no one had explained anything about me to him. Josue realized this and stepped beside me. He put his arm around my shoulder in a friendly fashion. "Don't worry, Mayo. Julio Antonio is completely trustworthy." He grinned broadly. "All that gasoline I gave to you so that you can leave, and the parts for your boat, like the bushings for the propeller? You owe that to him, not to me, because he's the one who brought them to us. This is a great kid."

Arturo's father looked at me still with an expression of fear, but relaxed a little. "Well, thank God he's on our side. He might be able to help us with our great problem."

We entered the hallway connecting the house with the workshop in back. "What's the problem?" I asked.

Josue pointed to a huge outboard motor in the middle of the shop that hadn't been there during my last visit. It was on top of a wheeled sawhorse. "This is the major problem Mayo has. It looks like the motor has been unused for so long that it's completely frozen. Even if we find the parts to repair it, which will be very difficult, it will take too long to overhaul the entire motor." He made a helpless gesture. "And I'm sorry, but I cannot do it. We're all prepared to leave tomorrow morning." He hesitated and looked me guiltily. "Do you know anyone with a similar kind of motor that would be willing to sell to Mayo? He's in a tight situation. The government has put a warning out on him, and if he doesn't leave the island within the next seventy-two hours, the G-2 will arrest him."

I furrowed my brow and squeezed my nose in thought. "I think I can resolve your problem on one condition."

Mayo replied immediately, almost begging, "Whatever you say. I need to get the hell out of Cuba and bring my family with me."

"I know, I know—I heard what Josue said. I know a family that has a similar motor, almost identical. They'd been planning to use it to abandon Cuba themselves, but they recently received a telegram from the government that gave them the authorization to leave legally. They'll be leaving everything behind, and that motor will be in the hands of the government." I stroked my forehead with the fingers of my left hand. "I think that if we offer them a substantial amount of money, they would be willing to sell it. Assuming, of course, that they still have it. If so, you guys have the problem resolved." I looked at Arturo, who listened by his father's side in silence to our conversation.

Arturo smiled and said, "Thank you very much, brother." Mayo repeated his thanks with a smile. I replied, "It's too soon to thank me. Let me go and see if they still have it, and we'll see how everything goes. If all is well, I will bring it back here. But my condition is that, whatever happens, if you guys get arrested or get in any trouble, you can never reveal where that motor comes from. Don't involve me in this at all. Invent whatever you want, but my name cannot be spoken in any conversation relating to this. Do you guys understand?"

Mayo said hurriedly, "Of course, of course. Claro! You have nothing to worry about. Offer that man whatever. I have over twenty thousand pesos that I won't be using once we leave, because they're no good off this island."

I shook my head cynically. "I've heard that before."

"You've got my word," Mayo repeated emphatically. "We will never mention your name."

"Very well," I replied, "I will take your word. If all goes well, I will be back here tonight and will leave the motor with Josue. If I don't see you guys again, I wish you a great trip and that God protects you on your journey."

Yaneba looked at me with pride and with a smile said, "When you arrived at the house and Martina screamed about a G-2 car outside, we thought that we were all going to be arrested for having Mayo with us. The authorities have been looking for him for a couple of weeks already." She opened her arms. "The end of the story—you who we thought was the danger instead might become the salvation for Mayo and his family!"

Yaneba's mother, Maria, asked, "Are you then going to come back here, one way or the other, and let us know the results of your inquiry? If it wouldn't be inconvenient, Yaneba can go with you if you're coming back anyway, because we forgot a small suitcase with Elena's clothes in her bedroom. Could you please bring it back?"

"For me, it's not an inconvenience at all," I replied. "On the contrary, it will be a pleasure. It could be the last favor I do for you guys for a long time."

"Thank you," Maria replied, "thank you very much."

After I said my farewells and hugged Arturo, I left the workshop with Yaneba following me. As we passed through the living room, Yaneba's little four-year-old sister, Elena, stopped me and gave me a small crystal heart and a kiss on my cheek. I smiled and thanked her, and we left the house. We passed Martina on the porch and returned her farewell wave.

We got into the Volga, and Yaneba grabbed my hand lovingly. She smiled and said, "Everyone in my family loves you. I like that very much—even my little sister, who is so tiny, can see you have a great heart."

I smiled and nodded. "God protect everyone."

She crossed herself. "Yes, God be with all of us. We will need Him more than ever to keep our enemies far away from us tomorrow morning." I looked at her sadly. Even if everything went well and they got away from the Cuban coast and arrived safe and sound at their destination, there was a great possibility that I would never see her again. She was taking my heart with her.

Perhaps she felt the same sentiment at that moment, or perhaps it was because of the look on my face, but she leaned over and kissed me on the cheek. "Don't worry—I have no doubts we will see each other again. You are the other half of my heart, and without you I cannot live anymore. I will wait for you, even if it's for a long, long time."

I shook my head. "No, no—you should not wait for me or anybody, ever. What if I die, or something happens to me, and you don't even know...."

She interrupted me by placing her hand on my mouth. Her eyes grew wet, and she said, "Please, let me dream. I don't want to hear or live any more in reality. I've been living in reality until today here in Cuba. This reality is too sour and bitter to digest. Let me dream once more." I kept my silence and spoke no more to avoid hurting her feelings.

We drove for a while, Yaneba resting her head on my shoulder. She put her arm around my right arm protectively.

When we entered the city, it was already dark, around 9:00 p.m. I drove downtown to the Vellez Caviedes, where the family who had the motor maintained their residence. A month ago, my older brother had sold the motor to an old friend of my father's, and I had accompanied him to deliver it to this gentleman.

I told Yaneba to wait for me in the car so that I didn't alarm these people. It would also be a lot easier for me to negotiate with them and put them at their ease. She understood and told me to go ahead and conduct my business. Knowing that the Volga might be a bad business card, I parked it a little distance across the street from the house. I walked to the house and knocked on the door.

A lady with a very aristocratic demeanor, salt and pepper hair, and in her late thirties or early forties opened the door. She nervously looked me up and down and smiled in recognition. "Julio Antonio, my son—how are you doing?"

"Good evening, Angelita," I said with utmost politeness. "Is Don Cristobal home this evening?"

"Yes, he is," she replied pleasantly. "Come in, come in." She moved away from the door to allow me inside. She turned around and said loudly, "Cristobal! The son of Leonardo del Marmol is here to see you."

A tall, thin man in his mid-forties with black, wavy hair came out to greet me with a grin. "How are you doing, Marmolito? Sit down, sit down," he invited pleasantly. After we were seated, he asked, "What good winds blow you into our home?"

I smiled. That was the same phrase my maternal grandfather used all the time. Don Cristobal was a Cuban of Sicilian Italian descent. His father had emigrated from Sicily many years before and had married a Cuban lady. He spent all his life and raised his family in Pinar del Rio. They had owned an import/export business, specializing in importing various Italian goods and exporting Cuban goods to Italy. He was a Mason of the same lodge as my father. He had assisted my father and personally contributed hundreds of thousands of dollars in bringing down the Dictator, like so many other Masons had. My father was the Great Grandmaster of the lodge and had convinced them to risk their lives to make the same Revolution that was now kicking all of them in the rear end.

He asked his wife, "Angelita, bring a Coca-Cola for Marmolito." I smiled, even though it bothered me slightly to be called that instead of being addressed by my name. Angelita walked back into the kitchen, and Don Cristobal asked, "How is your father? Have they already nationalized his business?"

"No, not yet," I replied. "However, I know for a fact it won't take too long. It's coming."

He shook his head in disapproving disgust. "Who could even believe that Fidel Castro would turn out to be a communist? Many of my friends warned me, but I never listened to them. I didn't want to believe it. I have nobody to blame, only myself." He looked at me up and down, taking in my uniform and pistol. "I'm sorry if I offended you, but I want nothing to do with communism. That's why I'm leaving the country and leaving them everything I've worked for all my life and all that my father had worked for in his."

"To be honest with you, Don Cristobal, you're not offending me at all. I'm a Revolutionary like my father and you, but a communist and an atheist—never! But please, keep this between you and me. I'm going to ask you to repeat this to absolutely nobody. You're leaving the country, but I'm staying here, and we're all surrounded by informants and spies everywhere."

He nodded. "Yes, you have every reason to be cautious. In here, we can't believe in anyone anymore. Things have completely changed."

I smiled. "Still, we have a few decent people that we can trust. If it had not been like that, I would not be sitting here right now, talking with you. The very little I've said to you is enough to make me no claro and an enemy of the government. This, in my position and with what I'm involved with inside of the military, could not just cost me my job but also my life. They would shoot me for treason."

Don Cristobal looked at me gravely and understood me perfectly. "You have nothing to worry about from me. First, I will repeat nothing of what is said here to anyone. And second, God willing, in a few weeks, I will be in Madrid, Spain, very far away from all this hypocrisy. But, my son, you haven't told me yet why I have the pleasure of your visit."

I leaned forward slightly in my chair and looked at him seriously in the eyes. "Do you remember the outboard motor my brother sold to you last month? You made my brother swear that he would never tell anyone you'd bought it?"

"Yes, and your brother kept his word, and you guys, too. Is there anything wrong with the motor?" he asked in concern.

"No, no," I waved my hand in negation. "Don't worry, no problems. I only wanted to find out if you still have it, or if you sold or gave it to another person."

"No, I haven't done anything with it." He pointed to the garage of his house. "It's there. Thank God I won't need it. Why do you ask?"

"Because I have friends who are in a jam and whose lives might depend on a motor like that. How much would you be willing to sell it for?"

He leaned back in his chair and looked at me dubiously. He stroked his chin, carefully assessing and weighing how he would respond. "The money, in reality, is not a problem. What do I want Cuban pesos for? But, if your friends have the misery of being arrested trying to leave the country with that motor, and somebody mentions my name, who is going to guarantee me that they won't involve me in this?"

I patted my chest. "I am. I guarantee to you and give you my word of honor that nobody will ever know where I got that motor. It's even registered in somebody else's name—you never knew, because we never told you. My brother made me swear that no one would ever know the name of the legitimate owner of that engine."

He was still filled with doubts. "Yes, but somebody could still see you taking it out of here and implicate me. They could accuse me of aiding and abetting an enemy of the Revolution in escaping the island. That could put me in jail for ten or fifteen years and ruin the possibility of my family getting out of here."

"Nobody will see me with that motor. I just came to say hello to you and bring you an exquisite dish my mother made for your wife. You pull your car out of the garage, and I'll drive mine inside. We'll put it in the trunk of my car, and nobody will ever know what we did in here."

He massaged his forehead and thought about it for several seconds.

"How much did you pay my brother for that engine?" I asked.

"Twenty-five hundred pesos. But that's not a problem,

like I told you before. What do I want with Cuban money? It would only make a problem for me, and it's no good—it's only toilet paper anywhere off of the island."

"Yes, I know that. Claro! But what if I pay you in dollars?" His eyes flew open. "Or even Spanish pesetas? Whichever you prefer."

"Where the hell are you going to get dollars and pesetas, kid?" he asked in surprise.

I relaxed in my armchair. "Don Cristobal, you don't have to worry about that. The less we know, the less we have to worry about. All you have to do is name a price for that motor, and in less than fifteen minutes I will be back here with the money. I'll take the engine off of your hands. It will only be in the hands of the government anyway—just one more thing you've worked for that they'll confiscate after you leave. You can use that money however you wish in Spain, and at the same time we both will sleep well knowing that it might save the lives of this family."

He scratched behind his ear. He hesitated a few seconds more and then leaned back. "OK. God help us and put our enemies far away from us. How about three thousand dollars? Will that be OK with you?"

"Absolutely fine," I replied. "We don't have anything more to talk about." I extended my hand to him, and we shook on it.

His wife came back in, completely unaware of what had been going on. She bore two glasses on a tray. "I made lemonade with honey for you guys. This is better for you—it's natural and healthier than a Coca-

Cola."

Don Cristobal exclaimed, "Ah, you and your health! We're all going to die, anyway. Lemonade, and no sugar?"

I smiled and said, "No, it's OK, Angelita. Thank you very much. You shouldn't have bothered yourself to work so hard for us."

"It's not a bother at all," she replied. "It's a very great pleasure." She looked meaningfully at Don Cristobal. "Even if some people don't appreciate it," she added with a playful slap at his shoulder.

After we finished our lemonade, I arranged with Don Cristobal to leave the car in the street and the garage door open. I left, telling him, "I will be back in ten or fifteen minutes." I walked across the street and rejoined Yaneba, who was anxiously waiting for me in the car.

"Were you able to resolve the problem?" she asked.

I raised my right hand and gave her an "OK" sign. "I believe the problem has been resolved after long negotiations."

She hugged me and kissed me on the cheek. "Thank God. You don't even know, but you've taken away a terrible weight off of my father's conscience. Can you imagine how happy they will be when they know? Arturo and his family won't be able to repay you ever, for what you've done for them today."

I smiled. "They don't owe me anything." I chuckled. "Ironically, if they want to feel any gratitude, they'll have to feel it towards Che." My chuckle turned into a laugh. "It's true what they say—whoever laughs by himself is remembering the mischievous things he's gotten away with."

She looked at me in confusion, not following what I was saying. "Are you going crazy, or what?"

I shook my head with a grin. "Someday, when we see each other again, I will explain to you and we will laugh together. Unfortunately, I cannot do it now. All I can tell you is that God works in mysterious ways." I smiled again and nodded this time. "Yes, my Lord, yes."

She still looked at me dubiously. "Well, remember the other saying: who laughs last laughs best. Yes, we will laugh later, indeed."

I stopped in front of her house and told her, "Go ahead and get what you need to get. I will be back in twenty minutes. I have to go get the money and complete the transaction, and then I'll come get you."

"Very well," she said.

I waited in the car until I she had gotten safely inside the house. I then drove the short distance to my house. I walked inside, said hello to my mother and one brother who were watching TV, and went upstairs to my bedroom. I double-locked the door, went inside my closet, and removed my shoes from the shoe rack. Then I raised the rack and pulled out the bag that had been in Che's briefcase. From the bag, I pulled out an envelope that was filled with cash from various nations. I went through the U.S. currency and counted out $3,500. I rolled the money up and wrapped it in a rubber band. I unbuttoned my shirt and rolled the bundle to the back, rebuttoned my shirt, and stood up to check myself in the mirror. After reassuring myself that there was no suspicious bulge, I put everything back in its hiding place, quickly replaced the shoe rack and my shoes, and left the house.

I drove very slowly, making sure I wasn't being followed. When I arrived at Don Cristobal's house, I saw he had followed my instructions to the letter. The garage was open and his car parked in the street. He was outside and signaled me to come into the garage. As soon as I was inside, he closed the door and I handed him the roll of money. I noted wryly that, even though he had expressed little interest in the money before, he now was carefully counting the bundle. The fact that they were genuine U.S. dollars clearly stimulated him to carefully complete the transaction.

He came over to me and said, "Marmolito, you gave me too much." He tried to hand me the extra money.

I raised my hand and said, "The extra $500 is a token of appreciation from me, not just for your trust, but also because of the aggravation this government has put you and your family through. For all the misery you've gone through there is not enough money in the world to repay you. But at least this will cover a couple of good dinners in a very fancy restaurant in Madrid."

He looked at me and grinned. "Thank you very much." He pocketed the $500 and said, "I knew you were good kid. When you left, Angelita was really worried when I told her what we're doing. She accused me of being naïve and went over to her sister's house a couple blocks away. She didn't want to be here when you came back with the G-2 to put me in handcuffs. This is why we can never tell anything to a woman, unless it's pleasant."

"Ah, ah, ah!" I exclaimed. "Not every woman is the same."

He laughed. "You must be in love!" He patted my shoulder. "When we're in love, we think that our woman is the best of the best."

I smiled without admitting anything. Between the two of us, we managed to roll the heavy motor from the hoist and slide it into the trunk of the Volga. After it was settled, we covered it with a very thick blanket.

After I said goodbye to him, I left the house and drove to Yaneba's place. She was already waiting for me, sitting in one of the rocking chairs on the front porch. As soon as she recognized my car, she took a small suitcase and a plastic bag and walked towards the car. I stopped by the sidewalk and kept the motor running. I got out of the Volga and helped her put the luggage in the back seat. We drove back to the Las Canas beach house.

We left the lights of the city behind us. I drove for a little while before she said, "Stop over here."

I looked at her in surprise and eased off on the accelerator. "What happened?"

She smiled mischievously. She opened the plastic bag and took out some towels. "Surprise, surprise," she said.

I pulled off the highway and onto the grassy shoulder. She pointed towards a small grove of palm trees that rose like an island in the landscape against the jungle. "Go that way, over there," she said, pointing. I drove the Volga very slowly until we reached the place she had indicated. I stopped the car on the grassy soil. She looked at me passionately, and we started to kiss for several minutes. We caressed each other's hair, and she unbuttoned my shirt. She caressed my chest and said, "I want our goodbye in a few hours to be something that you and I will remember for the rest of our lives. Do you have a blanket or something? I don't think these towels I brought from home will do it. We need something to put on the ground that we can lie on top of and be comfortable."

I looked at her with a smile, believing that I knew what she had in mind. I remembered the thick blanket that covered the cargo in my trunk. "Yes," I said, "yes—we have a huge blanket covering the motor in the trunk."

"Very well," she said. She pulled away a little from me. "Go ahead and take it out." She started to remove her clothes and place them on the dashboard. When I saw what she was doing, I hurried out of the car to get the blanket right away. I came back with the blanket, and she was undressed down to her underwear.

She got out of the Volga, took the blanket from me, and kissed me very passionately on the mouth. "Go take your clothes off," she said. I started to remove my clothes and sat down on the passenger seat. She draped the blanket across her shoulders and removed her undergarments, starting with her bra. She tossed them towards my face, taunting me. "Come on, come on," she said, flashing me teasingly with the blanket, "I'm waiting for you."

I rushed to take my clothes completely off and left the Volga to join her. She opened the blanket and embraced me, wrapping us both in the blanket. I was only in my underwear, which I then removed and tossed into the car. We walked clumsily wrapped in the blanket, laughing and joking as we went. We eventually tripped one another, landing in the grass in front of each other. We laughed at our clumsiness and then began to kiss each other with intense passion.

Just as things began to get heated, she put her fingers on my lips and said, "No, I've got something better." She helped me up, and carrying the blanket, I followed her where she wanted to go.

The highway was deserted; it was really a limited route, leading first to Las Canas and ending at the fishing port of La Coloma. During the day, one would see traffic; once darkness fell, however, no one used the road at all.

She stopped us in the middle of the road. "Right here, this is the perfect spot—the most romantic, as well as the most dangerous. A very unforgiving place."

I looked at her strangely and in complete surprise. We were in the exact center of the pavement, right on top of the white lane divider marked on the route. She spread the blanket on the road, squatted down, and motioned for me to do likewise. I followed suit, and we sat down on top of the blanket and then lay down. We pulled the excess area of the blanket over us as a cover.

To the music of the coastal insects and under the beautiful star-filled skies lit by a most radiant moon, we made love for a very long time, until my attention was attracted by the heavy klaxon of a ten-wheeled refrigeration truck that was evidently transporting fish.

"A truck!" I screamed. "Run!"

We snapped out of our romantic reverie, brought back to reality by the truck. We both ran naked to the car, abandoning the blanket in the middle of the road. It rolled under and between the large wheels of the huge truck while we hid as best we could in the grassy ditch.

I knew the driver had seen us running naked to the side of the road, because he blew his massive horn repeatedly as he drove by our place of concealment, giving us a kind of musical carnival to mark his passage.

Once the truck had passed by, I ran out in an attempt to rescue our blanket. The wind and the wheels of the truck had taken it a hundred feet from where we were. I wrapped myself up in it and returned to Yaneba's side. This time, I was the one to open the blanket and allow her to enter our little cocoon. We both laughed and walked back towards the Volga.

I said, "You really accomplished what you wanted. This is going to be the most unforgettable experience I ever had, because we almost got smashed under the wheels of that semi-truck."

"Ah!" she exclaimed, "Don't make so much about it. I saw that you kept one eye open to watch out for things like that. I was worried that you might lose your concentration and not be as good."

"Be thankful for that. If I hadn't been so distracted, things might have been different. The one time I let myself forget about my surroundings nearly cost us both our lives."

She looked at me and nodded. "Truly, you have all the reason in the world. Even in my fright, when I saw that gigantic truck so close, I felt the tranquility of having you by my side. I knew you were keeping your eye on the highway. I let myself enjoy it completely, because I knew I could depend on you."

I smiled. "Thank you for your trust in me, my love. But the next time we make love, please, I want to do it in a very comfortable bed or at least in a hammock, not with a truck coming up my ass."

"OK," she said, "I will promise you that."

After we dressed, we continued our trip towards the beach house. When we arrived, I left her in front as usual, while I drove behind, and Josue opened the doors of the workshop for me. I parked inside.

After the door was closed, I could see that Arturo and Mayo were still there, waiting for me impatiently. I was glad, because it meant more hands would be available to get that heavy piece of machinery out of my trunk. Putting it in had been easy, since we were able to slide it in. Getting it out, however, meant raising it completely, and it would be much easier with the extra people.

After I greeted everyone, I opened the trunk and said, "La! Magic! Houdini!"

Everyone laughed at my joke, and Mayo hugged me so hard that he lifted me off of the ground. He couldn't have been happier if he had won the lottery, and he jumped and danced around. He then went over to Arturo and hugged him exuberantly. He took a small grocery bag out of his pocket. "How much did you pay for it? I don't care how much you paid for it," he said quickly, correcting himself. "How much do I owe you?"

I looked at them all as Yaneba, her mother, Martina, and Elena walked in, feeling such great happiness for them all. I said, "Nothing. Absolutely nothing."

Mayo's eyes were moist with emotion. "Look, my son—with this motor, you gave me the ticket and passport the Cuban government didn't give me before, forcing me into the problem I have now. A few days from now, we'll be a long way from here. I have twenty thousand pesos that will be worth nothing, but they may be worth something to you. I know money isn't a big deal anymore, but you can at least buy your family something. Let me reward you for your good action."

Everyone listened in silence, but Yaneba said, "I know that it's possible you paid a lot of money for that motor. You told me you had to go get some money and you negotiated with someone for a long time. That means that motor is not a gift. Take that money from Mayo; you can use it for whatever. Don't feel ashamed; you did a good thing."

I said, "Yes, you're right. That motor was not a gift, and I had to pay money for it. But it's impossible for Mayo to pay me for it, because I paid in dollars, and I don't think that Mayo or most people have those anymore. Why don't we leave this as a little favor I did for you, Mayo, Arturo, and your family, and let's hope that when Josue checks the motor that it's in good condition and will take you guys to your destiny without any more problems."

Josue looked at me in surprise. "Where on Earth did you get dollars, kid?"

I raised my left hand. "Guys, guys, guys—forget what I said. And please don't even repeat it to your shadow. Sometimes I make the mistake of trying to make other people feel better, and I say things I should not. I want to rewind this, please, and beg you to keep this completely confidential. That will be the best form of gratitude that you can show me."

Mayo, his eyes still moist, lifted the bag he had offered me and said, "And what am I going to do with this money if you deprive me of the satisfaction of giving it to you?" I could see he felt guilty. "I was going to use this money to buy a motor anyway."

To everyone's surprise, I took the bag, turned around, and gave it to Martina. "I don't need this money, but Martina could possibly use it. You guys are leaving the country, and this good lady won't have a job. This could help her for a while. She might be able to put it to good use."

Martina said, "No, no, my son—I cannot do that, I cannot take this money. You brought the motor."

I held both her hands, placing the bag between them. I looked into her eyes. "Martina, you have very little family, you're by yourself, you're not a teenager anymore, and Heaven knows what's going to happen to you later. The government might even kick you out of this place. Please, take it. It's my gift to you."

She began to weep. "Thank you, my son, thank you. God bless you, my boy. You're right—now that everybody's leaving, I have to go and try to get another job. This money is really like it's coming from the sky to me."

"It probably is coming from the sky," I replied. "God is sending it to you. You deserve this, and a lot more, for all the years of love and devotion and great care you've given to this family."

The great and good black lady hugged me so

strongly she almost broke my ribs. She kissed my cheek so hard she almost left a mark.

Josue said, "Well, everybody is happy, and everything is taken care of—let's take the motor out of the trunk and make sure everything is fine. In a few hours, my family and I will be very far away from here. Let's do it!"

We all helped get the motor out of the Volga's trunk. Josue meticulously checked the motor and said to Mayo, "With the favor of God, a good wind, and the gas I gave you before, you can go all the way to China with this motor."

"No, no—please!" Mayo joked. "That is the last place I want to dock." Everyone laughed.

I drove the Volga out, and Mayo moved his Ford truck into its place. Mayo and Arturo, helped by Josue and me, put the motor into the back. We covered the motor with the same blanket that had already served so many purposes. They said goodbye to us and left, but not before Mayo and Arturo each gave me a big hug and repeatedly thanked me.

"OK, let's go and eat," Yaneba's mother said. "Martina has prepared a farewell feast."

We went through the hallway into the house. After we washed the motor grease off our hands, we all sat down at the large table to eat the delicious dishes Martina had spent the entire day working on: fish filled with shrimp, fish meatballs, pork and beef croquettes, meat-filled potatoes, and *platanos maduros en tentacion*[12]. As Maria told me, Martina had prepared a truly exquisite goodbye meal. A few hours later, we all sat down on the porch,

---

[12] Caramelized sweet ripe plantains

waiting for the night to get older and all of the neighbors go to sleep.

Josue said, "I don't want to tell you to leave, but I think you should go back to your home. The only thing we need to bring to the boat is a couple of boxes of food we're going to have on board for the trip. I don't think it would be prudent for anybody to see you around here if something goes wrong. I don't want to implicate you unnecessarily any more than you already are."

I smiled and looked at Yaneba next to me. "I will be with you until the last minute when you disappear into the waves of the ocean in the darkness of the night. If, by any chance, anything goes wrong and you guys get into any trouble," I gestured at my uniform, "perhaps this can keep you from getting arrested, and I can get you out of trouble. I might be able to invent some kind of excuse—we were going fishing or something."

Maria was close to him with Elena asleep in her arms. She held out her right hand to me in gratitude, and I gave her my left hand. With moist eyes, she said, "Thank you, Julio Antonio. You will make whatever woman you choose to be your wife very happy, because you have the biggest heart of pure gold I have ever seen."

Yaneba looked at me with a satisfied smile and took my other hand. We all stayed silent. Maria and Josue both knew what was going on between Yaneba and me—not completely, but they certainly realized the strong friendship and love we felt for each other. It was very unusual in Cuba for young kids to be sexually active like we were, but they certainly thought that we might have teenaged crushes on each other. They liked me so much that they simply turned a blind eye to any other implication that our obvious bond might lead one to believe, but they knew we were more than just friends. They had no clue, however, about the level of trust, admiration, and intimacy we shared due to our common enemy in form of the regime. We had realized it for ourselves, and that had turned our relationship into the deeply romantic one that it now was—all the more beautiful and sublime for it being mutually our first experience.

In silence, we both looked at each other, internally crying in sorrow at the coming separation caused by her father's determination to leave. It ripped apart our love-filled hearts. I mentally prayed to God for a miracle, some kind of divine intervention that would prevent that trip from happening—nothing that would harm her or her family, but something that would keep Yaneba by my side. At that moment, that was all that mattered to me. I looked at my watch and saw the minutes slipping away with each tick it sounded.

Josue interrupted my thoughts when he stood up and looked at his wristwatch. "Well," he said, "it's time."

Martina said, "Don't worry, I'll take the groceries and food supplies for your trip to the boat. You guys take care of the rest."

"There's nothing else to take care of," Josue said. "I've already loaded everything into the boat."

Yaneba and I looked at each other once more, and I could see the tears glistening in her eyes. "Let's go on ahead," she said. "Let's walk to the boat."

"Yes," Maria said, "you guys go ahead. We'll follow you in a moment."

Josue took a couple of duffel bags and threw them over his shoulder. I asked him, "Do you want me to help you?"

He smiled and slid them off of his shoulder. He jiggled them easily in each hand. "No, it's OK. They're both very light." He threw them back over his shoulder. "Besides, you've helped us enough, more than you should. You go ahead with Yaneba and walk to the boat. I'll wait for Maria, Martina, and Elena."

"Very well," I replied. Yaneba and I started to walk across the sand towards the mangroves where the boat was moored in the water. It wasn't too far from the grove where we had found the lobsters and had made such passionate and beautiful love.

We held hands as we walked in silence. When we reached that portion of the beach where the boat was anchored a little ways offshore, Yaneba could not control herself anymore and burst into tears. I embraced her tenderly and reached my arm around her to caress her blonde, wavy hair.

A couple of tears ran down my own cheeks; even I could not completely contain them. But I had to be strong and calm her down.

"You have to control yourself, my love," I said, gently detaching myself. "We don't want to attract the attention of the militia, nor do we want your parents to see you like this." This level of emotion could blow the cover of the nature of our physical relationship.

She looked at me sadly and sobbed as she tried to

regain control of herself. I took a handkerchief out of my pocket and offered it to her. She calmed herself a little and blew her nose several times. "Are you OK?" I asked after a few minutes.

"Yes," she replied, and we began to kiss passionately until we heard the footsteps of her family approaching us.

Elena was the first one to come to our side. Her extreme youth made her unaware of the danger we were all exposed to by being on the coast at such an hour of the night. She smiled and said, "Look, Julio Antonio—I brought you a little present." She handed me a tiny multicolored seashell.

"Thank you, Beautiful," I said. "You'll be the most beautiful lady in the family. When you grow up, you'll be a princess." I winked at Yaneba.

"Don't say that to her," Yaneba said with a smile. "She already thinks she's the most beautiful in the family."

Little Elena primped with her hair like a teenager and flirted with me. Yaneba and I both laughed, and I leaned in to give Elena a small kiss on the cheek and a hug. Maria and Josue were already nearby.

"Don't get in the water," Maria said to Elena, "your father will bring you into the boat. I don't want you to catch a cold by wading in that chilly sea at this hour."

Martina brought a box of food that looked a little heavy. Maria said to Yaneba, "Please, my daughter—would you help Martina with that box?"

"No, no," I said, "Let me." I went to take the box from Martina, and Yaneba came to help me.

Josue rolled up his pants, picked up Elena, and took her to the boat. Elena waved her little hand at me and let her father take her out there. A few moments later, Josue started the motor of the boat and backed it closer to the shore. I helped him load the box of food. After I hugged everybody, they boarded, save for Yaneba. We exchanged a long hug and a kiss.

"Yaneba, for the third time," said Josue impatiently, "come on! Let's go!"

I stayed on the shore with Martina, watching them slowly disappear into the dark night. Martina continually wiped her eyes clear of tears. After they were completely gone from sight, she put her arm on my shoulder and said, "Come, my son. Let's go back to the house. I will make you a hot chocolate before you go back to the city." She crossed herself. "God go with them."

We started to walk back towards the house. "I don't know why, and I didn't want to scare them by telling Maria and Josue, but I have a very bad feeling about this trip." She placed her hand on her chest. "I have a pain here that has not gone away for several days. I only have that when something really bad is going to happen."

"Don't think like that," I said. "You feel that way because you're sad, and you didn't want them to leave. Let's be optimistic and hope that they will be safe. God will protect them on their journey." I took the Caridad del Cobre that Yaneba had given to me a while ago. I gave the medal a kiss. "Please, Our Lady of Charity, protect her on her trip."

Martina patted me on the head. We walked across the sand in silence towards the house, Martina drying her tears with one hand while the other draped across my shoulders protectively.

The Women and I

The importance of women in general is they are a great complement to humankind and the most beautiful element in our life; from my modest point of view, they are the essence to our soul and mind.

The world is lost without the existence of women; to me, this can be like sitting at the dining table in front of delicious fruit tartlets, look up close to see but within reach an empty bottle of Grand Marnier. This, to me, is like an egg without salt, like a ship with no ocean, like love without crying.

What a waste!

Dr. J. Anthony del Marmol

The Havana Conspiracies

The shoreline at Las Canas near the house of Yaneba's family

Dr. Julio Antonio del Marmol

Chapter 8: The Diamond Connection

The next day I got up very early, even though I had gone to bed quite late. I hadn't been able to sleep all night. I tossed and turned in bed, thinking continually about the bad feeling Martina had about Yaneba's family and the trip. I decided to fight the feeling no longer and got up to take a hot shower. Afterward, I ate some fruit and a small portion of yogurt, and then I drove the Volga to the home of my dear, late friend Daniel's family to comply with his last wishes.

When I arrived at the house, I found Esmeralda sweeping the porch. I didn't even have a chance to say hello to her before she ran to me and embraced me, crying hard on my shoulder. Even as she did so, she said to me in between sobs, "How is it possible? I believe that God is the being of the greatest love—how can He be so cruel to take away my beloved boy? He was such a little angel! How could He do that? I'm so angry with Him!"

I tried to calm her down and said, "God knows what He's doing, better than any of us. Don't be angry with Him—be angry with those bad people and demons that created this situation that killed your son. Maybe you can't understand this because you're in such pain right now, but I assure you that wherever Daniel is, he's in a better place than the tremendous Hell this Revolution is converting our Cuba into. If Daniel is by God's side as I expect, just as he was an angel that was filled with love and nobility here on Earth, he will be so much happier sitting by the side of the Lord."

Still sobbing, Esmeralda stroked my face with her hand and tried weakly to smile. "Thank you, my son, from my heart, for those words so beautiful and full of love and for trying to comfort me in my sadness." She dried her tears with the back of her hand. "My sorrow is doubled today. When we received the notice that Daniel had died, my mother grew so distressed that she's completely collapsed. She's been inside the house, lying in her bed. She won't eat. All she does is cry all day long. Daniel was her joy. She's lost not only the will to live but her light in her eyes. It scares me, because she looks like a dead person. I don't know what I'm going to do to get her out of this state, but if I lose her, too, I don't know what I'm going to do."

"Calm down," I said. "She'll be OK. May I see her, talk to her?"

She dried the fresh tears in her eyes. "Let me ask her. She's repeatedly told me that she doesn't want to talk to anyone, and I don't want to upset her any more than she already is."

We walked into the house. She started to head into the bedroom and I raised my hand. "Before you go, tell her that I bring a message from Daniel. He told me to give it to you guys before he died."

Esmeralda looked at me in curiosity and surprise. She said nothing but nodded as she dried her tears yet again. She walked into the inside hallway towards her mother's room. I stood in the living room and waited for her to return. I put my hand in one of my uniform pockets and touched the Buddha figurines that he had given to me. A few seconds later, Esmeralda reappeared in the hallway. She gestured to me from there, and I walked over to her. I followed her into Doña Carmen's room.

Esmeralda said, "Mama, Julio Antonio is here, and he has a message from Daniel."

Doña Carmen tried to compose herself a little better in bed and opened her eyes. She reached out her aged hand to me. Esmeralda rushed to put a pillow behind her back to help the old lady sit up better. I took her slightly trembling hand. She reached out her other hand, cupped my free hand, and weakly drew me towards her.

I sat down on the edge of the bed and said affectionately, "You have to get out of bed and raise your spirits, because I'm very sure that Daniel is watching us from up there. I know he is in Heaven, because he is an angel. I don't think you're going to make him happy if he looks down and sees you the way you are right now, depressed and not wanting to eat."

She looked at me in recrimination and shook her head slightly. She did try to smile, but remained silent. I gently removed one of my hands, leaving her cupping my other in both of hers. I reached into my pocket and drew out both of the figurines. I put one in her hand.

"This is the Buddha of good luck, plenty, and security."

I handed the other to Esmeralda, who had been standing close by, stroking her mother's hair. They both looked at the figurines in their hands with the same compassion, love, and happiness as if Daniel were physically there.

Doña Carmen looked at me, and this time gave me a bright smile, as if that little figurine had given her an injection of energy, happiness, and optimism. She looked me in the eyes, and I could see joy shining there. She said at last with a pleasant smile, "What did he say to you when he gave you this?"

I returned her smiled and squeezed her hand. I leaned in close to her and kissed her withered cheek. "Daniel told me to tell both of you to be happy for him and give each of you a kiss. He also wanted for you not to separate ever from these figurines. They are supposed to protect you from all danger and will give you luck and plenty for the rest of your lives."

Esmeralda looked at her mother and smiled as she noticed the change. She looked at me in gratitude. "This is the first smile I've seen on my mother's lips since Daniel's passing. Thank you for bringing us his message, Julio Antonio, and bringing a little badly-needed happiness into our home."

"You don't have to thank me at all," I replied. "For me, it is a great satisfaction to be able to fulfill the last wish of my best friend. If, by doing that, I bring a little happiness to you, the compensation to me is doubled."

Esmeralda smiled. I heard a strange, guttural noise. We both looked at Doña Carmen. She swiftly grabbed both of my wrists with a strength that could not belong to an old lady. It felt like my circulation had been cut off; it was actually painful. Her eyes were completely lacking pupils, the same way they were at dinner the night she had predicted death for Lazaro and Daniel.

I looked at Esmeralda in confusion and pain, not knowing what to do. The old lady's grip continually grew stronger. Esmeralda looked at me in compassion, understanding my confused surprise. She signaled me to relax and remain quiet, that all was OK.

Doña Carmen sat straight up in the bed, fully in control and her arms resting dominantly against the bed. Her breathing grew almost labored as her nostrils flared. They appeared as large as those of an enraged gorilla. She threw her head back so far that the back of her skull almost touched her spine; it looked completely unnatural to me. From that position she said, "Much more death, more misery, more calamity. The enemy Lucifer is in power and in control of many souls on this island. He will fight with all of his demons to keep that control. Everyone on the boat of your friend will die. The death will arrive from on high, from the sky, and the beast will devour the victims. But your friend will survive to tell of the injustice and the crime. She will come to be a great warrior by your side, many years ahead. Later, from the sky, the gods will protect her and she will protect you from your enemies. You both have noble hearts, and so both of you will have long and turbulent lives, full of twisting roads, full of sadness and violent adventures. But in the end, the sun will shine and the gods will bring you happiness. They will bring a new seed from you for future generations."

Doña Carmen then began to scream and let go of my hands, clapping both hands to her face. "Be careful! Be careful!" She then ducked. "The beast—you will be face to face with him in the depths of the ocean after ten years of waiting. The same beast that devoured your friends on this night."

She removed her hands from her face and said in a sepulchral voice, "But the beast fears you." She laughed. "The beast won't attack you, he will run away from you," she said in triumph. She shook her head forcefully, like someone trying to wake up from a nightmare.

She looked at Esmeralda. "I'm very hungry, my daughter," she said in a normal voice. "You haven't been feeding me. Will you please make me something to eat?"

Esmeralda and I looked at each other in bewilderment. "Of course, Mama," she said, "Claro! I will prepare your favorite: *tamal en cazuela and pollo frito*[13]."

Doña Carmen looked as pleased and excited as a child who had just been told she was going to receive some chocolate.

I said goodbye to her, and Esmeralda and I left the room. She walked me to the door. I kissed her on the cheek and said, "This is the kiss your son told me to give you. I already gave it to your mother, and I give it to you now."

She smiled sadly and kissed me back. "I'm very

---

[13] Corn soup and fried chicken

sorry about what my mother said about your friends. Do you know what the spirit in her was talking about? Somebody close to you?"

"Yes," I replied, "unfortunately. I hope her prediction this time is wrong, for the well-being of that family." I shook my head. "I hope this one isn't as accurate as the one she made to Lazaro."

She put her hand on my face and said, "I'm sorry to tell you, but it's not her. It's the spirit inside her, and he has yet to be wrong to this day." She crossed herself. "Let's hope this is the first time."

She hugged me, and I left that place feeling much worse than I had when I arrived. A tight knot of pain and anguish gripped my chest. It occurred to me that it might be the exact same feeling Martina had been carrying for a while.

Very worried and depressed, I drove towards the ranch where I kept my horse to distract myself from all the sorrow I had experienced at that home.

When I arrived, the symphony of the dogs howling and barking escorted me all the way to the entry of the ranch house. I spotted my little Kimbo, the Akita puppy I had adopted after his mother and three siblings had been shot by soldiers on the side of the road.

Little Kimbo wasn't very little anymore; he had in this short time become a teenager. There was no doubt in my mind that he was a purebred, due to the rapidity of his growth. My good friend Leocadio, the caretaker of the ranch, had spoiled him rotten, giving him the best of all the treats in the house.

The faithful Kimbo

As soon as I stopped the Volga and got out of the car, Kimbo jumped on top of me, immediately recognizing me. I grabbed the bottle of Bacardi Añejo I had bought as a present for Leocadio. When I gave it to him, he grinned from ear to ear, and said, as he always did, "You never forget your old friend." He gave me a big hug.

Without my even asking, he said, "I'll go and saddle your horse." He bent over and opened an old chest on the porch and hid his bottle under some blankets inside.

Not long after, I left the ranch on Diamante, followed by Kimbo. The horse wanted to run free, as he evidently hadn't been ridden for a while. I held him to a walk, however, and enjoyed the scenery as I rode to the riverbank.

Without even realizing it, we reached the bridge that crossed the River Guama and led to the central part of the city, where Tite and his father Marcel had found me, bleeding and unconscious after my escape from the regiment following my theft of Che's briefcase. I looked up along the top of the bank, and saw Tite's house. By a small hill, I saw a long column of smoke from the charcoal ovens. I smiled slightly, thinking back on my ordeal there. While the outcome hadn't been perfect, it had been satisfactory. I turned my horse next to the grassy hill and followed the trail leading up it.

I arrived at the house and saw Marcel in the large front yard, working with a shovel by one of the ovens. He waved in greeting with a big smile. He dropped the shovel and came over to me. I dismounted and tied the horse on a low-hanging limb near the house, and we embraced.

"Great that you came over to see us, my son," he said to me.

I smiled. "Well, I'm here only by chance. I was riding my horse to distract myself, and I don't even know why I rode this way. Normally, I go in the other direction. When I saw your house from the river, I thought that I would come and say hello to my friend Tite and you guys."

"That is not chance at all," he said. "God brought you here because I've been asking Him to send you here. And finally He answered. Tite left Cuba almost a week ago. He's already in Florida; we received a telegram from our family in Miami. He is very well, and you'll be surprised to learn that he's registered with the military academy in Florida." Marcel smiled. "I think you are responsible for that. He saw you looking cute in that uniform and wanted to be like you." He grinned and added jokingly, "You set a bad example for kids."

"Don't blame me," I said. "Everybody does what they want to do, not because someone else told them to or showed them an example."

He laughed and said, "I don't know about that."

I heard his wife Fraya's voice. I turned and saw her in the door, both hands clapped to her mouth in surprise. "Thank God you came this way."

I grew curious, wondering why they hadn't come looking for me if they wanted to see me so badly. "Just today, we were talking about you!"

I smiled and stepped towards her as she came to me. We hugged and kissed each other on the cheek.

"Well," I said, "I expect that whatever you've been saying about me is good. My ears were buzzing strangely this morning." I wiggled my finger in my ear. "It was like somebody tore my skin off in pieces and made *chicharrones*[14] with it."

Fraya laughed and clapped me on the shoulder. "No, that's not true! We never talk badly behind your back. Everything we say about you is pure good."

Between the laughter and jokes, we went inside the cabin and sat down at the small table in the dining room. "Have you had lunch already?"

"No," I said. I looked at my watch and saw that it

---

[14] Fried pork skin

was 12:30.

Marcel was washing his hands in the kitchen sink. "Very well," he said affectionately, "you stay with us for lunch. In the time being, we want to talk to you. A few days ago, before Tite left the country, a couple of strange men came here. They identified themselves as G-2 and asked many questions about you. To be honest with you, they never told us the real purpose of their visit. It still puzzles me. They kept beating around the bush, but they never came to the point."

That caught me by surprise, and I stayed silent for a few seconds. Marcel sat down next to me. From the look in his eyes, I could tell he was worried. He asked, "Have you been in any trouble?"

"No," I replied. "Why do you ask me that?" An icy coldness settled into my heart, as this could only have happened on Piñeiro's orders, and the red-bearded security chief wouldn't act without consultation and approval from the Minister of the Interior, Ramiro Valdés. Clearly, I had people suspicious of me at the very highest levels of the government.

"I don't know. I just asked you, wondering."

"What did these men tell you, and what did they want with you? I'm curious."

Marcel replied with a grimace, "I don't know. They never told me, like I said, what the real purpose of their visit was. They asked me about you." He ticked each point off finger by finger with his index finger of his other hand. "First, how long have we known you? I said, we've known his family for a long time. Then they asked if you ever stayed here to sleep. I replied that you never had to the best of my memory stayed here overnight, but that they could ask you. I saw no reason for you to stay here when your own home isn't too far away."

Fraya, who was laying the table, looked at me with a raised eyebrow. "Would you like me to set a plate for you?"

I nodded. "But please—don't serve me too much."

"OK," she said. As she started to fill my plate, she looked at me first to see if I wanted any of the dish and then checked with me to see that she had given me enough before starting to put a different course on it. When she finished, she handed me the plate.

"Thank you very much," I said. "You're very nice, just like my mother."

Marcel had frozen his counting on his fingers. "Do you know what motive the G-2 would have to find all these details about you from us?"

I shook my head. "I don't have the slightest idea. I'll say for certain that you and Fraya don't have anything to worry about. The only person who saw me close to here after my disappearance was a young lady who is absolutely trustworthy. Not only that—she's not even in Cuba anymore. If she's not in Mexico, she's in Miami by now. I told you once, I will never open my mouth and say anything to anyone about what you guys did for me."

Marcel looked at me in embarrassment. "I know, I know." I could see fear in his eyes.

I picked up my knife and fork and began to cut into the Cornish hen in tomato sauce I had on my plate. "Besides," I continued, "all the time I was unaccounted for I spent with my brother in Las Martinas. That can be verified very easily by contacting my brother or his wife."

Marcel smiled, a little more relieved. I noticed his reassuring glance to Fraya. She sat down at the table and we began to eat the exquisite food.

"I told you, Fraya," Marcel said, "those pencil necks only came over here on a fishing expedition. But because the fish didn't open their mouths, they had to leave with empty hands."

As I ate, I thought about this turn of events. I didn't want to scare them, but I couldn't help but wonder what the reason the G-2 had to come and ask questions about me. I knew no G-2 agent had a crystal ball; somebody put them on the trail or said something. I had to find a logical reason to justify their investigation of Marcel and Fraya. Until I could discover that, I would have no peace.

At that moment, I remembered what Canen had told me. I thought that it could be true; Piñeiro and Raul might have put their plan in motion.

We all ate in silence. Every now and then, we looked at each other and smiled, but I noticed the pressure of the psychological terror was exerting on them, thinking that I might involve them in something that would cause the government to come after them. The kind of pressure that the government could exert on people could even eventually compel them to sign a statement that something false was the truth. It occurred to me how they must have felt, after being questioned by the G-2 and not seeing me for a week. The reaction they had when they first saw me was completely understandable. They weren't missing me; they were frightened out of their minds.

When we finished, we sat down in the small living room on rustic wooden chairs. They drank Cuban coffee, something I courteously declined like I usually did. Marcel said, "Well, I feel a little more at peace. All I wanted was to make you aware and put in your knowledge the questions they asked me and my answers. That way, if they question you, there won't be any contradiction between what you say and what we said."

I looked at him gravely. "Truthfully—you really feel more relieved now? You feel better, Marcel?"

He looked at me in surprise and nodded. "Of course I'm a lot more relaxed. Now that you know what we told you, nobody can trick you."

I raised my right arm and pointed up with my index finger. "I want to ask both you guys a favor. I don't want you to ask me any questions about what I'm going to say. Just listen, because I won't repeat it. First, I want to tell you that I've been trained very well to never break, no matter what this government or the G-2 put me through. It doesn't matter what accusation they want to drop on my shoulders; even physical torture won't break me, nor will psychological intimidation. The only reason I'm telling you this is so that you know you can sleep in peace at night. Hear me out very well. There will never be an accusation of you guys, unless you implicate yourselves. In that case, I cannot do anything for you. Like I said before, no one will ever know what you did for me.

"All I ask you now, please, is to take paper and pencil to write down those questions and answers you gave to the G-2 while they're still fresh in your memory and put the paper in a secure place. If those men come back one day, you'll be able to consult that paper and know exactly what questions they asked you and you'll be able to answer the exact same way you did this time without any contradictions at all. Is this clear?"

They had been listening to me very carefully. They both looked at each other and nodded seriously.

I rubbed my forehead. "I've lost my best friend—my father—the one I could trust without any fear to share any problem I had. Unfortunately, now he is completely brainwashed by the fantasies and false promises of this government to help the poor and the oppressed and give to all the people free medical attention and all of life's necessities. As you know, Fidel promised milk in pipes coming directly into the kitchen for everyone."

I smiled. "This is not only a Utopian dream, it's also physically impossible. Even if it weren't, it would cost trillions to accomplish it. Every day I lose another friend who leaves for another country somewhere in the world, looking for freedom and democracy. The only reason I'm telling you all of this is because you, now, as my confidantes, have become my family and friends. You're the reason I risk my life every day to bring back the Cuba and the society we used to have, with the respect every citizen deserves without the government telling them how to live their lives in the most intimate ways or face the firing squad. That is why I've been doing what I've been doing, and that is why I asked you to not ask me any questions. Please be assured that I would rather die than implicate you guys in anything that could bring harm to your family."

Marcel leaned back in his chair and crossed his right leg over his left knee. "I infinitely appreciate your words. You're making an effort to reassure us, and it's really appreciated. Once more I see your convictions and political feelings. Sometimes, we worry about it, and that takes away our ability to sleep at night. When I hear you talk like that, I feel like I can sleep again."

He stroked his chin, a little more relaxed, and placed the empty coffee cup on the center table. "I want to tell you something that you don't know about me." He smiled sarcastically. He tapped his chest with his left index finger. "For many years, I was one Fidel's best friends, both in the university and in private life."

I looked at him in surprise.

"Difficult to believe, true? But like you—" he indicated my uniform. "Who could guess what your feelings are and what is in your heart with your uniform, the car you drive, and the way you're living right now." He said emphatically, "I never sympathized with the regime of Batista. I only played the game." He relaxed and continued normally, "Knowing Fidel Castro as intimately as I did, I could predict ahead of time what would happen to this country if he got the reins of this country. We were all very young back then, Revolutionaries beside Eduardo Chibás."

He took Fraya's hands and both smiled in remembrance of their youth. He continued, "We fought by his side until Fidel corrupted himself and associated with the mafia. After so much sacrifice by all of us to maintain our ideals clean and pure, he convinced a small group to put themselves at the service of organized crime, what he called 'the good face of the mafia.' These people were old Sicilians that considered themselves morally correct. According to them, the younger Sicilian families were established in New York and other places in the New World; they rolled over and rebelled against the moral rules the old ones held as so valuable. The older ones in Sicily wanted to bring the younger ones back under their discipline."

I replied, "I'm sorry, but I don't think there's such a thing as the good face of the mafia. They are organized crime, and all that this represents is corruption, violence, and extortion, and none of this is good."

Marcel smiled and looked again at Fraya. "That is exactly what I replied to Fidel Castro when he tried to persuade me to swallow the pill and to brainwash me with this demagogy in the summer of 1947, when he personally executed the first attempted murder of the student leader, Leonel Gomez, who was at that time his opponent for the nomination as president of the Law School Student Federation. He shot him in front of a bunch of students. The crime was never prosecuted, because no one dared to show up as a witness against Fidel. Whenever someone contradicted him later on, he would raise his finger and say, 'Be careful, or I'll send you on a vacation with Leonel Gomez.'"

Marcel shook his head. "Not even a year later, he killed Manolo Castro, the president of the Student University Federation, gangster style. This time, one of the students accused him, and Fidel was arrested. But two days later, before he could testify against him, that student was found dead on one of the benches on the university campus, asphyxiated by Bacardi rum. Someone had forced him to drink the rum until he choked to death. There were no witnesses, and a couple of days later, they had to let Fidel go. Again, no one dared to be a witness against him."

He paused. "Nobody told me this—I was there! I had been there with almost twenty or thirty other students."

Marcel scratched his ear and crossed his legs again. "This event confirmed Fidel Castro as the strong muscle of the most powerful Sicilian mafia families at that time. He never had to kill with his own hands again. After this arrest, he began to order killings, planned by him, financed by the mafia, but executed by his trusted men, protecting him from being publicly exposed and allowing him to remain in the shadows like the Godfather."

He leaned back in his chair, stretched his legs out in front of him, and massaged his face with both hands. "Do you know why I've been telling you all this?"

I shook my head.

"I know you're playing cat and mouse with Fidel, Che, and all these criminals. You're too young for this game. I hope I can open your mind with these tales. I saw them happen with my own eyes. I want you to realize the tremendous danger you are placing your life in, because these men are all rice from the same sack. When they find out what you're doing, they will not just kill you; they will kill your family, they will kill your friends...." He pointed at Kimbo, who was lying at my feet. "They will even kill your dog! I'm telling you this today so you can realize what kind of criminals you're playing around with."

I looked at him gravely and replied, "I really appreciate what you're telling me, from the bottom of my heart. I know your intentions are very good. But I want to let you know something. You think those things Fidel did are terrible? Not to me. They're like this." I held up both arms and kept my index fingers about an inch apart.

"Now, the ambitions and plans to control the world, the massacres and destruction that he is planning to do is like this." I held my arms as far apart as I could stretch them.

"Somebody has to stop him and his group," I continued. "Fear only generates fear. That is what all of these assassins and mafiosos try to put in our minds. That cold sweat of fear. But we're capable of controlling it by remembering that all we can lose is our lives. It would be better to die a thousand times than to live with that fear.

"Only when we manage to substitute that fear with courage will we serve them the same cup of soup and give to them the fear they try to bring to us. And then they will feel in themselves something much worse than fear: terror. It is a terror to know they cannot intimidate us ever again, and that is the only way we can conquer and destroy them."

I stopped and looked pityingly at them. "Why do you think the firing squads have continued, every single day, from the first day the Revolution won? If it's not for one thing, it's for something else. Against all the protests from around the world, the UN and international nations around the globe, this government continues to execute women, children, and the elderly under the stigma of being counterrevolutionaries. In the beginning, they started with the followers of Batista, they followed with those disaffected by their arbitrary laws, and now it's anyone in the opposition. They will continue to kill people, because that is the only way they can continue in power, by injecting the same fear that Fidel Castro put into those students, mafia style, in his first two crimes. He learned many years ago like a good disciple of the mafia that this fear is the best weapon to control the masses. Psychological terror works this way: you kill one or two of your adversaries in public, in front of everyone, and everybody will fear you. No one wants to follow the same path."

"My son, you are so young," Fraya said tenderly. "You should not be involved in all of this, creating problems for you and your family. You should be dedicating yourself to study and having a good time with your friends. At your age, you should not be concerned about risking your life."

I smiled with a little irony. "My friends? What friends? Your son? He's in Florida. Every one of my friends who isn't already out of the country is in the process of leaving. Who wants to live in a place like this?" I leaned back in my chair and patted Kimbo on the head. "I believe we all have a destiny when we come into this world. I believe personally that mine is to try to stop these men from hurting innocent people, destroying and separating their families."

Marcel scratched the back of his head. "Maybe, maybe you have reason for what you're saying.

Somebody has to stay in front of the crazy horse running wild in the middle of the street. Someone has to jump in front of it to stop it, to keep it from destroying everything and killing innocent women and children."

He shifted in his chair, appearing uncomfortable with what he was about to say. He looked at his wife and raised his eyebrows. "I'm too old to serve as a ladder for another ambitious politician, to help him realize his dreams of power and be a witness to his broken promises. I'm too old for that. Do you know what Fidel Castro told me once in front of Haydée Santamaría while we were talking about the future of Cuba and ourselves?"

I shook my head.

"Fidel told us that his most precious dream was to come to be a global military leader on the level of Alexander the Great or Adolph Hitler, because after he passes away he wants people to remember and talk about him two thousand years later. His great purpose in life is to destroy the Catholic Church around the world by whatever means it takes, even, if necessary, taking the life of the pope. He wants to kill the faith of the millions of fools in the world who follow his stupid doctrines. He wants to create an organized public campaign to very cleverly expose any kind of immorality, the kind that exists in any large organization, inside of the Church, and the deception of all his followers will make them fall from faith by themselves. Even if it's only a handful, a few—he wants to use those instances to create a huge scandal to corrupt and smear the image of the church.

"When he was in school, his parents had enrolled him in a Catholic parish school, but because his family wasn't wealthy enough, he didn't receive any special attention from the teachers. They largely ignored him, and I don't think his ego could take that." He paused, and Marcel lightly stroked his face with his left hand. "The cynicism of this man! And to think that he is the political leader in control of the destiny of our country."

I shook my head in discontent. "If you only knew what this baby monster has transformed into over time, you wouldn't believe it. He's grown to a criminal mastermind whose ideas corrupt the world and destroy society. We have to remember people learn through experience and age, and they grow to be better or worse, depending on their own nature. Fidel Castro is no exception. If I have to tell you the truth, I don't hate him; I pity him."

Marcel looked at me seriously. "I have to tell you something truly out of my heart. I have deep admiration for you, because I've never seen anyone your age, or even older, who has the convictions you have. It's like you're a reincarnation of your great-grandfather."

I raised my hand. "Oh, God, don't say that! That's what my mother and family say all the time!"

Marcel shook his head. "I don't want to know exactly what you're doing or are involved in, but I'm going to ask you one thing. Fidel is not only vengeful, but he's also an unscrupulous, cunning fox. Be very careful with him."

"Thank you," I said, standing up. "I really appreciate your concern and your advice, and your stories about Fidel's early days. That helps me greatly.

The more we know our enemy, the easier it is to deal with him. I'm prepared to handle him and his group." I placed a hand on Marcel's shoulder. "For the time this fight lasts inside or outside of Cuba, I will give him a fair fight. By the way, in case anyone asks, the reason for my visit here today is that you invited me to lunch, as a courtesy and in reciprocity to the invitation I gave you to my sister's wedding."

They both nodded. They walked me to the door with Kimbo following us. I untethered my horse, mounted, and waved goodbye to them.

I rode back down the trail and turned along the riverbank to head towards Leocadio's ranch. As I rode, I could not help but wonder who had put the G-2 on my track and sent them to that house for questioning. It was one more thing for me to worry about, and I knew that I was going to have to find an answer, and soon.

It crossed my mind that the soldiers who had been attacking the girls might have been the same ones searching the road the day I protected Marcel, Fraya, and Tite. If so, it was possible they were simply harassing me as revenge for their comrades who had been arrested. It was a plausible explanation and the only one that I could think of at that moment.

I was so absorbed in my thoughts that I reached the ranch almost without realizing it. I left my horse and Kimbo in Leocadio's charge, got in the Volga, and drove back to my house.

When I arrived, I discovered to my surprise that my father had come home early from his business in Guane. I hadn't seen him much and was filled with joy to see him home. He saw me in my uniform, and in a voice filled with pride asked, "How is the leader of our Revolution doing?"

I smiled and answered, "Very well." I told him about saving Che's life in Caibarién, which made him even more proud of me. I then let him know that, because of that, Che had rewarded me with the Volga.

After we finished talking, he said, "Don't do anything to compromise that trust he's put in you. Don't defraud them of their loyalty. You have to prove to them every minute you've got the blood of the patriots in your heart from your great-grandfather."

I smiled, a little ironically, and nodded. I thought that if my father only knew the truth, he would probably collapse on the spot.

After we finished our conversation, I walked into the library where we had our telephone. I dialed the number of Chandee's house in Havana. Mrs. Xiang answered and told me no one was at home. Both of her daughters had gone with her husband to the Vedado district to do some shopping. I told her to let her husband know that I had a package of fresh vegetables, fresh eggs, and other produce from my brother-in-law's ranch and that he could send Chandee any time to pick them up, whenever it was convenient. I added that since it was produce, sooner would be better so that they received it still fresh.

After the call, I headed towards my room. As I crossed by the kitchen, I noticed that my mother had just made some fresh fried plantains. I picked one up, and she immediately filled an entire plate to take with me.

Once I reached my room, I ate my plantains. As I ate, I noticed my trousers and boots were stained white with the sweat from my horse, so I decided to change clothes. I pulled out a clean pair of pants and a white T-shirt, and I hung my pistol up in the back of my closet. I sat down on a bench next to the closet to change my boots.

I grabbed a pair of clean boots from my shoe rack and noticed that, in my rush the night before, I had not completely covered Che's bag with the shoe rack. The edge of the bag stuck out just past the edge of the rack. I started to fix it, but as I removed the shoes and opened it, I decided to organize things the way they had been before.

I put a towel on the floor, and emptied the contents of the bag onto it. I hadn't completely emptied this bag before, and was surprised when a folded piece of ocean blue velvet cloth fell out. I picked it up and opened it. The inside surface was lined with small pouches. I shook the contents from the pouches, and at least fifteen large diamonds dropped into my hand from different compartments. I put all but one of them back. I held it up to the light, and it shone like a rainbow in multiple colors. It was one of the most beautiful things I had ever seen.

I carefully wrapped it in a piece of toilet paper and put it in one of my pockets. I replaced everything exactly as it had been and this time made certain that everything looked normal under the shoe rack.

I combed my hair, and left both the pistol and the beret in my room. I wanted to be nondescript and left as much of my military appearance behind as possible. I was only dressed in uniform pants and boots, but all rank insignia and accoutrements of the Little Commander were not coming with me on this mission. I drove to the center of the town to La Zultana, the most prestigious jewelry store in town. The owner was a friend of my father's.

Mr. Aldemes' jewelry store, La Zultana

When I arrived, I asked one of the employees in charge, a tall, half-bald man with very respectable manners, for Señor Aldames, the owner. The gentleman replied to me, "Mr. Aldames went to the bank to make a deposit. He will return in perhaps half an hour or forty-five minutes."

I looked at my watch and saw that it was 4:30 in the afternoon. "Very well—I'll wait."

I went to a small waiting room and picked up a copy of Bohemia, from the magazine rack. It was a very thick special edition, and there was a story about *La Coubre,* accusing the United States of the sabotage.

Inside, they described the massacre in gory detail, complete with graphic photographs, and attributed it to a CIA plot. I shook my head in disgust. Even I couldn't believe how they could lie so openly without any proof and accuse the U.S. of anything. However, the press was completely in bed with Castro and his cadre, and they printed word as Fidel, Raul, and Che dictated to them.

About half an hour later, a tall, skinny man with thick glasses and wavy dark hair entered the store, announced by the small bell jangling over the door. I turned my head, and saw that he was of Arabic descent with dark skin and a hawk-like nose. When he saw me, he smiled affectionately and said, "Hola—how are you doing, Julio Antonio?"

"Very well, Mr. Aldames."

"What—your watch broke again? I keep telling you, you need a Rolex."

"I don't need a Rolex—my watch is so good that it chimes right in time with the bells of the church. I'm not here for that, though—I need a few minutes of your time in private."

"Of course, of course—come into my office." He turned to his employees, telling them, "Start to clean up. We'll be closing shortly."

He pulled a gold fob watch out of the vest pocket of his expensive tailor-made suit. The employees and manager began to clean the glass of the display cases and to pull the trays of jewelry out of the cases to place them on carts that would then be wheeled into the safe.

I followed him into his office. It was a beautiful room with thick, red curtains that hung from the ceiling and draped all the way to the floor. The furniture was very expensive. He offered me a seat and a drink, which I respectfully declined.

"Well, if you don't mind, I'm going to have a little Bacardi," he said. "It helps me unwind after a stressful day."

He went over to a small refrigerated minibar next to the safe. He picked up a glass with Egyptian figures engraved on the surface and put some cubes of ice in it. He picked up a bottle from among the many he had there and poured himself half a glass of the rum. He opened a small bottle of Coca-Cola and poured that into the glass. He sat down in front of me at his desk.

"Salud to you," he said and took a long sip. He then sighed and placed the glass on a silver coaster. "What can I do for you?"

I looked at him gravely. "The first thing I want to ask you is for your word of honor as a Mason that whatever we discuss here will be kept in confidence and that you won't reveal it to anyone else—not even my father. This is extremely secret, and if it's revealed, the lives of myself and some others could be put in jeopardy."

He raised his eyebrows in surprise, leaned back in his chair, and pulled his glasses down his nose to peer at me over the rims. "You don't have to worry about it at all. If that is the way you want it, I will give you my word of honor that whatever we say here will remain unknown by anyone. Excuse me one second."

He got up and opened the door. "Please don't bother me," he said to the employees outside. "I will be busy in here for a while."

He closed the door, locked it, and came back to the desk. "The only time I would ever repeat what we speak about today is if you come and ask me to be a witness to this conversation."

I relaxed slightly and smiled. "Very well." I leaned forward and a little to the left so that I could reach into my pocket. I searched around for a few seconds until I found my toilet paper-wrapped bundle. I pulled it out and handed it to him.

After he opened it and examined the diamond in the light, he removed his glasses and put a jeweler's loupe in his left eye. He examined it for a moment and gasped. He picked up a more powerful handheld loupe and scrutinized it more closely. He looked up at me in shock. He walked over to a flexible lamp with a magnifying glass and examined the diamond meticulously under it.

"Kid, where did you get this?"

I didn't answer.

He turned the rock over in his fingers as he looked at it, turning it admiringly to examine it from different angles. He returned to his desk and opened his drawer. He pulled out a square of black velvet cloth emblazoned with the name of his store. He put the diamond on the cloth and pointed at it with his left index finger. "In forty years as a jeweler, I've never seen a diamond as pure and without any flaw as this."

I smiled and nodded. I had no notion of what he was talking about; I only knew that a diamond's cuts, the way it shone, its coloration, and the number of facets all combined to give a diamond its price.

"What is the approximate value of this diamond, do you think?"

He leaned back and crossed his leg. With a small smile on his lips, he said, "This is worth so much that I don't think anybody in this city, the capital, or anywhere on the island, has the money to buy this. But, of course, to give you a more accurate estimate, we have to make a detailed study of this rock. In my professional opinion, based on my preliminary examination, I would conservatively say that you could construct many cities like this one and still have a lot of money left over."

That caught my attention. In surprise, I raised my eyebrows. "That much?" I asked.

"I have to be honest with you," he said in a calm, pleasant manner. "That's a very low-end valuation. It's possible that the right buyer would pay a lot more than that." He rubbed his forehead. "If you or whoever owns this diamond decided to sell it, you could not come to a better place. I've got buyers in New York and Europe who would give their right eyes to own a gemstone of such beautiful perfection like this. The only place I've seen such a beauty is from Sierra Leone in Africa. I would guess that this baby has the same origin, although this one is much larger than the stone I'm thinking of.

"What do you want to do with this?" he asked.

I shifted forward towards the table. Before I picked up the cloth, I asked, "May I keep this?"

"Sure, sure," he said.

I folded the diamond in the cloth and put it back in my pocket. "To be truthful with you, I don't know yet what I'm going to do with it. But if we can come to an understanding and do some business, as I told you before, this must be completely confidential."

He spread his arms wide and leaned back. "Claro, claro, chico! Of course. And I have to tell you, as a Brother Mason to your father, don't tell a soul that you have this, let alone show it to anyone. Men would kill for a lot less than this."

I nodded and leaned back in my chair. I relaxed and crossed my legs. I held my left hand out about waist high. "I've known you since I was this high. I remember how you would bring candies to our home when I was perhaps four or five years old. You always treated me with respect, and that is why you inspired this level of confidence in me. If I decide to sell these diamonds, I will need a partner like you who not only has the knowledge but also the experience and contacts to obtain the best result in that transaction."

He raised his right arm, took off his glasses, and put them on the desk. "Excuse me, but perhaps I misunderstood you or you expressed yourself incorrectly. But it sounded to me like you said 'these diamonds.' Plural."

I smiled. With my index finger, I caressed the small, white hairs of my peach fuzz mustache. "Neither one. You listened perfectly. 'These diamonds,' because there are several."

His eyes were large before; now, they positively bulged out of his face. "What?" He gulped. "What?" he said again. Very timidly, he inquired softly, "How many? If it's not creating any problems, can you tell me, more or less?"

"No, not at all—we're talking in confidence, it's not a

problem." I placed my index finger on my temple in thought. "I didn't count them out, but I'd say around fourteen or fifteen medium and large stones. There were a few that looked bigger than this one."

Mr. Aldames cupped his face in both hands and rubbed it, like the dreams of his life had just come to visit him. Feeling more confident in the conversation because of my candor and his growing curiosity, he still cautiously asked, "But you cannot give me their provenance?"

I shook my head. "No." I paused. "I don't even know what their provenance is. Let's just say that I found a treasure, and I'm not willing to give it to the government. That way, we'll both be more secure, since whatever we don't know, nobody can force us to say."

He looked at me a little unhappily, but he resigned himself to the situation. He smiled slightly, nodded, and said, "Well, at the end of the day, it's none of my business, so long as the provenance isn't a dark one. If we have no knowledge of it, however, it's not a bad one, since we don't know it."

I nodded my head in agreement.

"Thank God diamonds don't have serial numbers," he said, spreading his hands. "Whatever we don't know, que sera, sera."

I stood up and held out my hand to shake his. "How much do I owe you for your services?"

He also stood up. "Nothing, chico. Just let me know what you decide to do with this fortune. We could put it in the most expensive jewelry store in

Havana, but given the way this government is going, we should put it in Paris or New York. Let me know what you decide."

"Very well, we'll keep in touch," I replied. Before I left, I said, "I want to tell you that I really, really appreciate your honesty. I knew it was valuable, but I had no idea how valuable."

"You're very welcome," he said. "Honesty comes impregnated in our genes. You can't buy it in a pharmacy."

We both smiled and shook hands once more. At that moment, we heard a commotion from outside the office in the store. He turned and parted one of the curtains to look outside and see what the screams were about. Several masked men with automatic rifles were pushing and shoving the employees inside the shop. One of them held a gun up to the half-bald manager. Mr. Aldames, faster than a falcon on the dive, ran to the main safe, shut it, and spun the dial of the combination lock with vigor. He turned to me and gestured toward a sofa opposite the desk. "Behind the sofa!" he said quietly and covered me with the thick curtains. He squeezed my shoulder. "No matter what happens, don't come out of there."

"Don't worry," I assured him. There was a narrow gap in the curtain through which I could peer, giving me a limited view of most of the office, so long as I moved to change my angle of vision.

Aldames immediately took off his jacket. He rolled it and put it on the sofa, placing some pillows on top of it. He did the same with his vest, after removing his gold watch and chain, which he dropped into a planter by the refrigerator that was close to his desk. He removed his necktie and dropped it into one of the drawers of the desk and closed that. As he closed the drawer of the desk, someone started to pound on the door to the office. A voice on the other side yelled, "Open this door or we'll break it down!"

He unbuttoned his sleeves, rolled them up, and opened two or three shirt buttons at the neck. "OK, OK," he called out. He put on his glasses and grabbed an accounting ledger from the desk as he walked towards the door. He held the book under his arm like a baby. He unlocked the door and it burst open, knocking him to the floor. The men screamed obscenities as they trained their rifles on him. The one who appeared to be in charge put a pistol to his head.

Aldames, still on the floor, raised his hands in surrender. "There's nothing of value in here!" he yelled. "I'm the accountant! All of the valuables are in front."

The man said, "You open that safe at once, or you die right here. You're a lying old man—you're the owner! If you don't open it, this will be your last day, and they'll bury you in the safe."

Aldames continued to yell that he was the accountant. "You're wrong. The owner has left for the day. He took all the money to the bank on his way home!"

A fourth man entered the office and said to the man with the pistol, "We already loaded the jewelry in front. What do we do with the employees? Kill them?"

The leader with the pistol replied, "No. Tie them up

by the hands and feet, and put them in the back. Put the 'closed' sign up in the door. We'll leave in a few minutes."

The voice of the leader sounded familiar to me, but because of the way he was kneeling on the floor, I couldn't see his silhouette or general form, so I couldn't identify him. The other man left to obey his instructions.

The leader said, "OK, I'm going to count to three. Either you open that safe, or you die. We don't have any time to play around now. I know you're the owner. This is your last chance. One. Two. Three—"

"No, no," Aldames screamed, "I'm telling you the truth."

The man raised the pistol. It came down, and Aldames screamed, apparently as the pistol hit him in the face. From my angle, I couldn't see them at floor level. The man stood up and walked over to the sofa, right next to where I was hidden. He began to search the sofa. The first thing I noticed were his boots as he walked towards me. They had silvered metal toe caps on them. I had seen them before. They were unusual, especially on military boots. He was short and slightly overweight. I held my hand to my mouth to avoid making any noise.

I suddenly remembered Fausto Pijirigua's shiny boots with silvered caps on them, and this man's physical build resembled his. I knew I could be wrong, but if this was Che's assistant, what was he doing robbing a jewelry store?

He leaned back in front of the sofa and began to move the pillows around. I could smell his cheap cologne. Even though the ski mask completely concealed his face, it was too much coincidence. I could never forget that smell after those long hours inside the car on the way to Santa

Clara.

He found the suit jacket and removed it from the sofa. He then discovered and removed the vest. He examined the fabric and looked at Aldames' pants and laughed; the sound confirmed for me that this was Fausto.

"Son of a bitch, old man!" he said as he grabbed one of the pillows from the sofa, turned, and walked back to Aldames, who was still held at bay by two men. He dropped the vest and coat on top of him. With great sarcasm, he said, "Oh, you're the accountant, eh? I don't know the accountant that can afford such a high-class designer Italian suit."

He paused and scratched the side of the mask. "I will count again to three—but this time, I won't hit you. This time, I put a bullet in your head. This is your last chance. You got a second opportunity at life. You can go back with your employees if you open the safe, and you stay alive or you can buried with it. I've run out of time and patience. One. Two. Three."

He raised the pillow in his hand and put it over Aldames' head. There was a soft popping noise.

One of the other masked men opened the door and said, "We've got all of the jewelry out of here and in the car. We're ready to go."

Fausto said, "OK, let's get out of here. Goddamn old man—he preferred to die rather than to give us the combination of the safe."

The men rushed out of the office. I looked at my watch and waited five minutes. I couldn't be sure whether the bell on the door would reveal them leaving all at once, two at a time, or some other combination. After I'd heard the bell several times, a sepulchral silence fell over the store. I counted the seconds off in my head and as soon as I felt enough time had passed, I left my hiding place.

The first thing I did was lock the door, and then I ran to Mr. Aldames' side. His blood was already pooling next to his body. I took his pulse and discovered he was still alive—although unconscious and unresponsive. I whipped my T-shirt off and ripped it into shreds to improvise a bandage. I removed the pillow and saw that the bullet wound was on the right frontal region, so there was a chance that he might still survive. After I wrapped the improvised bandage around his head, winding it tight to stop the loss of blood, I used a pillow from the sofa to elevate his head. I didn't want to move him too much.

Shirtless, I went out into the store. The three bound men looked at me like I was a godsend. They had been gagged as well as tied up. I removed the manager's gag. "Where have you been?" he asked. "Thank God—we heard a shot. Are you OK?"

"Yes, but Mr. Aldames is not. You have to call the police and an ambulance immediately. Can you handle this? I need to go home. If you need me for anything, you tell the police. They can come to my house and I can give my declaration there. I'm extremely distressed and need to get back. I don't understand—why didn't Mr. Aldames open that safe in the office? You guys had all the jewelry in the front. Why didn't he give that to them?"

The man smiled. "He has all his savings and all of the most valuable things in the store are in there. Everything out here is insured, but what he has in there isn't." He held out a hand to me. "Don't leave like that. Come here." He went over to a closet and pulled out one of his spare dress shirts. "It's too large, but at least you won't be wandering shirtless in the street like some urchin."

The only thing in my head at that moment was to leave before the police arrived. My legs were shaking with the urgency to get out of there, and a huge knot grew in my stomach. I kept thinking that if only I'd had my gun with me, Mr. Aldames would not be lying on the floor, wounded and bleeding right now.

By the same token, God had been with me, because the only reason I had remained behind that curtain was the knowledge that I had no way to defend myself. I had seen only four men, but the employees informed me there had been a total of six. I thanked God for protecting me yet again.

As soon as I got to my house, I told my parents what had just happened, telling them that I had gone to the store to have my watch repaired.

My mother got up out of her chair, walked over, and embraced me. With my head against her stomach, she exclaimed with tears in her eyes, "My God, my son—why do you always have to go through these terrible things and witness all this horror? Why don't you go to your room and change out of that huge shirt? You look like a scarecrow. I will make you a tilo tea to relax your nerves."

My father had been silent during this. "Are you OK?" he now asked me.

"Yes, I'm fine," I answered. "I'm just a little pissed because I left my pistol here in the house."

My mother crossed herself at that. "Thank God you left it behind. What would you have been able to do against that many men with automatic weapons? If you'd had that pistol, they would probably have killed you."

"Maybe," I said, shaking my head, "but at least I would have been able to do something to defend that poor man, rather than watch this horrible crime in silence."

This time, my father stood up and walked over to me. He put his arm on my shoulder and squeezed it. I had seldom seen him this emotional, but my story and my distress and had brought this usually inexpressive man to such a state. He was typically inscrutable, but I had touched a nerve, and it took me completely by surprise.

In a voice cracking with emotion, he said, "Don't blame yourself; there was nothing you would have been able to do in those circumstances. You did what Mr. Aldames told you to do. He was probably thinking of one of his sons, and he wanted to protect you. There will be no way I can repay him for what he did for you. As a brother Mason, I would have done the same for him. If you'd had that weapon with you, would probably have done something crazy without regard for your own life. That is part of the principle you live by, and it is why you now feel this guilt." He clenched his jaw. "I'm very proud of you for the way you handled the whole thing." He nodded approvingly. "Do you know what hospital they took him to?"

"No," I replied. "I left him in the care of his employees and rushed back home. I wanted to get out of that place as soon as possible."

"OK, OK," Mima interrupted, "you already told us the story. We can talk some more later. Go and wash up and put on clean clothes."

My father still had his hand on my shoulder. He nodded in agreement and released me. "Yes—go and do as your mother says."

The first thing I did when I got into my room was to take that diamond out of my pocket and hide it with the others. I washed my face and changed back into my uniform. I grabbed my cartridge belt and fastened it around my waist. I felt a little better now armed with my knife and pistol.

I went down into the dining room, where Mima already had a huge cup of tea for me. I took a couple of sips; it was supposed to have the properties of a muscle relaxant and nerve tranquilizer. We all sat in silence. As I drank my tea, I thought about how lucky I was to have such great parents. My father got up and went into the library. I could hear him dial the phone.

"Oh, they took him to a private hospital?" I heard him ask. "I see—*La Colonia Española*[15], yes, yes—in what room?" There was a slight pause. "Room twenty-nine? Intensive Care Unit? OK, thank you very much. You've been very helpful."

He came back into the dining room and sat down. "Poor Aldames—they say he's in critical condition. His chances of making it are very slim, but at least he's still alive."

"Do you want some tea?" my mother asked him.

---

[15] The Spanish Colony

He grimaced and shook his head. "Tea? No! Give me a double espresso."

My mother shook her head and smiled. "Your father doesn't like to relax. He likes to put his feet all the way down on the accelerator."

My father smiled and shook his head. "Mima, Mima, Mima."

"That is typical Cuban macho," Mima said. "Too manly to drink tea!"

We all laughed at that. Silence fell again as Mima and I drank our tea, and Papi drank his espresso.

Chapter 9: The Other Side of Sandra

In Havana's Capitol Hill, my ex-girlfriend Sandra was following strict instructions from the top Commander of the Naval Academy for Counter-intelligence.

Only a few months earlier, she had broken up with me by means of a letter she had left behind at my sister's wedding. In it she explained that she was leaving the following day for the Nautical Superior Military School in Moscow. The letter also contained what could have been construed as a veiled threat against me, accusing me of treason to the Revolution and warning me to "walk carefully."

Years later, Sandra told me that she had in fact never gone to Russia. That story was only a decoy; they didn't want anybody to know what school she was actually attending.

Her training was taking place at a stadium in what once had been a private country club in the middle of the wealthy Miramar district of Havana where the most prominent people used to live. The area was surrounded by cypress trees and the gardens were decorated with Roman statues. There was a tower with large windows at one end of the stadium. With the recent remodeling, it looked more like the kind of arena where gladiator games had taken place.

Through the glass, one could see officers bearing rank insignia that identified them as Cuban Intelligence. Sitting in the middle of them, the red-bearded Manuel Piñeiro was talking with the director of the school, a masculine-looking, heavily muscled woman named Marivela. Everyone was equipped with binoculars and waiting expectantly for an event that was about to take place. Marivela was not happy with Piñeiro's plans for her star athlete.

Piñeiro asked Marivela, "When will this start?"

"Very soon," she answered. "The twenty finalists are just entering now."

They looked down at the stadium and saw ten boys and ten girls between the ages of twelve and eighteen. They lined up, alternating by sex, all ready to participate in the training competition. They were all dressed in camouflage black uniforms, monogrammed on the left breast with an emblem that had a white background with a black dolphin in the center, bordered on the edge by a circle of gold.

"Our girl, Sandra, is already qualified," Marivela told Piñeiro with a smile. "A-1 in every single exercise. The Soviet and German trainers are completely fascinated by her. They propose to give her more advanced training in the Soviet Union and send her to represent the Socialist Bloc in the 1964 Olympics in Tokyo."

Piñeiro violently shook his head and clucked his

tongue. "Absolutely not. I have other superb plans for our Dolphin in some matters of global importance."

Marivela grimaced sadly as the G-2 chief unfolded his plans.

"I don't want anybody to know who she is or the extraordinary qualities she has. She will be our Master Dolphin, the head of espionage around the world. She will make a mark in history and live in memory as the greatest power of Cuban intelligence who ever existed. She will be tearing down whole regimes, not winning silly little games. Just the mention of the Dolphin will terrify the heads of state in all the nations."

He stroked his beard and shifted to a more comfortable position in his chair. He smiled and said, "You tell the Russians and the Germans to limit themselves to do what they were hired to do, and we will pick who will go to the Olympics and who will do something else. Sandra belongs to me and the plans of the International Proletariat Revolution."

Marivela smiled and nodded in agreement. "Very well. I will do exactly as you order, Commander Piñeiro. I will mark Sandra's file 'Classified, Sealed, and Reserved for the Government.'"

"Very well understood, Comrade Marivela," Piñeiro replied. "When the games finish, bring me the file and I will sign it myself before I leave."

He raised his right arm and declared, "Anyway, before I leave the school today I will brief her on her first and most important mission. But since this is the final competition, I don't want to deprive myself of the pleasure of watching her perform. She graduates in one year. This mission will turn her into a complete professional, with no emotions for the common people, her family, or any other kind of attachment. She will be solely focused on our purpose, willing to make the greatest sacrifices for our cause."

Piñeiro removed his hat and scratched his head. "This will be the last test she has to pass before she graduates."

"I'm very sure that our Sandra will pass that final test with flying colors," Marivela said with complete confidence. "For her age, she has the most extraordinarily mature political and ideological education that anyone can imagine."

Down on the stadium floor, a tall, blonde, green-eye man stepped forward. He looked like a European athlete. Around his neck hung a large whistle on a blue, red, and white ribbon. The competitors were ready to start. He raised the whistle to his lips and blew a shrill, piercing blast. All of the competitors started to run around the stadium.

The first obstacle they encountered was a tall wall formed from vast utility poles tightly bound together. They stopped at the foot of the wall and removed from their backpacks small devices that looked like spurs. They bent and fastened them onto their boots. They then put on special gloves with small spikes in the palm. They scampered up the wall like mountain lions, as all of the big shots in Cuban intelligence watched them through binoculars from the tower.

Once over the top, the competitors scrambled back down in the same way. As they came down, Sandra and a tall, dark-skinned boy with a mole on his upper lip were in the lead. Halfway down, one of the other young boys lost his grip with one hand and nearly fell. He was able to recover his equilibrium and continue.

The second obstacle was a crocodile-filled swamp bordered by barbed wire. Sandra was the first one to reach it. She removed her spurs and gloves and rapidly re-stowed them in her backpack. She dropped to the ground and took a small, adjustable *garrocha*[16]. She extended it to its maximum length of eight feet. Inside it was a mechanical spring that would increase its flexing energy to that of a pole of twice its length. Placing the butt of one end against the ground, she used it to pole vault into the area. She landed in some muddy water, almost on top of the crocodiles. She avoided them as they tried to bite her. She hit one or two with the pole, while adroitly sidestepping some of the other reptiles.

She jumped into the next pool while some of the crocodiles attempted to follow her. She walked down the slope until she was neck-deep in the water, and then swam to the other side until the opposite slope was shallow enough for her to walk back out.

She found another spot to plant her pole to vault over the barbed wire. This time, her pants caught on the wire and a small strip of the fabric tore off. A trickle of blood ran down her leg. When she got to the other side, she looked down at the rip and shook her head angrily. She knew it would cost her some points, and that motivated her on to a fresh effort. She put her head down and ran even faster this time, now

---

[16] A pole used for jumping

leaving even her nearest competitors far behind her.

Sandra stopped at the border of a large wall, about 150 feet high. A knotted rope hung down. At the top of the wall was a one-hundred-foot-long pole, supported on the opposite end by second wall with another rope. No netting was laid out beneath the pole. The object was to climb up and walk along the pole like a tight rope, and then climb down the opposite side. She pulled her spiked gloves back out of her backpack. She tied her backpack even tighter and began to ascend the rope. She ran across the pole. By the time she was on the other side and back on the ground, the young man who was nearest behind her was only just beginning his climb up the rope. She took off her gloves, replaced them in her pack, and ran to the next obstacle.

The fourth obstacle consisted of muddy slopes up and down, with barbed wire about two and one-half feet off the ground. At a height of three feet was continual .50 machine gun fire—with live ammunition. At the bottom of each slope were pop-up targets armed with paintball guns. In each slope the targets popped up at different angles, some concealed, some in the open.

Before she began this course, she stopped to strap spiked pads onto her elbows and knees. She had to avoid getting hit while shooting each target with her own gun. After clearing the last slope, she tossed a grenade into the pillbox that controlled the machine guns. The firing stopped.

She had squirmed through the trap without any real difficulties then sprinted towards the next obstacle course. She smiled as she heard the machine gun fire start up for the next competitor, knowing that she was now far ahead.

She began to remove her clothes in preparation for a swim. She stripped down to her swimming suit. The fifth and final obstacle was an Olympic-size swimming pool. Scuba diving gear was waiting for her in a sealed plastic bag. Using a knife, she quickly slit the bag open and put on the equipment. She looked at her wristwatch and jumped into the water. She swam to the opposite side, climbed out and removed only her swimming fins. Three hundred feet away was a vast, man-made lake. She ran across that distance. Before she entered the lake, she sat down on the shore and removed from her waist some leather harnesses and wrapped them around her arms.

She made some guttural sounds and three dolphins came over to her. She gave them something to eat and patted each head. She then tied a harness to each dolphin—small explosive devices were attached on top. She got into the water and swam, the dolphins following her into the deep water.

When she reached the far side, she made more noises, and the dolphins swam to a small boat that floated in the water. One by one, they dove under the boat, gently tapping against the keel of the boat. The tap released a cunning catch on the harness, leaving the device with a red light blinking in the hull of the boat. The dolphins returned to her. She fed them and patted them again. She got out of the water and removed her swimming gear, depositing it tied up in a secure container. She started to walk toward a building where Marivela was waiting with a large bathrobe and a huge grin on her face.

"Congratulations, Master Dolphin," she said. She gave her a hug. "I'm very proud of you—you broke another record today."

"Thank you," Sandra replied as she returned the hug. "I need to improve. I had a little glitch."

"Don't be so hard on yourself, for God's sake. Go and take a shower. Commander Piñeiro is waiting for you in the conference room." She looked Sandra in the eyes. "You did great!"

Sandra nodded, still not very satisfied. "Thank you."

She headed toward the shower. After she showered and put on her uniform, she went out into the corridor where some of the other competitors had just arrived. They congratulated her on her performance. The young man with the mole on his lip waited until the others had left before coming up to her as she walked towards the conference room.

"How is it possible that no matter how hard I try I'm always in second place?" he asked. "I believe strongly you are made with other material—maybe you're crossed with aliens or something like that."

Sandra put her hand on his shoulder and smiled. "Julian, we are half-siblings. We both share our father's genes. All you have to do is give a little more effort and maybe you'll be even better than me. It all depends on you and how badly you want to make it happen."

Julian smiled. "You're so kind and so sweet—but better than you?" He shook his head. "Never. I would be pleased to be like you, that's all."

"Ah, ha!" she said. "That is your problem! You can't beat me because you don't think you can do it." She gave him a kiss on the cheek.

Julian raised both hands in the air and waved them in surrender. "OK, whatever you say." He shook his head in disbelief.

She shook her head and smiled as she left him and entered the conference room. Piñeiro sat at a huge table, several photographs scattered in front of him. She stood at attention and saluted him. He returned her salute.

"Sit down, sit down," he said. "Congratulations on your extraordinary performance today."

"Thank you, Commander."

"That said, I have your first mission for you." He picked up one of the photos and dropped it in front of her. "I have the most terrible suspicions that the Commandantico is the spy we've been looking for—the one we call the Lightning—or at least that he works with that spy directly. He disappeared right after Che's portfolio was stolen. A few days after he reappeared, we confirmed with his brother that he had been staying with him. But we received contradictory information from his brother-in-law, Guerrero, that he had seen him in the proximity of the house of Marcel, the charcoal man—at the same time the Commandantico said he was with his brother."

Sandra leaned back in her chair and nodded, remembering a ride she and I had taken in the jeep. The charcoal man had been stopped by the soldiers in search of contraband liquor.

Piñeiro noticed her nod and looked at her in surprise. "What?" he asked gravely. "Something I said reminded you of something?"

"No, not at all," she answered. "These are very serious accusations, and I believe the Commandantico is very close to the Commander-in-Chief."

"Yes, yes," he replied, "but Raul and I don't want to even bother Fidel with questions until we accumulate enough conclusive proof to accuse him. If any of it is true, we'll hit the jackpot, even if the Commandantico is only a link in that chain."

Piñeiro spread out several more pictures of me standing with the soldiers on the riverbank.

"Last week, we interviewed the sergeant who was arrested on the charges of attempting to rape some young ladies by the river. He told us he had tried to search the man's wagon for liquor, but the Commandantico wouldn't allow him to do so. It's extremely strange, because everyone in this town knows that the charcoal man sympathizes with the Dictator and is not very fond of our Revolution. I would dare to say that he's probably on the side of the worms, because all of his family has left Cuba, including his son."

"I was there that day," she said.

Piñeiro shook his head in surprise. "What are you saying?"

"I was with the Little Commander when that happened," Sandra said. "I questioned why he interfered in the search and protecting Batista's worms."

Piñeiro took even greater interest. "Ah! You were there!" He put both arms on the table and leaned forward. "How did the Commandantico reply when you asked him that?"

Sandra scratched her neck. "He said that different

political opinions didn't justify the harassment of innocent people. All they did was work hard every day just to put food on the table for their family. Instead of persecuting them, he said we have to conquer them intellectually to bring them to the side of the Revolution."

Piñeiro leaned back, a little disappointed. He stroked his beard. "Uh, huh. That's what he told you, eh?"

"Yes," Sandra said in firm assurance. "I have to tell you, my Commander, Julio Antonio del Marmol is the strangest person I've ever met. He has his own way of thinking for himself, like all great leaders have. He's not a follower."

She leaned forward and placed both elbows on the table. "I have to tell you honestly my personal opinion from a political point of view. I don't think he ever has been or ever will be a true communist, because people like him don't follow any doctrine. They have their own way and their own mind to themselves. But it's also my personal belief that he would never be a spy. This kid is too loyal. A spy requires a double face and great ideological conviction. I don't think he will follow anybody, ever. He is on the side of the truth, and he will speak the truth, even if it risks his life. But again—that is my opinion."

Piñeiro said, "Well, your first and most important mission is to discover the truth."

"We're not on good terms anymore," she said. "I left him a letter when I started this scholarship that I never wanted to hear from him again."

"Why?" he asked.

She replied, "Because of his personality."

"That has to change. You have to get close to him again. Every time you get out of the school to visit your family, you have to stick close to him like glue and find out every single movement he makes. You will prove to me and the Revolution how effective you can be. If he is the person we are looking for or even has any connection with that person, this will be the greatest accomplishment for you. You will report to me directly, and I will report to Raul Castro. Remember, no one can know about this mission. We don't want to be wrong and have a fiasco explode in our faces. I want you to make me as proud as your father and Raul are proud of you. It is a great honor that we entrust this mission to you, and to you only, Comrade Sandra—Master Dolphin." There was a knock at the door. "Come in," he called.

Marivela entered and put a folder in Piñeiro's hand with a picture of Sandra on it. He signed it. He opened a container and gave something to Marivela, who walked over to Sandra and pinned a beautiful medal on her chest.

"This is the highest honor for any intelligence officer," Marivela said, "and you haven't even graduated yet!"

Sandra stood up and hugged Marivela. She saluted Piñeiro and said, "Comrade Commandate Piñeiro, I will make all of you very proud of me, as I assure you that if the Commandantico is that spy you've all been looking for, I will serve to you his full confession on a silver plate. If there's anybody he trusts, it is me."

She paused and squeezed her lower lip with her left hand, "I want to ask you, Commandante Piñeiro, one thing that has been bothering me. Why did they give the name of the Lightning to this sophisticated spy you're looking for?"

Piñeiro grimaced unhappily. "His first two most important missions were done during thunderstorms, and he strikes so fast that we have no way of determining who inside our most elite military circles is doing these things. He is probably as good as you are—or even better, as he's been in the game since before you even started it. Somebody trained this spy very well."

She nodded her understanding. She suppressed a smile at Piñeiro's reference to the Liting being possibly even better than she was. Piñeiro exchanged salutes with the newest, youngest agent in the Cuban intelligence group called the Dolphins. Then they shook hands and sealed their pact to attract, entrap, arrest, and place before the firing squad the spy known within intelligence circles as the Lightning.

Sandra left Piñeiro and Marivela behind in the conference room. She walked into the hallway and closed the door behind her. She leaned against the wall with an expression of distaste as she digested the information she had been given and what had just been asked of her. After considering it briefly in displeasure for a moment, she slowly walked down the corridor, still absorbed in her thoughts. Julian walked up to her, startling her out of her train of thought.

"I'll give you a peso for your thoughts," he said with a worried expression. "What about it? Did your interview with Piñeiro go unpleasantly?"

Julian had been watching her all the while and observed her initial reaction. Sandra smiled without an answer. She showed him the medal she had just received. His eyes widened in surprise and admiration.

"Ooh, la la!" he exclaimed with a smile. "My God, you haven't even graduated from school, and you've just received the highest commendation this institution awards! Apparently, intelligence knows how valuable you are and wants to grab you. Piñeiro is a fox, and he wants to have a grip on you."

Disappointment crept over his face. "Well, I have to say goodbye to any possibility of reaching your level. If I had any doubts before, this medal has completely shown me that it's utterly impossible to aspire to your rating." He let go of the medal and shook his fist in the air.

He smiled once more and continued, "Nevertheless, I'm very proud of you, Sandra." He leaned in and gave her a kiss on the cheek and a big hug. "With all my heart, I congratulate you. There's no one else here who deserves that award more than you do for your efforts and diligence. You deserve a lot more, in fact."

Sandra smiled and kissed him back. "Thank you, brother. I know you said that with love, with all your heart. Believe it or not, this medal will probably bring to me more jealousy and resentment than satisfaction and pride. I know a silly medal really means nothing. But the angry looks and envious comments behind my back will be daggers that will produce a lot of pain for a long time."

Julian hugged her once more in support and love. He could not understand her apparent feelings of sorrow and regret, and he leaned in to whisper in her ear. "What is wrong? You know you can trust me."

She turned away slightly to conceal the involuntary tears that escaped her eyes. She tried to wipe her eyes with the back of her left hand. Julian realized that she was crying and said, "I'm sorry. The pain you're feeling right now, I feel as well." He put his hand over his heart. "If you don't want to tell me what's going on, that's fine. But let's take a walk in the gardens to get some fresh air. Maybe that will make you feel better, and maybe it will give you a little time to decide whether or not you want to tell me what have happened in that office just now."

Sandra still didn't reply to him. She simply put her arm around his shoulders and started to walk with him down the corridor, nodding her head.

In total silence, they walked into the gardens until they found a private, comfortable spot away from the installation. Sandra stopped and sat down on a granite bench. She patted the bench to invite Julian to sit with her. He sat down next to the bronze statues of Cleopatra, surrounded by cypress pines, bougainvillea, and other luxurious flowers.

Sandra looked deeply into her brother's eyes. "No matter how much dedication and sacrifice I put forth to make our father proud of me, and no matter my pride in the Revolution and our political and ideological sentiments, my love for Julio Antonio del Marmol is stronger than all of that. I've given every effort I could muster to remove him from my head and rip him from my heart, but it's impossible. The more I try to forget him, the more the gentle, tender, loving memories we shared continue to grow and make it more difficult to forget him. He is very deep in my heart."

She smiled sardonically as she shook her head in frustration. "Piñeiro told me that he and Raul Castro believe that Julio Antonio is the dangerous spy we've been trying to discover—the Lightning—or at the very least, this spy's contact. This destroys my heart, but to make things worse, he asked me to squeeze Julio Antonio for information to bring him before the firing squad!" She raised her arms in impotent anger. "I love that damned man with all my heart! This is the kind of thing that could only happen to me!"

Julian put his hand on her shoulder. "I can assure you that Julio Antonio del Marmol is a crazy rebel, and he will always call it the way it is. But to think he's a spy or helping a foreign spy...." He shook his head. "No, no, no—nobody will ever convince me of that. Besides, if Piñeiro had any proof of what he said to you, for certain he wouldn't tell you and send you behind him."

He tapped his temple with a finger. "Just think about it, Sandra. First of all, you and I both know that the Red Beard has a very nasty reputation in this country as being an ass-kisser to Fidel. I think what's behind this is a tremendous envy Piñeiro bears against the Commandantico. Julio Antonio is very well-respected and admired in Fidel's circle as well as the other leaders of the Revolution."

"That crossed my mind. But lately Julio Antonio has kind of confused me with his attitude and criticism of the Revolution's methods. He doesn't consider them fair and is really against the idea that we cast out those people who don't sympathize with the Revolution, cut them off from their work, and persecute them, even though they are our enemies."

Julian smiled. "Well, I don't sympathize with that idea, either. I don't think it's fair. We started this Revolution to make things equal and fair for everyone, even if they don't agree with us ideologically. Instead of bringing our enemies onto our side, persecution only forces them to break the law and live illicitly. Everyone has to live and eat, Sandra.

"We're also obligating these people to leave the country, which does not present a great image of the Revolution to the world. This is bad politics. We should treat them fairly so that they'll come on board with us and help us build the Revolution.

"The only difference between Julio Antonio and me is that I don't share my feelings with anybody out of fear that someone would classify me as a worm and a counter-revolutionary. Maybe he, being who he is and feeling secure in himself, doesn't have the same fear and so will tell anyone what he feels, just as he's told you—things that no one would dare speak out loud. But telling the truth is far from being an enemy to the Revolution and even farther from being a spy."

Sandra looked into her brother's eyes and remained silent for a few seconds. Finally, she smiled. "Yes, there's no doubt at all that he defends his point of view and expresses it in a very loud voice without any fear of any criticism or consequences it could bring him. It's very possible that these comments have come to the ears of Commandante Piñeiro, who of course doesn't know him as well as we do—his personality and rebel character towards any injustice—and so could have come to the ridiculous supposition that he is a spy or the associate of one."

Julian asked, "How did you answer Piñeiro when he told you all of this?"

She replied, "What do you think? I told him not to worry about it at all and that I would make sure that if the Commandantico is actually a spy, I would find out and bring him to Piñeiro on a silver plate."

"Bravo!" Julian replied. "It could simply be a final exam for the Master Dolphin, to test your loyalty and verify your reactions, gauge your emotions. Besides, this is all too strange. If this is as Piñeiro says, that the Commandantico is under investigation of being a spy, why take a chance on telling you? We all know you're very close to him and probably still have an emotional tie to him. Would they really risk that you blow the whistle and allow that spy to fly out of their hands? Then the investigators tracking him down would lose all of their work. Doesn't that seem strange to you?"

Sandra made a grimace of ambivalence. She thought about it for a moment, her thumb on her jaw and finger on her temple. "You know what, Julian? You'll be a better spy than me, because I didn't even take that into consideration." She smiled at the irony. "Maybe Piñeiro told me all of this and is going to sit down to wait and see how trustworthy I am. If I run and tell Julio Antonio all of this, then I fail his test."

Julian nodded. "This is one of the possibilities in a group of possibilities to take into consideration. Of course, I don't want to say one hundred percent that this is the right one, but this has the most likelihood of being accurate."

He shook his head once more and smiled. "Is it not also strange to you that the precise day they give you this medal for your accomplishments, they drop this bomb on you?"

Sandra nodded once more. "Yes, it is extremely strange that they chose this day. I still have to be extremely prepared, though, because even though the possibility of Julio Antonio being a spy is remote, at the end there may be some foundation for it. Piñeiro has a lot more experience than we have at this, and he may just be looking for a way to confirm his suspicions. He doesn't want to make ridiculous accusations towards the Commandantico before Fidel and the others without any evidence or valuable content."

Julian shook his head and clucked his tongue. "No, no, no—I don't believe that. Put that possibility at the end of all the other ones. I assure you that you won't regret it later on."

He paused and stroked his chin. "What I can tell you for sure is that you cannot tell the Commandantico any of this. He'll be very pissed that his loyalty was questioned, and rightly so. He'll talk to Fidel, Che, and the others about it. Piñeiro will come up with an excuse and find someone else to blame for it, like all the leaders do under similar situations, and he will continue in his current position. But your career as a spy will be over. Red Beard will never trust you again and will destroy and discredit you as disloyal towards his intelligence corps. If you really want to protect your career without putting at risk all of your effort and hard work, don't breathe a single word of any of this to the Commandantico.

He held up his hands. "But if, on the contrary, none of this is important to you or your future, you trust him one hundred percent, and the love you feel for him will endure for a very long time, then the risk will be worth revealing this to him in confidence. If you don't and you one day wind up marrying him and having his sons, he may one day learn of this plot. Having concealed it will create an emotional barrier that will destroy not only his trust in you but also the relationship between you. The most important thing in our lives, my sister, is our family. If that is your plan with Julio Antonio del Marmol, to make him a member of our family, then my opinion is this: to Hell with Piñeiro, the Revolution, and all the rest!"

He spread his hands. "But what do I know? That's only my personal point of view."

Sandra leaned back, her eyes wide in astonished disbelief. After a few seconds, she smiled in surprised satisfaction at her brother's words. She reached out and stroked his chin with her hand, then leaned in and gave him a kiss of gratitude on his cheek. She straightened up and tightened her lips in displeasure.

"You are completely right, my brother. Family is the most important thing we have in our life, and if we are disloyal to them, who then can we show loyalty to? I consider Julio Antonio del Marmol a part of our family already. And even if our destinies take us in different directions and I marry another man, I will continue to love him all my life until I die." She emphasized her point by tapping her heart with her finger.

Julian smiled in pleasure. "I'm glad I managed to

relieve your sorrow. I see you feel better now."

"Yes, I feel a lot better now." They both stood up and walked arm in arm out of the garden.

Dolphins working with their trainer

Dr. Julio Antonio del Marmol

The Beauty in Your Soul

Beauty in a human being lies not in the physical; it is in the soul. To have the capacity to understand the suffering of others, even when you are going through the worst moments in your life yourself, to make a pause and take the time at that moment to console those in need and to offer to them help, compassion, and love, forgetting momentarily about your own interests and personal pain, is the truest sign of a really beautiful soul.

Dr. Julio Antonio del Marmol

The Havana Conspiracies

Chapter 10: The Final Link

There was a knock on the door of our house.

"You guys finish your drinks," Mima said. "I'll go and answer it."

Without waiting for Papi or me to stand up, my mother quickly left to see who was at the door. She returned and said, "A beautiful mulatta is looking for you, Julio Antonio! She's sitting in our living room. She says she's a friend of Yaneba." She looked at my father. "Your son has the most wonderful luck I've ever seen. The most beautiful girls always flock around him like bees in the honeycomb."

Papi smiled and shook his head. "Mima, leave it alone and don't be jealous. You are his only love."

She raised her hand and clucked her tongue. "These girls don't leave him alone. Between them and the Revolution, he doesn't have time to study anymore!"

"Don't worry," Papi said, "he's very smart. He'll catch up."

I finished my tea and walked quickly into the living room to find Marlina sitting in one of the armchairs.

She stood up, giving one of her beautiful smiles. She gave me a strong hug and a kiss on my cheek. She whispered in my ear, "Chandee is here in Pinar del Rio. She asked me to bring you to her."

"Oh, good!" I said, remembering that I had called her. I was a little disappointed that she wasn't here with news of Yaneba. "Let me say goodbye to my folks, and I'll be back in a few seconds."

She nodded her head, and I went back into the kitchen to let them know I was leaving. I came back and the two of us left the house, heading for my Volga parked across the street.

"Drive to the central park," Marlina instructed me. "Do you know anything about Yaneba's family?"

"No," I replied. "I believe it's too soon. Do you know anything about them?"

"No," she said. She crossed herself. "God protect them. That ocean is so immense, and so many things could go wrong."

I took my right arm off the wheel and reached over to pat her on the left shoulder. "In a few days they'll be eating ham and chewing gum."

She smiled. "You always are so filled with optimism," she said with a worried expression. "I hope it will be like that. By the way, thank you very much, and give my greatest gratitude to your brother-in-law, Canen, for putting all of those would-be rapists behind bars like they deserve."

I smiled. "You don't have to thank me. It was all done in the name of justice."

She made a sour expression as she shook her head. "Justice? The Cuban people don't know the meaning of that word anymore. From the beginning of the triumph of the Revolution and the Castro brothers taking power, that beautiful word died. Such a shame! Don't you think so?"

I nodded and replied, "The only word that can compete with justice is freedom, but I think both have been buried by the Castro brothers. Those two words should be holding hands like those people." I pointed at a couple who were walking hand in hand on the sidewalk.

The central park was a huge circle filled with beautiful trees and groves. It was a custom for couples to take long, romantic walks through there or to sit for hours on the benches. In the summer, especially, when the fragrance of all the flowers filled the air and the stars shone like diamonds in the black velvet of the clear nighttime sky, the park was an irresistible location for young people seeking romantic seclusion. There were more of them on the weekends, but even in the middle of the week one would find several couples there. It was also common for the couples to slowly drive around the park, following the old trails established for horse-drawn coaches in the previous century, or for single kids to find a pickup for the night. With only three movie theaters in town, most of the kids found great entertainment in this. As a result, finding a parking space there could be like finding a needle in a haystack.

As we approached the park, Marlina spotted someone leaving. "Look, there! A spot is opening up!"

I quickly zipped into the spot and parked the Volga. "Good eye," I complimented Marlina.

She took my hand and said, "Follow me—I'll take you to her. She's on the other side of the park."

We walked through the multitude of people in the park. Chandee was sitting on one of the benches with a tall, good-looking young man. As soon as she saw me, she stood up and ran towards me. When she reached us, she hugged me and kissed me on the cheek. The young man looked to be of mixed Asian descent—about seventeen or eighteen years of age, black-haired, and dark-skinned. He stood up, bowed, and introduce himself.

"Mucho gus—" he began before pitching forward with a bullet hole in the right side of his forehead. He fell practically at my feet. Everyone froze in confusion.

I yelled, "On the ground, now!" Dirt spurted up in three different areas near us. We dove into the grass near the poor kid.

"Oh, my God!" Chandee said tearfully, "Poor Chantel!"

The people walking by us froze for a few seconds in confusion. Some started to run in different directions. I took the pulse of the young man next to us and shook my head at Chandee and Marlina. "He's dead. Let's get out of here!" We crouched and tried to run, but more shots sang out above our heads. I pointed at a dump truck about a hundred feet away. "Let's try to make it over there. On three. One. Two. Three!"

As we ran, we heard more bullets whine past us. Some bullets created sparks as they struck the concrete of the sidewalk, while others hit trash cans with a loud clatter. One of the ladies who was trying to run was shot in the chest and fell at our feet as we ran by. As the rate of fire increased, panic spread, and people started to run in greater numbers. This helped us, in a way, as the confusion gave us cover. We reached the truck without great difficulty. Sparks from the bullets struck the steel bed of the dump truck. There were more wounded people, innocent victims of what was going on there.

"Be careful," I said. "It looks like there are two gunmen on the rooftops."

The truck's tires were hit, and the air hissed out of them. We were caught in a crossfire, and I realized that we were still exposed. Our position was observable to at least one of the gunmen. I took out my pistol and cocked it. I gestured to the girls not to move from my right side. I looked at the roof for the muzzle flash of the weapon shooting at us. I could see in the flare the silhouette of someone moving on the rooftops and could determine what direction they both were taking.

"They've been shooting from those two roofs," I said, pointing. "When I start to shoot, you guys get to the other side of the park, where I left the Volga." I tossed the keys to Chandee and held out my pen. "Hide this where nobody can find it. This is what your father asked for."

"OK," she said.

"Where did you leave your car?" I asked her.

"It's not around here. I left it at the Interprovincial Bus Terminal."

"Very well. Leave Marlina at her house, leave the

Volga at the terminal, and leave the city immediately. OK?"

"What about you?" she asked me.

"Don't worry about me. The important thing is that you get the hell out of here with that information—and that you get your friend here out of danger."

Chandee squeezed my hand. "Thank you. You take care of yourself, OK?"

"Don't worry, I'll manage. I'll pin them down for you guys. When you hear me start to shoot, you both run away while I cover you."

"Please, please—be careful, OK?" she pleaded with me.

"Go in peace," I told her. "I have nine lives like a cat. Ready?"

I slowly slid up. I could see one of the silhouettes on the roof still shooting at the truck. I aimed my pistol and yelled, "NOW!"

I started to shoot while the girls ran through the grass of the park towards the side near where I had parked. I saw the form fall. I couldn't tell if I had hit him, or if he had simply jumped down or ducked.

The other guy started to shoot at them, and I moved slightly around so that I could see his flares and opened fire on him. Marlina screamed in pain. I looked around and saw that she had fallen. Chandee helped her up onto her feet and helped her limp away, leaving that scene behind them. They were soon lost among the trees.

People were still running around the park in panic, some falling as they were shot. Some were running from tree to tree; one stood still and screamed. I remained for a few seconds behind the truck. I looked down at my cartridge belt and looked for my spare clips. I opened the pouch and made certain that they were still there. Finding that I had sufficient ammunition, I returned my attention to the rooftops.

A shot took out the window of the truck, spraying my hair with shards of broken glass. After a few seconds, there were no more shots. I stood up and looked again. Both of the guys were moving from roof to roof to a vantage point at which they could shoot at me directly. I reached inside the truck, opened the door, and slid inside onto the seat. I stayed low, quiet, and unmoving. I peered through the windows of the truck and watched their motion.

Once they had taken up their positions opposite from where they had started, I slid to the other side of the truck, opened the door, and began to fire upon their positions before taking off at a run towards a grove of old pine trees with nice, thick trunks. I could hear bullets pass over my head as I ran through the grass across the park. I ran past a trash can attached to a tree, and it gyrated in a weird dance as multiple bullets struck it. I dove into the grass once I reached a more secure spot. I was just in time, as several rounds hit the tree where my head just had been, showering me with pieces of pine wood.

Lying on the darkened ground, I brushed the glass and wood splinters out of my hair and checked myself to make certain I hadn't been wounded. Once I reassured myself that I wasn't bleeding anywhere, I crawled through the grass to the next grove of trees on the other side of the sidewalk. In an attempt to throw off my enemies, I went in the opposite direction. When I cleared the grass, a couple of people almost tripped over me, since they couldn't see me in the dark. I crawled to the next large pine tree and stayed there motionless. I heard no more shooting. Several people jumped out near me. Each time, I trained my pistol on them, scaring the living daylights out of the poor people. In the distance, I could now hear the sirens of police cars and ambulances.

Still crawling along the ground, I managed to reach the tree. I carefully stood up and looked around to see what these guys were doing. I could see two shadows on the rooftop where the gunfire had aimed at Chandee and Marlina. I could hear one yell to the other, "Be careful! I think he's in those bushes over there!"

I shot several times in that direction. This time, I ran towards where the Volga was supposed to be, leaving behind that side of the park entirely. I was drenched in sweat, not only from all the running, but also from my adrenaline rush. I wiped my face on my shirt sleeve and kept running, pistol still in hand.

As I ran, I scanned my surroundings in all directions. I arrived where I had left the Volga. To my surprise, it was still there. I looked around, hoping to find Chandee and Marlina. They needed that car more than ever, since Marlina had been wounded. I thought quickly and realized I couldn't stay there for long. I reached into one of my belt pouches and pulled out a spare key to the Volga. I looked around to make sure no one was watching the car. I got in, started the engine, and scanned the sidewalk looking for my friends.

A couple of police cars and ambulances passed by me. I drove very slowly, looking through the multitude of people running around in confusion. Some people had stopped half a block away, talking in the middle of the street about the shooting. Some were pointing at the park. I was worried; I couldn't think of where they could possibly go.

I was almost six blocks away from the park but thought about turning around. This was the way to Marlina's house, but it was possible that they had gone the other way, towards the bus terminal and Chandee's car.

I turned towards my left in preparation to turn the car around when I heard Chandee's voice. "We're here, Julio Antonio!"

I looked in my interior rear mirror and saw both of them gesturing towards me as they stepped into the street. I hit the brakes and put the car in reverse. I backed up about seventy feet close to the sidewalk. Without stopping the engine, I got out and helped Chandee bring Marlina into the back seat of the car.

"Is she hit bad?" I asked.

"She wasn't hit," Chandee answered. "She twisted her ankle while we were running."

"Thank God!" I exclaimed.

"You don't know how painful this is," Marlina moaned.

"Don't complain," I said, "it's better than being shot in the leg."

I got back into the driver's seat and drove quickly away from there. I hadn't any idea who was shooting at us or why and wanted to get away from there as quickly as possible. "Why didn't you guys take the

Volga?"

"There were two suspicious looking guys parked across the street from the Volga," Chandee explained, "and we didn't want to take a chance. We decided to mix with the crowd and get away on foot, in case they were with the shooters."

"You don't know how worried I was when I saw the Volga still there," I said. "It crossed my mind that you guys had both been taken."

Chandee said, "I'm sorry I worried you, but I wanted to take the most minimal chance."

"I understand," I replied. "You did very well. I still don't know who that bullet that killed your friend was intended for. As I was going to shake his hand, you were beside me. It could be either one of us, from the angle the shot came from." I thought about it for a while. "I simply can't think who is behind this. It could even be Marlina that they were trying to kill."

"For a minute, I thought it might be friends of those soldiers you had sent to jail," Chandee said. "But it doesn't make any sense. For something like that, people don't kill people."

I could tell she was trying to alleviate the tension and divert from Marlina the type of business Chandee and I were involved in.

"Poor Chantel! He was supposed to get married next week. I cannot believe he is dead, and it's all my fault. I asked him to come with me to the park so that I wouldn't call attention to myself by being alone. I didn't want to be bothered by a bunch of guys trying to pick me up while Marlina went to get you. This is terrible!"

I reached out and squeezed her left hand as it rested

on the seat. "Don't beat yourself up—it's over now, and we're all alive. I'm sorry about your friend. He looked like a good kid."

Chandee nodded sorrowfully. "Yes, he was a great kid. God take him in Heaven with Him."

In the backseat, Marlina crossed herself and prayed silently.

We arrived at Marlina's house, and as she got out of the car, I asked, "Are you sure you don't want me to take you to a doctor and have that ankle checked out?"

"No, no, it's fine," she said. "I only want to ask you one thing. If you ever come to my house, don't mention a word of what happened tonight. Even though everybody will be talking about this all around town tomorrow, I'm going to ignore that I was there tonight. Please. If my parents find out, they will never, never let me go out or associate with you guys again."

We all got out of the car to say good-bye. "Listen, I don't care what you guys are involved in, but I'm not an idiot. You should be careful. Tonight we all three had the Grim Reaper very close to us, ready to chop our heads off. Just ask yourselves if it's worth it to risk your lives this way. I love you guys anyway, and whatever I see or hear stays sealed in here." She put her hand to her chest. "I'm not an idiot. But I'm not brave like you guys."

She turned very serious. "I nearly crapped in my pants and will want to check there in case something unexpected happened. But when I was running and twisted my ankle, I could no longer hear the shots. All

I could hear was my own farting, and it was like a machine gun. I got confused whether I was hearing shots or my gas!"

Chandee and I tried to keep straight faces. However, after only a couple of seconds, we both burst out laughing. We both turned simultaneously to her in apology.

"I'm sorry," I said.

She was still serious and slightly embarrassed at our laughter. However, it was only a couple of seconds before she started to laugh as well.

She turned her rear towards Chandee. "If you don't believe me, touch the muzzle of the machine gun. It's still warm!" She put her hand on her rear.

We all three laughed so hard, the stress releasing itself through that laughter.

Chandee and I said goodbye and left, but not before Marlina advised us a couple of more times to be very careful. As we drove towards the bus terminal, I related to her the conversation I'd had with Canen. "I need to know immediately from where Canen has knowledge of the General and what kind of game he's playing with me. Immediately. I want with all my heart to trust him, but I need to know to what extent I can do that and if I can depend on him in an extreme emergency."

Chandee assured me that she would get that information as soon as possible and bring it to me.

"Communicate to the General and my uncle that I have discovered a very valuable treasure inside the other treasure," I told her cryptically. "The value, though, is beyond my skill to assess. I will discuss it personally with them as soon as circumstances change and we are able to safely meet once more. It could be of the utmost importance to them, as it will allow us to detour and follow up on some of their foreign operations. I wouldn't relay that information to anyone until I am given the green light in person, though I might use some of those resources according to my best judgment. It has already been a great help in facilitating the exit to freedom of some of our dear friends."

We were passing the private clinic where my father had been told Mr. Aldames had been brought. I said to Chandee, "Do you mind if I stop in here for a few minutes? I'd like to check in on a friend. I'll tell you later what happened to him and the other crazy thing that happened today that put him in intensive care."

"Of course," she replied. "I'm in no rush."

"I won't take too long," I reassured her, "I just want to see what his current condition is."

I turned in and drove through the vast concrete entry arch and parked outside the intensive care unit. I got out of the Volga and walked up to the small booth by the entryway to speak to the admissions nurse stationed there. When I greeted her, she explained that she wasn't supposed to let me in, as there were only certain hours designated for visitation. However, she would bend the rules for me, since the shooting had just happened today and I was obviously worried about my friend.

"If the charge nurse asks you anything," she finished, "you tell her that you're very close family, OK? That way they won't kick you out. I can give you five minutes."

I was sure that she allowed me in for no other reason than the uniform I was wearing. At that time, the Cuban people were still fascinated by the army and those who served in the Revolution. The stars on my epaulette meant I was one of the leaders, and she didn't want to make any trouble for herself.

I smiled and thanked her. Once inside, I looked around the pavilion and found room number 29. Mr. Aldames was covered by a plastic oxygen tent. Two nurses were at his side, checking his IVs and blood transfusion apparatus. I greeted them and asked, "How is he?"

Both shook their heads sadly. The older nurse said, "We've been working hard to save his life. The doctors have operated, and he's now under heavy sedation. All we can do now is wait and pray—it's in the hands of God at this point."

I nodded and asked sadly, "Did he ever regain consciousness? Or has he been out ever since they brought him in?"

The younger nurse said, "No, he's been unconscious throughout our initial treatment and the surgery, and now the sedation is keeping him under. We have to let him rest. The next seventy-two hours will tell us whether he's likely to pull through. Let's just hope he responds to the medication."

I walked over to his bed and looked at him through the oxygen tent. He didn't stir.

"I don't know, my friend, if you can hear me or not," I said sorrowfully, "but you have to be strong. No matter what, I want to thank you for saving my life. I hope you have enough will to live, because I need a partner. God be with you. I will check on you soon."

I thanked the nurses and said goodnight. I left the room and walked through the pavilion. On my way out, I also thanked the admitting nurse for her kindness. I said to her, "When I come back, I will bring you a tiny gift of appreciation."

"No, no," she protested, "that's not necessary."

I raised my index finger in the air and said, "I will." I shook it at her. "You are a nice person."

As I crossed through the gardens and back to the Volga, I saw a flash of light. I turned and observed two men sitting in a relatively new 1959 dark green Buick—so dark a green that it was almost black. The driver was lighting a cigarette. What really caught my attention, however, was the reaction of the other man. He very abruptly and quickly tried to pull down the cigarette and knock the match out of the driver's hands. Both men wore dark baseball caps.

I continued walking but also maintained my surveillance of them, crossing by in a wide arc on my way to my car so that I could look inside their car. They both ducked their heads down so that I couldn't see their faces. I put my hand on my pistol and unsnapped the peace bond on my holster, anticipating the worst after all that had happened to me that day.

When I got to the Volga, Chandee asked me, "How is your friend? That was literally a doctor's visit you gave him—very short."

"Yes, there's not too much to say to him," I answered. "He's still unconscious and in very bad shape."

I drove towards the bus terminal to drop her off. After we crossed several streets, I kept my eyes nailed to the interior rear-view mirror. Chandee noticed this and pulled down the visor on her side to open the vanity mirror on it and look behind her.

"We have a tail, eh?" she asked.

"I believe so, but I'm not sure. We'll find out very soon. Brace yourself."

I made an abrupt left turn onto a small side street and headed down a very steep hill.

The car behind us did the same thing. I stroked my chin with my right hand, while with my left I palmed the wheel to the right and did the exact same thing onto another street. This street went by one of the largest men's clothing stores in the city called *El Fuego*[17]. I slowly pulled over, switched the lights off, and parked. I turned the engine off and told Chandee to wait to see what happened. I drew my pistol, cocked it, and placed it on the seat beside me.

Chandee looked at me in worry. "Oh, no! Again?"

I put my finger on my lips to motion for silence. I leaned back in my seat and tilted the mirror so that I could still see outside. I motioned for her to do the same, so it would look like the car was empty. She complied, and we were virtually lying down. I kept my eyes glued to the mirror with my hand resting on the grip of my pistol. A few seconds later, the Buick passed by us. The men looked at our car closely, the driver almost sticking his head out of the window in his attempt to peer inside the Volga. They drove ahead about three hundred feet. They

---

[17] The Fire

found a space to park and switched their brake lights off.

"These individuals are definitely tracking us," I said. "After what happened today in the park, I don't want to leave you alone in the terminal without any way to defend yourself."

Chandee smiled mischievously and raised her skirt flirtatiously. She had a .25 pistol attached to her leg by a strap.

"Whoa!" I said. "You're not only sexy, but you can defend yourself! You aren't as defenseless as you appear!"

Chandee said, "Do you really think those are the same guys and the same car you saw at the hospital? You're not overreacting because your adrenaline is high and you're stressed?"

I raised my eyebrow, straightened my seat and looked her in the eye. "Absolutely, without any doubt."

She also straightened her seat and pulled her small handbag out. With her right hand, she took out the pen I had given her.

"Well, the only thing that is really compromising us right now is this pen. If you're sure, I think the best thing to do right now is to get rid of it." She looked around and noticed a small trash can on the porch of the clothing store. "It's really a pity, but if those men are from the G-2, it'll be too dangerous to keep this with us."

I thought about it for a moment, squeezing my upper lip. I looked to my left and stared at the trash can she was thinking about using. "Why don't we make sure before we throw away this valuable information your father needs so badly?"

"How?" she demanded. "How much more do you want to push it? The next time, we might not have an opportunity like this to throw it away. What are you cooking in your crazy head?"

I smiled and replied, "Tighten your seat belt and grab whatever you can so you don't break your spine. I'm going to make sure I remove this thorn of doubt from my neck."

I started the engine, turned the lights on, and slowly crept out of the parking space. I looked up and noticed the sign that indicated this was a one-way street. I let a couple of cars pass by me first by pulling into a new empty space. Once they had gone by, I pulled out into the street, noticed that no one was coming in the rear view mirror, put the car in reverse, and stomped hard on the accelerator. The tires squealed in protest and smoke rose from the pavement and wheel well as the wheels spun to gain traction. I put my arm over the back of the seat and turned around so I could see where we were going, and we sped out of that street in an attempt to get to the corner before another vehicle reached the intersection. Chandee crossed herself and clung with one hand braced against the roof and the other clutching the frame of the window.

Perhaps two hundred feet before we reached the corner, two cars turned onto the street. To avoid colliding with them, I tried to squeeze myself all the way towards the line of cars parked on the right side of the road.

"Hold on tight!" I yelled and sped even faster.

Sparks flew from both my car and the other one as we scraped not only each other but also the parked cars on either side of the street. As we squeezed past the first car, leaving behind pieces of metal and paint, the second car stopped completely and hugged the left side of the row as much as the cars parked there would permit in an attempt to avoid colliding with us. It wasn't enough, and more sparks flew as we scraped against each other. Chandee was gripping the dashboard so tightly that I thought she might leave behind dents. She turned to me with a terrified expression.

We cleared the second car and thought we were home free when a large eighteen-wheeled truck with a trailer attached entered the intersection. When he saw us speeding towards him, he slammed on his brakes. I knew we would have no chance in that collision, so I also slammed on my brakes. We still hit hard enough to jar our bodies in the compartment, but it was a much gentler hit than it could have been. Both external rear view mirrors were now hanging uselessly by the side of the car, and the driver's side mirror fell onto the street. I spun the wheel hard, went up onto the sidewalk, and sped off into the night. I could see in my rear view the driver of the truck get out and gesticulate wildly at me.

We left the commotion behind, and I asked Chandee, "Are you OK?"

Her eyes were still abnormally open, and she smiled nervously. "Yes, yes," she stammered, "I'm fine."

It was a relief to still be in one piece. "You blew

your cover tonight for sure and lived up to your nickname. When I saw the sparks flying off both sides of the car, I thought you were crazy and that I'm even crazier to be here with you tonight. If those men didn't already know, you showed them who you are. I wonder what must have crossed their minds when they saw all that white fire coming from both sides of this Volga. My God, *le prendistes fuego al fuego*[18]!"

In spite of all this stress, I had no choice but to smile at that. "Well, let's see how persistent these guys are."

We only drove a few blocks when the Buick reappeared on my right at another intersection. It sped ahead of us, trying to cut us off. I stomped on the accelerator, ran the left wheels up onto the sidewalk, and zipped through before they could do it. The pedestrians ran away to find a safe place and stay out of the way. The other rear mirror fell off and rolled across the cement sidewalk like a baseball. I tried to avoid hitting pedestrians as best I could.

Not only had I managed to zip through, but I also cut ahead of several cars by continuing to drive half in the street and half on the sidewalk. The drivers of other cars, seeing what was happening behind them, pulled over and stopped, allowing me to pass ahead. I floored the accelerator and maneuvered in an attempt to get out of the congested traffic. I turned left at the next major intersection onto Velez Cabiedes, which was the same street with the police station and the jewelry store.

Chandee knew this wasn't the way to the terminal and asked, "What are you doing? Where are you going?"

---

[18] You burned the Fire with fire

I smiled impishly. "We're going to the police station. What better place to go, even if the ones following us are G-2? Even they will not want to shoot us in front of the local police."

She nodded, her expression showing her agreement.

Another car came out from another intersection. This time, it was a 1958 light mint green and white Chevrolet. I easily avoided this cutoff attempt, since I was already halfway through the intersection when he appeared, and I made a half-circle to get around him.

I could see in the rear view both of the cars in pursuit. The driver of the Buick passed the Chevrolet; he apparently was really upset and wanted to get to us first. We were about two hundred feet from the police station when another car managed to cut us off, forcing me to slam on the brakes and come to a stop only a hundred feet from the station with the motor running and the lights still on. Side spotlights hit us through the windshield; it was apparently an unmarked police car. Large trucks were parked on either side of the street, eliminating my previous option, and the two cars behind cut off retreat. The car that was before us was a dark 1959 Ford.

The occupants got out, placing a revolving red light on the roof. Chandee and I looked at each other as we watched the four men scramble out with weapons drawn. They yelled at us to leave the car, and we worried about them being G-2 as well. The two cars pulled up behind us. Leaving their lights on, as well, the occupants of those cars got out with weapons drawn.

Chandee grabbed the pen in her right hand and asked me, "Can you please give your handkerchief quickly?"

I snapped my head to her. Without a word, I quickly gave it to her. She snatched the handkerchief and cleaned the pen carefully. She moistened both ends of the pen like she was licking candy. She held it in the handkerchief and looked at me with an unpleasant expression.

"Well, goodbye to my virginity. At least you will be my witness, whenever I decide who my future husband will be."

I was stunned in shocked silence. Without thinking twice, she opened her legs, put both hands behind her skirt, and with a pained expression, she leaned back in the seat, gently easing the pen inside her. I was filled with revulsion at what she was compelled to do even as I was stunned at her willingness to commit such a sacrifice for our cause. With an expression of extreme discomfort it was done. She brought the handkerchief out—it had bloodstains on it.

I looked at her in utter disbelief. "What did you do that for? Maybe they won't even search us."

She looked at me, shook her head and clucked her tongue. "We can't take that chance. Our lives are worth a lot more than my virginity."

I felt incredibly guilty. A knot rose in my throat, and I almost cried. I knew what that meant in our culture—it could even ruin her prospects of marrying well. I looked at the bloodstained handkerchief as she slowly and meticulously folded it and concealed it in her handbag.

"Don't worry—I'll buy you a new one."

I said, "Please—who's thinking of that right now? Forget it!"

I took the pistol from the seat, a round still chambered, and holstered it. I did not, however, fasten the peace bond. I told her, "I'm going to get out of the car with my hands up, but I'm leaving the motor running. As soon as I'm out, jump in the driver's seat. If they shoot me, gun it, and hit them, even if it means you have to hit me, as well. Get out of here as fast as you can, and reach your destination."

She held out her hand to try and restrain me, but I didn't give her a chance. I opened the door and put my hands up, stepping out into the street. I yelled, "Don't shoot, don't shoot! It's me, the Commandantico!" I walked towards the unmarked police car in front of us. After I took a few steps, I yelled once more.

One of the guys recognized me and said, "Don't shoot! It's the Commandantico! What's going on here? He's the brother-in-law of Guerrero."

I continued walking towards them, shielding my eyes with my left hand so I could see who was speaking. One of the men got on the radio and said to one of the other men, "Back up! H10 calling H13. The subject is not an enemy. He's a friendly subject. It's the Commandantico! Who the hell gave the order over the radio to shoot to kill? *Quien cojones*[19] sent that code over the radio?"

---

[19] Who the hell

The cars behind reversed and left. Several other cars from the police station arrived, this time marked units. Guerrero got out of one of them and came up to me. After greeting me, he said, "What the hell happened here? You OK?"

"Yes," I answered, "I'm still in one piece. For a minute, I thought those cars behind us were counterrevolutionaries and were going to cut both me and my friend into pieces."

He replied, "I've been looking for you for hours! I went to your house, but your mom and dad told me you had left on a date with a friend."

"Yes, but the date wasn't a good one, after all. The entire day has been bad, in fact, since one friend is dead in the central park, and another is in the hospital, practically dead as well."

He stepped up to me and put an arm on my shoulder in sympathy. "I'm very sorry. Somebody called a code over the radio to all the patrol cars, saying that your car had been stolen. They even gave the license plate number of your car, and said that this car was a part of the shooting in the central park, and was the same car parked in front of the jewelry store this afternoon when the robbery took place."

"Yes, the car was parked in front of the jewelry store and the central park because I was in both places when they happened."

"They also said over the radio that the same car wrecked many other cars by the Fuego store when they tried to detain it."

I shook my head. "I cannot believe this. Somebody has been trying to kill me. The two men were shooting at us in the park only a few hours ago, and those guys following us had the opportunity to approach us when I parked, and they never did."

"What guys? What car?"

"The ones that were behind us!"

"I saw cars, but I thought they were police."

"No, they were civilian—a '59 Buick and a '58 Chevrolet."

He scratched his head and looked worried. "I'll investigate this incident personally. It's very strange. But I need you to come with me to the station so I can take a statement from you about the jewelry store and everything that's happened to you. Actually, the employees at the jewelry store said you were a witness but left before the police arrived."

"Yes, and I told them that I would make my statement later. I'll come back in a little while. I have to drop my friend at the bus terminal, and then I'll be back."

"Go ahead, I'll be waiting for you here." He signaled to the other cars that everything was under control.

I went back to the Volga and opened the driver's door. Chandee was still there. She was about to slide to the passenger's side, but I told her to go ahead and drive. "I need to relax for a little bit and let my nerves calm down after this crazy day. I need a tilo tea to unwind."

Chandee drove towards the terminal, and I told her about the strange alarm that had been sent over the official channels that had put the regular police and the DTI[20] on high alert. "We were exceptionally lucky that they didn't shoot us on sight with that kind of order over the radio," I concluded. "We were classified as armed and dangerous. We would have been dead, and they would have excused it later on as a mistake or a confusion, just like Commander Cristino Naranjo."

"Yes, you're right," she agreed. "Maybe that's what they wanted to do—get rid of both of us."

I squeezed her hand encouragingly.

Chandee looked at me and said, "Thank you. You made the right decision when you decided to get out of the car with your hands up. If you hadn't done that, and we had remained inside the car, neither of us would be speaking right now. We have to be very careful from now on. Evidently someone is after our heads; if not mine, they're at least after yours."

We reached the bus terminal and she parked near her car. She looked at me with compassion. "Do you mind staying with me for a few minutes?"

"Of course," I replied, "for as long as you want. What do you need?"

"Nothing, only your company." She took her wallet out and removed my handkerchief with her left hand. She reached out for my hand with her right. I took hers in mine, and she reached between her legs with her left hand. With an expression of extreme pain on her face, she gradually worked the pen loose and removed it. She let go of my hand. With both hands, she wrapped the

---

[20] *Departamento Tecnico de Investigeciones*, or the Department of Technical Investigations.

pen in my handkerchief and returned it to her wallet.

"Thank you," she said with a grateful smile. "Thank you very much for staying with me a little longer."

"Please, you're welcome. It's no big deal." I took her hands in mine and said with a sad expression, "I'm truly very sorry, and I thank you for your sacrifice. I know what this meant to you—your honor, the most valuable thing any woman has to offer to the man she picks to be her husband and share her life forever. It was your choice and election to give your honor to our cause, something I admire profusely. Your extraordinary altruistic act can only come from a woman like you."

She grimaced as she choked back her emotion, tears glistening in her eyes. Bravely, she tried to smile. She opened the door and stepped out of the car. I did the same and walked with her to her car. We gave each other a big hug. She grabbed my face and said, "Please, take care of yourself, OK?"

I took her face in my hands as well and said, "You, too, OK? And drive carefully home."

I watched her car until it disappeared into the traffic. I drove the Volga back to the police station, where Guerrero, two other officers, and a sergeant took my statement. I explained in detail what had happened, leaving out those things I considered unnecessary for them to know. When we finished, Guerrero walked me out to the Volga.

He looked at the disaster both sides had become. "Oh, my God! What a pity!"

I smiled ironically. "After watching a friend die at

our feet with a bullet in the head and then seeing the shooters running along the rooftops, I think you would have done the same with this car if somebody tried to stop you and you didn't know who the hell they were."

"Of course," he said, "I would even destroy a brand-new luxury Mercedes in order to save my life in the same situation. I'm not recriminating you, just expressing what a pity it was." He patted the roof of the car. "This is the most prestigious car any leader of this government could drive. This all can be fixed," he added dismissively. "Death, however, cannot be fixed in a body shop."

We both smiled and said goodbye. I drove to my house. When I arrived, I noticed a brand new 1960 Oldsmobile parked in front with two soldiers relaxing in it. I slowed and stopped the Volga behind them. The soldiers saluted me as I got out of the car. Their faces looked familiar to me. When I came into the house, I discovered drinking a Cuban coffee and speaking with my mother and father none other than Fausto Pijirigua. With a grin from ear to ear, he said, "Thank God you are here already, Commandantico. I've been waiting for you for a while. Your folks told me you were out on a date with a beautiful mulatta, and I figured that you wouldn't be back until much later."

I shook my head distastefully and said, "She's a friend of mine. There's nothing between us."

He smiled ironically and answered, "Sure, sure. I have a lot of those friends." He drained his cup and handed the saucer to my mother. "Thank you very much, Mrs. Marmol—this is one of the best espressos I've ever had."

I looked at his boots and recognized them as the same ones I had seen through the curtain at the jewelry store. I could even see a dark stain on the back of his uniform pants, near the elastic band at the hem—dark enough to be blood. As he crossed his legs, he could see me looking at his boots and noticed the stain. "Oh, I think I spilled some of your great coffee on my pants."

My mother, polite as ever, offered, "If you like, I can bring you a little towel and soap so you can clean it up before it stains your pants."

"Oh, that's all right—these are old clothes, and I have to take them to the laundry anyway. Thank you, you're most kind!" He stretched in his chair. "I'm here because Che sent me to pick you up to bring you to the capital with us. Tomorrow afternoon, you have an appointment in the office of the French ambassador."

"Very well," I said. "When do we leave?"

He spread his hands. "As soon as you're ready. I'm at your service and waiting for you."

My mother handed me my travel bag which she had already packed for my trip. "They've been here for a long time waiting for you," she said. "I used the time to prepare your bag—which I haven't even had a chance to empty since you came home."

She said it very diplomatically, but I could see from their wincing expressions that Fausto and my father knew precisely what she meant.

He stood up and said, "Don't worry, Mrs. Marmol, he will be back here very soon. I don't think this will take much time."

Mima shook her head skeptically, though her smile didn't leave her face.

My father also stood up. "Do you have money with

you?" he asked me.

"What do I need money for?" I pointed to Fausto. "With these guys, you never have to pay for anything. Even when they try to give people money, they won't take it!"

Fausto nodded. "It's true." He turned to attempt to console my mother. "Don't worry about it. He'll be in good hands with us, and we'll bring him back soon."

We said goodbye, my father very proud and smiling at his son being picked up by the personal assistant to Che Guevara. My mother wasn't as happy, and she kissed me saying, "All right, but you rush right back home, OK? You're getting so far behind in your schooling."

We walked outside, and Fausto took one look at the Volga and said, "Oh, my God! What happened to this car! Are you OK? Were you involved in a big accident?"

"I'll tell you all about it on the trip, but someone evidently tried to kill me today. They killed one of my friends, but apparently they couldn't touch me. The only wound is the Volga. We have to take it to the hospital."

Fausto shook his head and put one of his arms around my shoulder. "Well, the important thing is that you're OK." He turned to one of the escorts and said, "Olerio—follow us. Drive the Volga, and we'll leave it at the regiment so that they can fix it. We'll go by there on the way to Havana, anyway, and if it takes longer than we expect in the capital, it will be fixed by the time you get back."

I nodded and said, "Thank you. I hadn't even thought of that. I've had such a crazy day." I lifted my leg and reached into my uniform pants, removing the key, which I gave to Fausto. "You're on the ball, Fausto. Thank you, that's great idea."

He smiled, flashing his rotten teeth. "You're welcome. That is what I'm for. I never have bad ideas. That's the reason Che picked me out from among all these bums and brought me close to him—because I have good ideas."

We left my house, stopping on the way out of the city by the regiment to drop the Volga off at the body shop there. I thought about my poor mother, holding in her opinions out of respect for my father. She knew that whatever protests she might make, my father would attempt to justify my leaving home again in the company of men she felt were not good examples to me.

A few hours later, we reached the capital, and Fausto asked me if I was hungry. "Yes," I replied, "I haven't eaten dinner yet."

"OK, let's have a first-class meal with refined flavors," he said.

"Where are we going?" I asked. "To the Cordon Bleu?"

"No, to the Hilton. Well, not the 'Hilton'—no Yankee names in Havana anymore. Now it's the Havana Libre—the Free Havana. It belongs to the people. It's true what they say—nobody knows what you're working for. The gringos gave us a fine, five-star hotel! By the people, for the people."

I smiled slightly, as I mentally rephrased that by replacing the word "government" for "people." He noticed and said, "What are you laughing about?"

"I'm laughing at what you just said. Who would

have thought before that you would be able to eat in these places? You were probably born in the middle of the jungle, no?" I asked teasingly.

"You're not kidding, Commandantico—my scenery was only a few banana trees on the patio!" He pulled out a bunch of vouchers that looked like a book of food stamps. "We have to make good use of these—they expire next month. With these, we can eat lobster, shrimp, and all kinds of great food. I'll be extremely sad if we let them go to waste."

The Havana Libre Hotel, formerly the Havana Hilton

We drove into the valet parking of the hotel. Between our uniforms and brand-new car, we were received like royalty. I thought to myself as they opened the doors and gave us all their reverence that the old class had disappeared, but the new class, the government, was born.

After an exquisite meal with numerous dishes, Fausto paid using the vouchers, without leaving a tip.

I asked him, "You're not going to leave a tip for these people after all the attention and service they gave us?"

He raised a hand. "No, no—no tips. That is part of the capitalist way of humiliating people. That is one of the things we have to eliminate in our new society. It makes the waiter look like a beggar or a slave."

I shook my head. "No, the tip is not a humiliation."

"Of course it is, Commandantico! Waiters are like any other workers. They get a salary, they do their job. Why should they expect anything more?"

I raised my eyebrow and shook my head. "I don't agree with that at all. The tip is only a stimulus for them to provide to you excellent service, so that when you come back you'll not only receive the best service but will also be received with cordiality and joy. If you don't do that, what is the incentive for these people to serve us the way they did today?"

He replied sarcastically, "If when we come back here they don't serve us the way they did today, we call the manager and they lose the comfortable job they have. Then we send them to cut sugar cane or dig for potatoes or whatever. Then you will see, after a few months of sweating their asses off in those fields, you won't need a tip any more to stimulate them. Their stimulus will be their concern about keeping the job they have now in air conditioning. Forget it, no tip!" He turned around and started walking to the door.

I reached into my wallet and pulled out a couple bills, ten-peso and five-peso notes, and placed them under my water glass. A waiter saw me do that, winked at me, and said, "Thank you, and go with God."

"Thank you very much, and thank you for your service." I followed them out, feeling embarrassed that I didn't have more to leave for them.

A little while later, we arrived at the beach of Boca Siega, not too far away from the city, perhaps twenty-five to thirty minutes. To my surprise, we walked into a mansion I had never been in before. As we walked through the house, multiple soldiers let us in as they recognized us.

We walked through to a luxurious terrace overlooking the beach. I saw three men, two of whom I recognized. One was Jack Ruby. The other looked like Marko. They were sitting with Che amidst the beautiful scenery and planters, drinking rum and smoking Habanos cigars.

After I greeted everyone, I said to the one I had thought looked so much like Yuri, "How are you doing, Marko? Are you back in Cuba, or did you never leave because you love the Cuban women so much?"

Everyone remained silent, including him. He looked at me in surprise without the slightest hint of recognition. He looked at Che and Jack, and I thought for a moment I had said something inappropriate. Che looked at me and shook his head. "This is not what you think. This is another friend of Jack's. His name is Marcelino. He's an Italian gentleman who will be working with us on a future project."

"I'm sorry," I started to reply.

Che cut me off. "Marcelino, this is one of my

intimates, one of the most trustworthy men we have around. He is the Commandantico, and one of the future architects of our international Revolution—the brightest and greatest man of the future."

Marcelino stood up and held his hand out to me, saying in perfect Spanish, "Much gusto, Commandantico."

"The pleasure is all mine."

He was the spitting image of Marko and Yuri. I wondered where they had the mold that they were using to make these people. They looked like they were coming out of the same factory.

The other man sitting by Jack was dressed like a mafioso or FBI agent, with a raincoat, a hat, and a pocket handkerchief that perfectly matched his tie down to the same design and color. This man didn't speak Spanish as well. In a very heavy accent, he said, "Mucho gusta. Mi nombre is Alfonzo Machi."

I held out my hand and replied, "The pleasure is all mine, Mr. Machi."

"Call me Al—like Al Capone."

Che stood up, his Habanos cigar in his right hand, and said, "Well, let's hope that everything continues to march the same way it has been marching until now."

Jack and the others stood up when they saw him stand. Jack repeated, "Claro, chico!"

Che smiled and slapped his shoulder in friendship and gave him a hug. He pointed to the floor with two thick black portfolios, both of which had chains and handcuffs secured to them. "Don't forget your deposit slip."

Jack signaled to Al and snapped the handcuff on Al's right arm. He spun the dial on the combination lock on it. He attached the other one to Al's left arm and similarly scrambled the lock. Jack removed his hat and scratched at his receding hairline. "Well, our mission is finished here. Who will be taking us to the airport?"

Fausto said, "Right here, sir. We're ready for you right now." Two guards followed Fausto and the three men out of the terrace and into the house.

This concludes the second part of Rites of Passage of a Master Spy. Julio Antonio's adventures and trials continue in Volume III, The Dark Face of Marxism. For even further adventures of the Lightning, visit our website, www.spymasterspy.com.

The Havana Conspiracies

What Is Your Country?

Your country is the place you learn to love; it is in your heart. That piece of land, to you, represents more than soil. It represents your dreams of justice, love, and family values, where the water tastes sweeter, more so in your mouth than it does for anyone else. The place where you feel at peace and where you know you have respect for your God. Your country is not the place where you were born sometimes; occasionally, you are born in the wrong place or time. Your country is that land where you live in harmony, where you build your family and your life, where you have your friends, and what you are willing to shed your blood to defend. That land you love so much that your heart aches with pride and you think there is no other like it.

It is not a piece of paper that any government can create; it is the love and the feeling you have for it, where you are happiest, have the love and respect of your brothers and sisters, where no persecution or discrimination exists from anyone for your political views. That is the land you make your country; defend it with your nails to the death if need be from any who seek to destroy it because after all, my friends, in the eyes of God we are all citizens of this Earth; and that, my brothers, is an undeniable fact.

Dr. Julio Antonio del Marmol

Dr. Julio Antonio del Marmol

Copyright Credits

Submarine Base Entrances
Copyright: <a href='http://www.123rf.com/profile_samum'>samum / 123RF Stock Photo</a>
Copyright: <a href='http://www.123rf.com/profile_samum'>samum / 123RF Stock Photo</a>

Mercenary soldiers training in terrorist tactics
Copyright: <a href='http://www.123rf.com/profile_kaninstudio'>kaninstudio / 123RF Stock Photo</a>

The mansion given to Daniel, Lazaro's father
Copyright: <a href='http://www.123rf.com/profile_apalmero2000'>apalmero2000 / 123RF Stock Photo</a>

Havana's Old Chinatown district
Copyright: <a href='http://www.123rf.com/profile_epokrovsky'>epokrovsky / 123RF Stock Photo</a>

The damaged *La Coubre*
Copyright: <a href='http://www.123rf.com/profile_ocipalla'>ocipalla / 123RF Stock Photo</a>

Damage to harbor facilities
Copyright: <a href='http://www.123rf.com/profile_digitalsun'>digitalsu

n / 123RF Stock Photo</a>
    Copyright: <a href='http://www.123rf.com/profile_dollapoom'>dollapoom / 123RF Stock Photo</a>

    The faithful Kimbo
    Copyright: <a href='http://www.123rf.com/profile_tdjoric'>tdjoric / 123RF Stock Photo</a>

    Mr. Aldames' jewelry store, La Zultana
    Copyright: <a href='http://www.123rf.com/profile_dotshock'>dotshock / 123RF Stock Photo</a>

    Dolphins working with their trainer
    Copyright: <a href='http://www.123rf.com/profile_hbrrbq'>hbrrbq / 123RF Stock Photo</a>

Dr. Julio Antonio del Marmol

Other Works by the Author

Cuba: Russian Roulette of the World
The Cuban Lightning: The Zipper

Rites of Passage of a Master Spy Series
Cuba: The Truth, the Lies, and the Coverups

Forthcoming in this Series
The Dark Face of Marxism
The Deadly Deals
The Evil Rituals
JFK: The Unwrapped Enigma

www.ingramcontent.com/pod-product-compliance
Lightning Source LLC
Chambersburg PA
CBHW031308150426
43191CB00005B/132